BROWNSTONE INSTITUTE

THE MARKET LOVES YOU

Why You Should Love It Back

JEFFREY TUCKER

The Market Loves You
Why You Should Love It Back
By Jeffrey Tucker

Physical ISBN: 978 1 63 069590 3
Digital ISBN: 978 1 63 069589 7

Design: Vanessa Mendozzi

THE MARKET LOVES YOU

Why You Should Love It Back

JEFFREY TUCKER

BROWNSTONE
I N S T I T U T E

Praise for The Market Loves You

"Economics, love, and life — these are all the same topic in the creative intelligence of Jeffrey Tucker. His writing sweeps you into a world of beautiful stories about the material world, infused with his gift for seeing the underlying human element in every exchange (as well as the brutality of the political means of social control). His new hymn to market forces brings what economics too often lacks, a vivid celebration of life and love as real human beings experience it. To see the world as Tucker does is a gift that few writers in economics have ever possessed."

— Helio Beltrão, President
Mises Institute Brazil

"If you want to understand the plain sense of real economics, as against the fairy tales of fake economics, Tucker is your main man. In scores of charming little essays, free of pomp or pretense, he brings you to understand how a free people can live without coercion. He's a liberal 2.0, a sweet egalitarian, a generous, open-hearted spirit, yet realistic and tough-minded, too."

— Deirdre McCloskey
University of Illinois at Chicago

"Jeffrey Tucker is always a delight to read because he understands and appreciates the market's invisible heart as well as its invisible hand."

— Art Carden
Samford University

"Jeffrey Tucker writes with a rare mix of economic understanding, historical awareness, philosophical depth, and unaffected humanity. And oh, also on display in these pages is a fearlessness in going to wherever the logic of his reasoning brings him. I learned something important from each of the 91 essays collected here."

— **DONALD BOUDREAUX**
George Mason University

To My Mother Janeice Tucker,
who has loved unceasingly

CONTENTS

Section 3 - Government

Section 4 - Technology

Section 5 - Money

Section 6 - Stuff

Conclusion

Introduction to the Second Edition

This book was written in the Before Times. Looking back through it, I'm reminded of what I cared about before the world fell apart with lockdowns, mandates, and the ensuing existential crisis of civilization itself. I wondered at first if this book mattered anymore but now I'm sure it does. My theme is meaning. Not big meaning but meaning in small things. The meaning of everyday life. Finding friendship, mission, passion, and love in the course of working out one's life in the framework of a commercial society, which should not be narrowly construed as only a way of paying bills but rather should be seen as the instantiation of a life well lived.. We were not doing a good job of that, so my thinking was to inspire people to come to love what we take for granted.

A conversation I had with a smart 20-something early after lockdowns hit still haunts me. I asked why she and it seemed like her whole generation were so eager to comply. They were living a good life but then signed up full on with all the lockdown nonsense even though the data was clear they were not among the vulnerable. They all could have risked exposure – as we all must do every day in all normal times – and shaken it off with an upgraded immune system. Why did they all go along?

"Because for me and everyone I know, this is the first thing that has ever happened to us."

Happened. What does that mean? Well, her whole life so long as she could ever remember had been scripted. Her earliest memories were learning how to sit in a chair and listen to an authority. That early memory became her whole life from 6 to 18 until college, which then was just a four-year vacation from reality at her parent's expense. Next came the internships, all of which were designed to snag the highest-paid position with social standing. What was the goal? Keep the money flowing, hang out, fuss around with the Internet, dress well. Or something.

So, yes, not much happening. Where is the challenge? Where is the drama? Where is the struggle against adversity? There was not much if any at all.

Nothing big, nothing important, ever happened to her. What goes for her goes for multitudes of others. So the visit of a virus seemed like something glorious, something at least different. Something that required sacrifice, belief, conflict, struggle. It was existential. It was meaningful. Lockdown ideology was a replacement for a life without meaning.

I do not believe that bourgeois civilization must be this way. But we have constructed it so. Weve caged the kids for 12-16 years. We have bureaucratized the office. We have cartelized industry and markets. We have denied many the chance to get ahead. We have segregated and classified the whole population. We have made safety a religion and obedience to authority a creed. We have demonized difference. We have canceled dissent. All of this was true in the Before Times.

In the crisis of 2020, the anger, the frustration, the nihilism, the loss of direction, and the resentment against the caging and life in the system all boiled over and were redirected toward a single goal: pathogenic avoidance. There was a clear message, a clear dictate, and a clear goal with numbers to back it up. All the other complications of life faded into the background as the population rallied around this one purpose. It gave multitudes of people meaning.

It's impossible not to notice that the people who avoided the frenzy and panic were older and tended to be religious. They had more life experience and they found a source of meaning outside of civic culture. They had a North Star and it was not the CDC. So they were less susceptible to manipulation. The rest, not so much. And so vast swaths of the population behaved like cartoons from history: flagellants, Red Guard enforcers, Prince Prosperos of the laptop class, scolds and scapegoaters. It was painful to watch.

Would this crisis have afflicted us had we as a culture believed in something more meaningful, something such as freedom and all that we did within those freedoms? Doubtful. This is one reason that the crisis of 2020 and following shocked me so much and why I ended up writing one of the first books opposing lockdowns and another thousand or so articles. I simply could not figure out how it was that so many were so confused and easily led. As I look through the essays of this volume, I can see now why I was so alarmed. I was completely unaware that the foundations of a meaningful life had already crumbled under the feet of so many people.

This is why this book is in a second edition. The purpose is to illustrate what it means to fall back in love with life, including its arts, professions, creations, challenges, excellences, friendships, uncertainties, mysteries, and dreams. These are all matters of the heart – the individual heart. There is no escaping them. No grand project dictated to us by government, media, and Big Tech can substitute.

My only discomfort with the book is the title: the use of the term market. I like it but I'm aware that it might come across as too centered on economics alone, narrowly construed. That is not what I mean. My purpose here is to say that markets and life cannot be separated. Abolish one – we ended up trying that – and you radically diminish the other. The CDC and Twitter are not replacements for a life well-lived.

This book also serves as a good goal for me too. The pandemic response changed us all. We cannot help that. It's fine if it makes us wiser and less naive. What we do not want is to allow them to gut us of joy and optimism. Rebuilding is in fact possible. There is a sense in which this book might help point the way forward. It is dedicated to my mother because it is she who has always done that for me.

Preface

In most places I shop today, I'm asked if I want to round up to the next dollar to support a charity. Sometimes I say yes and other times no. You do the same. What's interesting is how the choice is offered to us. It's made possible by financial technology that allows instant processing of payments and careful allocation of funds through mathematical algorithms. The technology ends in directing resources to good causes that might otherwise not be funded.

The transaction ends with both me and the cashier saying those magic words, thank you. Each of us offers thanks to the other because we've both benefitted, slightly better off than we were before. We express our gratitude for each other's presence in our lives. Where is the benevolence in this event? Some would say it takes place only when I round up to give to charity.

I would go further. Benevolence characterizes every aspect of this sale, and not just this sale but also the millions upon millions of other transactions that enable the store to exist at all, and not just the store but the existence of all the products on the shelves, each of which embeds complex human relationships that extend all over the world, involving potentially billions of people.

Every unforced decision to trade represents a spark of insight, a hope for a better future, and the instantiation of a human relationship that affirms the dignity of everyone involved. Sometimes that relationship is personal; it is even more awesome to consider the enormously complex impersonal relationships that make up the vast global networks of exchange that make our lives wonderful.

We take the results for granted because they are so much part of our daily experience. If they suddenly went missing, any aspect of what we depend on to live a better life, we would experience demoralization and even devastation. The lights go out. The gas stations close. The shelves are empty. The doctors run out of medicine. There is no one to fix the plumbing, no one to repair the heater, no one to do the surgery on my heart. This is a world that is less lovely than the world of plenty we've come to expect.

Or imagine finding yourself in a position in which you can no longer find a market for your personal talents. No one is willing to pay you to be you. Permanent unemployment. Your personal connection to the matrix of exchange has been severed. This is a dehumanizing condition. You feel unloved. Few would disagree. I want to take this one step further to say that the presence of a vibrant commercial society in which we are personally involved is a major reason we feel the presence of love in our lives. And it's not just about a feeling; it is about the practical realization of love.

I was two semesters deep in an economics major in college, steeped in curves and mechanisms of large-scale statistical aggregates, before the reality dawned on me. Economics is about human life. Exchange is about forming human relationships and connections, so that everyone benefits. Social order is an extension of these relationships.

The more complex these connections are, the greater the chance for wealth creation, reparation of social and personal problems, and the realization of the good life. To love and feel loved — there are so many layers to what that means, so much more than the common use of the term denotes — is at the foundation of what we call the good life.

The institutional setting in which human relationships become real in our lives is the market. This does not entail reducing human life to dollars and cents. It is about the recognition that our value as human beings is bound up with our associations with others, our trading relationships, and the opportunities we have to value and be valued by others.

Looked at this way, the moral aesthetic of the market is lovely. It fosters love. It needs love.

This is the theme of this book. It nowhere makes a comprehensive much less irrefutable argument for what appears to be an implausible claim. I've learned to leave that way of writing and thinking to others. I can only ask the reader sincerely to consider my impressionistic account of the immense contribution that commercial society makes to our hearts, souls, and lives.

The market desperately needs defense against those who would undermine it. Property must be secure. The right to accumulate wealth must be intact. The freedom to innovate and associate at will cannot be put at risk.

The need to protect markets against invasion dates back to the ancient world. Consider the Ottoman region's continued popularity of the Nazar amulet. It is a blue charm with a white dot in the middle and another shade of blue, finished off with a dark blue dot. It's a bit strange looking and basically unknown in the West outside those who travel and come back with souvenirs. It looks kind of like an eye.

What it is? It is a foil to the evil eye. The theory is that when someone resents you for your success, this charm looks right back at the person and wards off the dangers of envy.

When you travel in Turkey and Greece, you see the charm everywhere: airports, cars, boats, shopping centers, houses and so on. Why such prominence for this item, which has no religious basis and emerges entirely from a folk tradition? It has ancient origins, originally designed to ward off resentment people feel toward a cute and healthy child.

As time went on, wealth took other forms. The Ottoman region is one of the oldest commercial regions in the world, a place where the rise of wealth began to appear in the course of one generation during the 16th century. To keep others away from your just earnings was certainly a priority. It still is. It is particularly important to keep envy at bay.

If markets are love, envy embodies a form of hate. It observes the excellence of others and desires it to stop. It sees the fortune of another and aspires to punish it. Envy is actively destructive of another's successes as an end in itself. It is not even the case that the realization of envy brings happiness to the person who wants to harm others. It merely achieves the goal of satisfying the anger you feel when looking upon the happiness of others. It tears down. It harms. It hurts. It crushes, smashes, and kills. It begins with resentment against others' achievements and ends in the infliction of personal harm.

In Judaism, the rabbis taught to favor instead the "good eye" (*ayin tovah*) which calls for us to rejoice in the fortune of others as an expression of love. The relationship between markets and love is mutually reinforcing. The more we practice peaceful human cooperation, the more we come to depend on and value the presence of others in our lives, and the more we are incentivized to respect their rights. It is through a deep understanding of and appreciation for markets that we find our way toward believing in and living the good life.

Søren Kierkegaard tells the story of two artists. The first looked in vain for the perfect face to paint and gave up his craft because he could not find it. The second artist looked for beauty within every face and concluded: "I have not found a face so insignificant or so full of faults that I still could not discern in it a more beautiful side and discover something glorious. Therefore I am happy in the art I practice."

My hope is that the essays herein will inspire us all to be that second artist and see the beauty and love all around us.

• • •

Nearly all of the essays herein were composed to my times at the American Institute for Economic Research, founded by E.C. Harwood in 1933 with an incredible ideal in mind. He sought to create an institution independent of government, academia, and pay-to-play interests so that creative and earnest researchers, scholars, and writers could speak to the public in ways that rise above the current winds of politics. Being given the honor of directing editorial affairs at AIER has been a tremendous source of grace in my life. And I believe it has inspired the best writing of my career.

I would like to express my gratitude toward my colleagues Max Gulker, Pete Earle, Phil Magness, Richard Ebeling, Donald Boudreaux, and all the regular writers at AIER whose insight inspires me daily. The staff at AIER has been unfailingly generous and helpful. AIER's president Edward Stringham, whose wit and wisdom set the tone of our work here, and who certainly deserves the moniker great, has done the hard work to bring this institution into the 21st century and set the highest standards for rigor, research, sincerity, and progress.

As I'm finishing this introduction, early Monday morning, Edward just walked in the office, dressed to the nines, and is making rounds. I'm listening to all the delighted conversations taking place in the hallway, the greetings, the laughter, the congratulations, the inside jokes, his careful attention to every person who contributes to the life of the institution, everyone on a first-name basis, and so, of course, the idea of love again strikes me. I do feel it here and everyone does. This is the basis of a great enterprise and the realization of a mission rooted in an ideal, not just at AIER but all over the world.

Markets and Life

Markets are About Love

There's this nice woman who works at the local Goodwill who is always happy to see me come in the door. She thinks she knows what I'm looking for and enjoys running to get things that recently arrived at the shop: bookends, or cufflinks, or a small lamp in a classical style. Together we revel in the bargains. When I purchase something, she feels a sense of joy. My patronage supports the work of the store, which is charitable. I too feel joy. It's a special moment, of the sort that brings joy to life and makes what sometimes seem like a dark world just a bit brighter.

The context is commerce, the source of an endless stream of such personal encounters. We should take note of them and learn the lesson. Realizing the full extent to which commerce brings us delight and generally fosters the kind of human connection we all seek — one in which we discover dignity in others and they in us — has the potential to change the way we think about markets themselves. They are an indispensable foundation of a society built on love.

These experiences are not always personal. Last week I took a couple of hours, in the middle of the afternoon, to be amazed and thrilled by an action-packed movie, shown in a theater built for me though I never requested it, a movie that required a production structure of thousands of people, with some of the most skilled talent in the world, all for the purposes of delighting me. Others too. What these people wanted from me was $7, in exchange for which I received an adventure experience that would have been unattainable anywhere on the planet just a few decades ago.

I felt loved. It's an interesting kind of love. I don't know any of the people who did this for me. But that they did it for me, I have no need to doubt, because as a consumer I possess the power to affirm or decline to affirm their every effort.

I had to wait until the end of the movie during the credits to even know their names. They don't know my name either, even though everything they do in their lives is targeted toward my interests. So it's not personal love. It's more like structural love, a system-wide devotion to mutual benefaction based on giving and getting.

I had ordered cheese popcorn. I didn't know that eating a small bag would effectively give me a second skin on my hand made of cheese powder. It took lots of scrubbing in the men's room to remove it. I returned to the concession to get some regular popcorn, and, in passing, mentioned my issue with the cheese. The person at the counter was mortified and offered to give me my money back.

I assured her that this was not a disaster really, and that I was perfectly fine. But I could still tell that she was truly upset, genuinely concerned that I was not entirely pleased. We exchanged a series of assurances that all is well. We smiled at each other. We wanted the best for each other. I walked off with a sense a happiness that comes from courtesies of these sorts. I didn't know her and I might never see her again, but there was still love there: a mutual affirmation of the inherent dignity of the other.

These stories might sound trivial. They happen to all of us every day, and are a part of every commercial encounter. Yes, sometimes things go wrong: a clerk is rude, a customer gets too demanding, there is some misleading or manipulation going on. But that's just the point. We recognize this as the exception, and we work to fix it because we know it can be fixed. The driving ethos and ideal of commercial exchanges is that sense of affection, even devotion, to the ideal that everyone is better off.

This is the etiquette, ethos, and ethics of the commercial spirit. It is about love.

Is that too strong a word? C.S. Lewis famously distinguished four loves organized by their intensity: *storge, philia, eros,* and *agape.*

Storge he describes as affection, a type of love. This is the core of what we find in commercial life. It is uncoerced and mutually regarding. "The especial glory of Affection is that it can unite those who most emphatically, even comically, are not; people who, if they had not found themselves put down by fate in the same household or community, would have had nothing to do with each other," he writes. "Affection is responsible for nine-tenths of whatever solid and durable happiness there is in our natural lives."

What he is really describing here is a feature of the regular course of events of capitalism, which is best thought of not as a system but a network of human relationships based on exchange.

Clearly, for centuries, the whole point of capitalism has been missed. It is not about material greed, much less exploitation and exclusion. Its fundamental theme is love of this special sort. That is its driving energy and ethos. This love permeates every aspect of its operations. It requires love. It rewards love. It elicits love. It lives on love.

Think of the fundamental unit of capitalism: the exchange. You own and I own. We could keep what we possess. But we are attentive to bettering our lot. We discover something remarkable, namely that if we cooperate we could both be better off. I want what you have and you want what I have. You value mine more than yours and I value yours more than mine.

We come together in trust. We exchange, out of choice. Though nothing has changed about the material world, we have created value and wealth, something we know by reflecting on our inner sense of well being. It's an act of love.

This act of love takes place trillions of times a day all over the world. The act can be as simple as exchanging money for a cup of coffee or as complex as a multi-billion dollar company changing ownership. In substance, these are the same acts. It is all about the giving spirit: you give me value and I give you value. We discover that in our mutual association, in the act of giving to get and getting only when giving, that our lives are improved.

We need each other. We trust each other. We are lovers. Indeed, the rarely used Latin term commercium literally means sex, but came to be more commonly used in medieval spiritual writing to refer to the incarnation: God becoming flesh in a wondrous exchange (O admirabile commercium) between time and eternity, one that ends in the ultimate act of love (agape). This is the root of the term commerce. Love — even the divine love that leads to a new creation — is present in every exchange.

It is easy to see how *storge* can lead to *philia*, which is friendship. Think of your co-workers, business partners, long-term customers, and other relationships. They begin in the affections that are a normal part of commercial life but then intensify as these relationships persist. You need each other and therefore become more deeply concerned about each other. You celebrate birthdays. You cheer moments in life like weddings. You weep together over sad turns of events.

Commercial relations turn into social occasions and deepening friendships. There are dinners, drinks out, backyard parties. Social circles begin to be organized around them. They become centers of mutual learning and more benefaction. Philia extends outward from them. We all know this from experience. Commerce may not form the basis of a permanent bond but it can be its introduction and foundation, the occasion for coming together and growing together through the years.

The next form of love spoken about by Lewis is *eros*, and this meaning is well known, and the most common meaning of the term love today. It is known to create in the human mind something extraordinary and even biological. It gives the heart a lift and affects the way we see the world. Through eros, old things take on a new shape. We are inspired to imagine new possibilities. We see things in our mind that previously had not existed. Through eros there is a blossoming of the human spirit, a conviction that the world can be made new. It feels like a new dawn, and we wake every day with a sense of possibility. This is the work of eros.

Where do we find this in the world of economics? If you have ever known an entrepreneur with a dream, and you have listened to this dream and watched as it unfolded, you see the realization of eros. The entrepreneur is a lover of something he or she can see that does not yet exist, and from this comes the inspiration to take wild risks and work unfathomably hard to see that love realized. And where is this love directed? Toward the discovery and service of others' needs, because it is the consuming public that is in a position to say whether it was all worth it.

Eros in the classical world was known for its capacity to lead to the overthrow of whole kingdoms and becoming the force for the turning of history. In the world of commercial capitalism, eros becomes a source of new shopping centers, new technologies, new software applications, new fashions and style — all things that cause the material world to avoid the natural trajectory towards decline and instead give a lift to life itself. Eros is the source of progress because it inspires us to depart from what is and believe in what could be.

It is easy to wonder sometimes why it is that merchants and entrepreneurs do what they do. Why spend the time, the resources, the energy, the risking of reputation and credibility, all in the service of a goal that is statistically very unlikely to ever really result in profits? It truly is a form of beautiful insanity — precisely that kind of insanity that is the foundation of every romance. Entrepreneurs are lovers.

These forms of love are woven into the fabric of the voluntary society where exchange flourishes and creates new value, where commercial relationships lead to deep friendships and networks of mutual aid, where dreamers breathe deeply the air of freedom and imagine the possibility of creating worlds that do not yet exist and commit their lives fully to see them come to fruition.

To be sure, the market is not a path to *agape;* they do not and cannot create a connection between time and eternity, nor pave a salvific path to immortality. We should not expect them to do so; that fourth type of love requires more than the material world can offer. For this supposed failure, markets have come under fire and their displacement sought, inevitably, by politics that promises to usher in a new age of the spirit. It's a delusion that threatens to circumscribe and cut off opportunities all of us have within markets to experience dignified lives full of voluntary human connection.

Love is an affair of the heart. It extends from our fundamental right to choose. It is instantiated only through the exercise of human volition inspired by our own values. These features of love are realized not only in friendship, and not only in sexuality, but also, and in the most common and socially beneficial way, through the material world, in the ceaseless effort to grow the bounty of wealth for us all.

And so it has been for 150 millennia, from the dawn of time to our time, the longest and most cumulative story of at least three forms of love working themselves out in the course of human events, drawing us out of the state of nature and always into a future full of promise, all with the dream of a world of unbounded plenty. The story of this material rise, and the commercial relationships that give us so much of what we need and want and hope for in the future, is a story of love.

Free Enterprise Combines Self-Interest and Love

Try to imagine a frozen-over train station in Hudson, New York, at 6:00 p.m. on a Sunday night on a holiday weekend. The interns and I had hoped there would be taxis there. We were wrong. It was a bad mistake. We had a 40-mile drive to make to get to the stone house at the American Institute for Economic Research.

The weather was not cooperating. All flights had been canceled. The roads were frozen over. The thermometer registered 7 degrees Fahrenheit. This was not a night on which you wanted to leave your home for any reason.

We tried Uber. No drivers. We tried again. No drivers. We started examining the benches at the train station to see if they could be used as beds. But the heating in the train station was not good. The forecast said that the temperature overnight would fall to 30 degrees below zero. We would wake with frostbite. Hey, it would make a good story.

I tried Uber one last time. Someone picked up! The car was on its way. Be there in 15 minutes, said the app. My goodness, what a world. Uber was only legalized here about a year ago. Now it is a lifesaver.

Right on time, a man's car drove through the desolate parking lot, the tires crunching through the frozen snow. We left the station to go outside, put our bags in the trunk, and drove off, slowly and carefully because there was no point at which the tires met the road. This would be a perilous journey. We made it safely home. Seeing the warm lights shine through the windows as we drove up to the house was a beautiful sight.

The Calculus of Compassion

I'm so grateful to this nice man, this stranger who saved us, and the Uber app that made it possible. Along the way I asked about the motivation. I pointed to the money. He said that he will only make $30 but he is glad to help. That touched me, so I began to dig deeper, trying to find out what led him our way.

He said that he saw the first two requests. But he was sitting by the fire with his wife, safe from the storm. Why bundle up in such conditions? When the third request came in, he felt a pang of conscience. There are three people waiting at a desolate train station. They need help. He bundled up and set out on the frozen roads to be valuable to other people.

It's a beautiful reminder: there are human beings behind these mobile apps. Drivers can reject or accept. It's up to them. No municipal taxi was running. To come out on a night like this approaches a heroic enterprise. My initial assumption that the driver did it for the money was wrong. The money is nice but doesn't motivate heroism. There is something else going on. He wanted to be valuable to others. He wanted to help.

Here we observe an interesting example of the complications of human drive and its interaction with the economics of the material world. Might the driver have shown up without the profit motive? Maybe. But how would he have known about our plight? We used a profit-making app that was built and is maintained through a system of profits. What's more, it does in fact make sense that this driver would be compensated for his work.

Enterprise, this story shows, is moved forward through a complex set of human motivations that include the desire for money but also the desire to serve and be valuable to others. The material means to provide for ourselves and the desire to be useful to others are both crucial here, and they are not in conflict.

Greed and benevolence work together. Material acquisition and love of one's neighbor are harmonious. It's the combination of the two that makes up the driving force of economic progress.

I'm thinking of another case from the Hudson train station. There is a snack bar. The people there sell coffee, candy, muffins, and tea. I ordered a beer. The woman said they don't carry it. I asked why not. She said it's because the snack bar is run by a local charity and so they don't think serving beer is a good idea. I asked what it means for a snack bar to be run by a charity. She said it means that she doesn't get paid. She is just there to raise money by selling things to people so that all the profits (however meager) go to the charity.

Realizing this changed my whole outlook on the enterprise. But for love, compassion, dedication, commitment to the well-being of others, travelers could not get coffee and snacks. Because people are willing to commit their time without pay, it is there, not as a profit-making enterprise but as a charity, helping on both ends: tending to the needs of travelers and also raising money to help the community.

Here again we see the fusing of economics and love. It comes together without dictate, without mandate, without central direction, without a top-down command to care for others. The motivation comes from within. But here again we see on display this essential but often unrecognized motivating force: the need to be valuable to other people.

The first time I realized just how essential this is was the day I stupidly languished in jail because of an unpaid traffic violation. I felt it keenly. I was suddenly not valuable — not to anyone in my purview. It shocked me. It didn't last long, thank goodness. I could never again go a day without being grateful for the opportunity to serve others, because serving others imparts value to me. You can call this selfish if you want. I find that term unhelpful. It's all about the desire to make a difference in the world, in big and small ways.

Strangers and Love

Let's return to my driver and the mobile app that brought his services to us. He was a stranger. I had never met him. Never will again. And yet we had a beautiful experience together, all thanks to technology and enterprise.

There are political arguments about this. Is Uber putting out of business the taxis? Is it paying drivers enough? Should drivers have to submit to a great degree of regulation? Because of these questions, cities have banned Uber in many parts of the world.

Think of the human loss, the missed opportunities to bring people together for mutual benefit, the forgone chances for people to serve people. This is what enterprise is all about.

Those who do not understand this miss the whole point. Economics is not just about making money. It's also about a chance to be valuable to others, to the world, to yourself. Banking money and showing love can and do exist in a harmonious relationship. Bring them together under just the right conditions, and you feel the same inner warmth we all felt when finally arriving back home in safety, preparing to sleep well with the knowledge that thanks to free enterprise, we would wake without frostbite and our wonderful benefactor would wake knowing that he both did a good deed the night before and made just enough money to say it was materially worth his time.

3

Liberty and the Search for Meaning

Let me propose a question to you. What is the strongest objection to the idea of liberty, markets, and a self-managing society? We've been subjected to vast numbers of them recently. Which is most compelling?

Some people say the key objection is the problem of inequality. In a free society, there will always be unequal outcomes, and even unequal opportunities. Human experience eludes identification with mathematical equations. Some people can't tolerate that. They want social upheaval to end it.

Others say that markets deal insufficiently with accidents of birth. Being the product of a family with assets in a beautiful, peaceful town, with great educational opportunities, naturally grants certain life advantages relative to those born into poverty and raised in a world of crime and ignorance. Freedom, they say, doesn't deal well with this. My problem with this idea is that no system apart from freedom has successfully dealt with it; certainly, any state-managed system only ends in exacerbating and entrenching accidents of birth.

You can multiply these objections, most completely baseless, without limit: monopoly, economic instability, public goods, greed, the poor, streets, you name it. In times when we are experiencing the beautiful productivity of markets more than ever before, we are being bombarded by unending attacks on the whole idea.

What Does It Mean?

My own opinion on the top objection to liberalism, classically understood, concerns something a bit more opaque and philosophical. People say that the idea of freedom does not do well to address the great human problem of the search for meaning. This has historically been the most politically effective critique. The opponents of liberalism have long derided the market society as pointlessly consumerist, nihilistically materialistic, and hopelessly mired in moral emptiness.

Freedom is not a system that gives our lives meaning, they say; in fact, freedom distracts us from finding meaning. Trading, working, accumulating, investment, acquiring nicer toys, getting along ever better with others, living in a better home, raising a family, carving out ever more pleasurable forms of leisure — what is the point of all this? This path of life is too linear, too predictable, too undramatic, too boring!

The two most effective assaults on bourgeois liberalism have followed this script. Karl Marx posited in the 19th century that this system was inherently reactionary because it failed to come to terms with the dialectic of history which, he said, was inexorably leading to socialism — via some huge class struggle — and eventually communism in which property, family, religion, class, wages, capital, and so on, would be rendered obsolete. His vision was compelling because it infused the passage of time with direction and purpose, whereas the market society is only about living a better life within the world as it is given to us. His solution was a mighty struggle against capital and a dictatorship of the proletariat as led by a vanguard in charge of the state apparatus so long as is necessary.

A different spin on this theme came in the 20th century with the work of Carl Schmitt, whose works are experiencing a huge academic resurgence today. It is said that he was the most effective critic of liberalism in the 20th century (and never mind that he was a Nazi). His main point is that the life of trading, peace, and prosperity is lacking in anything epically meaningful. The glorious classical virtues include bravery, being part of something giant, participating in the seismic shifts of history. None of this is possible with liberalism.

Schmitt heaped unrelenting disgust on the idea of merely getting along with others and getting more stuff. He demanded to know: what could life possibly mean under these conditions? Just getting along with others, as liberalism suggests? No, no, this approach will utterly deracinate you from your identity, whether religious, racial, sexual, linguistic, or ancestral. What you need for meaning is some sense of attachment to something larger — larger than your life and larger than your times. You need a struggle, and an agent to represent you in this struggle.

These days, most critiques of freedom from the left and the right do not achieve much more than riffing on these Marxian and Schmittian themes. Choose your critique; it all comes down to the dreariness of life under liberalism. The opponents of liberalism demand that we drop all this bourgeois nonsense about just getting along with people and instead engage the dialectic of history as real players, ushering in the new age of you name it.

Note the similarities between the same proposition for a new sense of meaning. Both insist that meaning involves something outside your own mind and experience. You cannot define it for yourself. Meaning is made operational by virtue of your attachment to the collective, which is why this critique always devolves to populist forms of political organizing. But reality also dictates that a collective cannot truly act or think; it will always be fractured into parts. The champions of collectivism decry this as social division, fracturing, a society rendered into parts. This is true on the left and right, and they see it this way because their imagined ideal society is always about groups on the move in the context of a grand struggle; this is what gives life meaning.

The Machinery of False Meaning

And what represents this great collective? For both the left and right, the answer is obvious. It is the state. Only the state has a plausible claim to represent the purposes of the collective. Both socialism and nationalism depend on this idea. Donald Trump stated the point directly: "The nation-state remains the true foundation for happiness and harmony." Alexandria Ocasio-Cortez echoes the same themes with her call for "a new national social, industrial and economic mobilization on a scale not seen since World War II and the New Deal."

Others on the religious right are pushing the same theme: Daniel McCarthy has written for *First Things* a sweeping rejection of economic liberalism and a call for it to be replaced by "refocusing on the American citizen as the basic unit of the economy. This is the essence of a nationalist political economy," failing to consider that economy itself is not about forced collectives but rather human choice. And the now-famous rant by Tucker Carlson echoes the same theme, thoroughly putting down the idea of letting society evolve on its own without decisive direction from the center.

What's behind all this is, of course, the struggle to control the direction of the monstrous, wealthy, and powerful federal government in the interest of the particular desires of intellectuals and politicians. The intellectuals and pundits who put down the idea of freedom as inherently meaningless are, unwittingly or not, feeding the politicization of society and the beast that benefits from collectivist ideology. Neither side will finally win; the struggle to control the state will never end and the rest of us will be caught in the crossfire.

Meaning within Freedom Itself

There is another school of thought that sees freedom as completely barren of meaning in itself, an empty vessel that we must fill on our own. I see the point here, but it seems to disparage the meaningful component part of freedom such as individual rights, the opportunity to live a better life, the incentive and need for human cooperation, the resulting prosperity that comes from trading, the courage that it requires to be entrepreneurial in the face of an uncertain future, the opportunity to create something new. These are all meaningful things, even virtuous things, and they flow from the opportunity and energy that freedom provides. The state cannot provide a substitute.

And this is the point that the statism of meaning always overlooks: every state action, every program, every nationalized priority, every vision of what we are supposed to be doing together that depends on some form of enforcement, all comes down the same thing: the imposition of violence. There is no true access to genuine meaning at the point of a gun; meaning is replaced by fear and compliance.

The kernel of truth in the idea that freedom is an empty vessel is this: meaning is individual. It flows from the individual heart, mind, and soul. That does not mean it is disconnected from others. Our communities do indeed have the most profound impact on our perceptions of whether we are living good and valuable lives or live in desperate loneliness. Nonetheless, it is up to each of us to find it, interpret it, and apply it.

The Failure of Top-Down Meaning

For at least a century, we've constructed public institutions that have sought to provide a higher sense of purpose than we can find on our own. The state has invaded every area of life: education, family, culture, the production and distribution of everything. The whole machinery has let us down because the project was mistaken to begin with. It has only left carnage of broken lives, shattered dreams, dependency relationships with bureaucracies, a pathetic but credentialed ignorance, and a loss of sense of personal responsibility. Rather than abandoning the idea that we can find meaning through the state, many citizens have entered into a cycle of abuse, inexorably drawn to whatever nostrums are being sold by the left or right. Others have taken a different route of forging their own paths, and hence the wild popularity of Jordan Peterson.

Let's finally turn to Victor Frankl, the author of what might be the most profound reflection on meaning ever written. The text is forged from time in a concentration camp, and therefore written from the vantage point of a failed experiment in imposing meaning via state control. He utterly rejected the idea, as should we all.

"Ultimately, man should not ask what the meaning of his life is," Frankl wrote, "but rather must recognize that it is he who is asked. In a word, each man is questioned by life; and he can only answer to life by answering for his own life; to life he can only respond by being responsible."

The search for meaning must begin with the individual human mind; it becomes operational through individual volition and voluntary cooperation with others, which is to say, through freedom. No substitute is possible.

4

What Self-Ownership
Means and Why It Matters

I've been thinking about this idea of self-ownership, a concept almost universally assumed to be a foundation for human rights and the civilized life. At the same, this idea is constantly threatened by political ideologies that presume it not to be true.

Here is what got me thinking.

In the final episode of season two of *The Americans*, Elizabeth Jennings, a Soviet spy in America during the Cold War, is given a message from her Moscow-based handlers. The KGB expects that her teenage daughter Paige — who believes that her mother is a humble travel agent — will also become a spy. This is her destiny.

The mother profoundly objects. Elizabeth explains that she chose this life based on her commitment to communist ideals. Her daughter ought also be permitted to exercise such a choice. It strikes Mom, even though she is a committed communist, that denying her daughter volition over her life destiny would be inhumane and even ghastly.

Her Moscow handler disagrees. Her message: "We don't belong to ourselves; we belong to the world." Of course the "world" needs an institution to mediate the meaning of such audacious belongingness. That is the Communist Party. The vanguard of the dictatorship of the proletariat is the party elite, who are chosen by the workers and peasants to lead the way in ushering in a new world without capitalism.

All of which is to say that her daughter, now only 15 years old, has no choice about it. She will be trained to be a Soviet agent in America, just like her mother. It is up to Elizabeth to facilitate the transition as the child gets older. That is to say, Paige must be convinced to make the right "choice." Doing the convincing is a test of loyalty and ideological commitment. You must be willing to give up your own child, because there is a sense in which nothing is yours. Everything belongs to the world, which is to say the Soviets.

The Core Moral Issue

The Americans is a seemingly endless show with fully six seasons — a total of nearly 75 hours of watching! In what I've seen so far — the brutal assassinations, the betrayals, the struggles over loyalty, the political machinations — the drama over the fate of the daughter is the most emotionally gripping. She is being denied the essential idea of self-ownership, which is to say that she is born a slave to the communist cause and the state that embodies that cause.

It's deeply painful. It gives rise to profound reflection on how much we take self-ownership for granted. Communism in practice has to deny it. Many other political ideologies share that view. Racial nationalism demands that your biology determines your tribal loyalties. Religious nationalism insists that the belief structure in which you are born determines your life destiny. Geographic nationalism says your first loyalties are bound up with citizenship.

At the same time, in the modern age, we've come to believe a different idea. The French historian Ernst Renan explained the contrary position in 1882: "No one has the right to go through the world fingering people's skulls, and taking them by the throat saying: 'You are of our blood; you belong to us!'"

So too for familial loyalty. An essential component of the liberal idea is that as a child matures, he or she gains the capacity for making choices over life destiny. The job of a parent, as the custodian and caretaker of the child, is to prepare that child to make grown-up choices when the time comes. They must be real choices: over marriage, job, living arrangements, religion, and so on. Parents can and do influence, but with maturity comes this essential human right even when it takes place in defiance of familial and community expectations.

John Locke

I would say that most of us assume self-ownership to be self-evident. As a concept, however, it seems very much tied to the liberal tradition. This is for a reason. It was denied in the ancient world, where one's birth and social standing were fixed. Only with the birth of modernity and the rise of social mobility in the late Middle Ages did we gain social consciousness of the notion that each of us should be able to choose our life path, that we are owners of our own bodies as much as our minds and hearts.

John Locke's Second Treatise on Government makes an elaborate argument concerning private property, and you can agree or disagree with his analysis here. What matters is that this argument begins with a statement he finds self-evident. "Every man has a property in his own person: this nobody has any right to but himself."

When does this happen? It is an embedded part of human life, and one begins to exercise it upon maturity. Children's "parents have a sort of rule and jurisdiction over them, when they come into the world, and for some time after," writes Locke. "But it is but a temporary one. The bonds of this subjection are like the swaddling clothes they are wrapt up in, and supported by, in the weakness of their infancy: age and reason as they grow up, loosen them, till at length they drop quite off, and leave a man at his own free disposal."

You don't have to rely on Locke to believe it. Marcus Aurelius presumes it when he implores man to preserve that "spirit which is within him, from all manner of contumelies and injuries," and "wholly to depend from himself and his own proper actions." Jesus presumes it when he implores his followers to leave their parents and communities and follow him. The Declaration of Independence postulates that every person has a right to life and liberty. And so on. There is a sense in which every philosophical outlook that focuses on what a person should believe and do presumes that the juridical center of control is located with the individual.

Do We Believe It Really?

Obviously the communist overlord in The Americans disagrees with this theory, and the result is the most morally alarming part of the show. And yet, think about many features of regular life today. Think of times when it suddenly struck you that you are not really being treated as if you own yourself.

I feel it when I'm stopped by the police for some traffic violation. Even if the policeman is nice, even if there was a good reason to stop me, I'm profoundly aware of my lack of choice when he or she is standing outside the driver's side window and demanding documentation. I must have my papers in order. I must answer with the right words. I must not make any sudden or strange movements. If I do the wrong thing, I could be arrested and caged or even shot. In the blink of an eye, I'm no longer a self-owner; the police officer owns me.

I've also been feeling this recently when traveling internationally. There have been big changes in how one is treated at the border. It's been normal for at least 100 years that you can't just walk into another country without a checkpoint; I get that. But more recently, it's become more difficult even to leave one's own country. I've three times faced an exit facial scan when leaving the U.S., with the implied threat that if I don't pass, I would become a prisoner in my own nation-state.

I faced a strange situation when recently leaving Bermuda to return to the U.S. After you go through security, you enter into U.S. territory, controlled entirely by U.S. border police and the Transportation Security Administration. I was going through the passport check and they took my passport. You cannot object. I was put in a holding room and not allowed to leave or ask questions. After 45 minutes, they called my name, gave me back my passport, and I was waved on.

You might say that this is no big deal, but it was actually very alarming. There were mediators standing between me and my ability to get home — that is, to use a ticket for a plane for which I had paid. My right to travel hung in the balance. I never found out why they had detained me. They are under no legal obligation to say. Protesting that I own myself would only end badly, I presume. In fact, in that situation, I had no rights.

Act on What We Believe

The notion of self-ownership is bound up with modernity's understanding of what liberty is all about. The idea of slavery, which for thousands of years was believed to be essential to social order, we now rightly find morally disgusting. No person can presume without consent to possess the right to control the body and choices of another person, thus denying him or her the volition that lies at the core of what makes us human.

And yet we are terrible practitioners of the idea of self-ownership. We have built huge states in almost every country that exist and grow based on denying it. They necessarily must. Any ideology that proposes to support and expand the state implicitly denies it too. That is true whether the ideology is communism, socialism, nationalism, or any other ism that proposes to submerge individual rights to the higher claims of the political community.

They try to inspire us to give up what is ours, in the name of living according to higher ideals, being part of something larger than ourselves, submitting to the demands of the community. Some people want to do that. It should be their choice to do so. It should also be their choice to decline.

It's not that we as a humane culture reject the idea of self-ownership. It's that we don't take it very seriously in our politics. Everyone believes it; no political system practices it. We should. But if we do, prepare for dramatic structural changes in the composition of our political communities. You will have to get used to the idea of being free.

5

If You Love Progress, Embrace Markets

At some point in the 1990s, my father said he wanted to Xerox something. I recall being a little perplexed. It was the word used by several generations, from the mid-1960s and onward, for what was later called simply photocopying. This great company somehow managed to unite the brand with the technology itself, and gain the full monopoly over a verb. That's marketing genius right there.

And like all great marketing, it was backed by something real. The Xerox machine, however huge and expensive, represented a massive upgrade over what came before. That would be the Spirit Duplicator, sometimes confused with the mimeograph. One of my earliest memories was of this machine, which we called the "Ditto Machine." It used a messy, smelly purple ink to roll out copies from a stencil. This was public school, and the place was using this machine long past its prime.

By 1960, a new technology was made available to high-end offices that could afford it. Instead of ink, it used photography, or what was branded xerography. The word from the Greek roots means dry printing; no more wet stinky chemicals. The show Mad Men features a scene where office employees gain their first experience with a Xerox 914. It weighed 648 pounds and took up vast space. It made one copy every 26 seconds. But it was amazing. It was the new center of the office. And it was constantly breaking and in need of service — just like the machine in your office today.

Even then, the xerox machine lived side-by-side with typewriters and carbon paper, which remained the cheapest way to make a copy. I can recall even from typing class using this. One wrong key stroke and you had to start over. So, yes, Xerox was an amazing thing to behold and the company earned its dominant position.

But in a vibrant market for technology, in which no one person or institution knows what's next and so no one institution can maintain dominance forever, Xerox lost the race with the personal computer. Its first model was marketed at $16,000 in 1981 — a price way out of line with what was already developing in the industry. Xerox was never able to gain traction.

And now finally the moment has arrived. Xerox has sold what remains of its company to FujiFilm, thus turning the verb into a piece of history. In a world of Google Docs, endless forms of cloud computing, distributed networks, infinite forms of text-based communications, not to mention a thousand companies begging for customers with their audio and video technologies as well as print-on-demand books that require no more inventory, there is just no more place for a print-based monopoly.

This is just the latest step in a long trajectory of improved publishing technology that dates to the 3rd century. Wikipedia publishes an extremely helpful (and instantly accessible) timeline. It begins with the use of the woodblock in 200AD. Those remained in use throughout Europe, along with huge teams of scribes who worked in monasteries to make copies on parchment and vellum. Within the walls of the scriptorum, there was more value than in all the castles, simply because the books contained the most valuable thing: human knowledge.

Knowledge has always and everywhere been more valuable than power. When you look at the history of printing technology, you see the relentless march of progress, seemingly unencumbered by leaders, regimes, kings, and wars. Technology has proven to be the indefatigable thing because it lives mainly as ideas that belong to no one person or sector in society. The tendency is for the ideas behind technology to spread and defy every attempt to stop them. The successes of one technology feed the innovation of others, as people emulate success and spread it ever further.

At each stage, the warning goes out: this new technology is going to ruin everything. When the printing press appeared in Europe, and created a new frenzy for book buying, the scribes who had enjoyed the highest scholarly and intellectual status worried for their future. Some monasteries banned printers. Scientists warned of the spread of false information. Moralists created apocalyptic scenarios in which we no longer know what is true, we lose our memories, and our reverence for wisdom fades. Even after the invention of mass printing of books in the late 19th century, there were panics. The kids were no longer going outside. They are wasting all their time reading junk novels.

The technological panics continue to this day. Video games, texting,

Snapchat, Facebook, Twitter, smartphones themselves, are wrecking a whole generation. Streaming music and movies are making art unprofitable. The panics over piracy began 25 years ago and continue to this day. Even I have the vaguest memory of a massive controversy over video-tape technology. Surely it will ruin television as we know it.

But at every stage, technology proves impervious to attempted blockades. It is always improving in the interest of making life better for you and me and everyone. This is what the market test achieves. The market finds technologies that make life better at the least cost and rewards them, even as new and better ways displace that which came before. The result is a beautiful tapestry of invention that stretches back to the beginnings of recorded history and will continue long after our death.

As we think back on our own lifetimes, we find that the tools that we used in our daily lives have a larger impact on how we think of our lives than presidents. I remember the first time I saw a color television show. I think Nixon might have been president but it hardly matters. Maybe you remember your first look at Pac Man but whether the Republicans or Democrats controlled Congress at the time has no relevance at all.

I daily marvel at the glorious ways in which my life has changed. I have a vision of myself as a young boy scouring the LP section of the grocery store, looking for the latest recording of Brahms string quartets or vibrating with excitement over the latest Elton John album. I can today conjure all that music up with a few words directed at my Google Home, who seems to provide me with unrelenting, unconditional love. What happened to my huge speakers, my stacks of components, my walls of albums and CDs? It all went away.

People in office places of the early 1960s probably never imagined a time when the Xerox machine would be seen as a museum piece, or a time when the very word Xerox itself would carry no cultural currency at all. Despite all this nonstop progress, we are all still habituated to believe that whatever technology we are using today is about as good as it gets.

The most exciting innovation in the world today is a brilliant successor to the need to record, document, and spread innovation. It is the distributed network that eliminates the need for a central authority and provides a means of porting immutable information packets that cannot be censored or tampered with at all. Who is going to benefit from this? Absolutely everyone.

Let me pass on an example that hit my email yesterday. It is from Mother Cecilia of the Benedictines of Mary, Queen of Apostles in Missouri. The sisters are building a new church, and they are behind on fundraising. Out of nowhere, they received a $160,000 donation in Bitcoin. They still have a long way to go on their fundraising. But the sisters are new fans of the newest technology available today!

People talk often of how technology is disruptive. That's only part of the story. Technology also serves the oldest values and the most ancient aspirations of the human experience, and does so in a way that is organically peaceful with how we live. It's the much-maligned market economy that makes it all possible, and does so without elections, speeches, legislation, and scary leaders we don't like. We should love markets more than we do. Their proven benevolence forms a beautiful narrative history of our lives, connects the generations, and points to a bright future.

6

Society Does Not Need Unity

A fundamental historical and economic fallacy is back in a big way. The claim is that society needs homogeneity to be orderly, just, and free. It is a core claim of the alt-right and its sympathizers, and, in a different way, of the left too. It's too easy to dismiss this claim as a political tactic. What's at issue is the structure of society itself.

Conformism is the watchword. Everyone is in the mood to cast out the dissenters, drive out the other, coerce our way toward unity, in the name of creating "high trust" or "social justice," depending on your ideological orientation. The absence of unity is what leads the right to reject freedom as a path forward and embrace state control of demographics, and the left to condemn "hate" speech and un-PC utterances as a threat to decency and equality on earth.

This longing for some kind of unity is not only completely wrong; it is highly dangerous. If you have ever been confronted with this claim, I'm writing this article for you.

Freedom and Diversity

Here's an anecdote from my past. Before his death, the now-famous "social nationalist" writer and theorist, and self-proclaimed fascist, Samuel Francis and I were talking at some luncheon. I was prattling on about liberty as usual. And he interrupted me and said (paraphrasing): "Human rights and liberty are slogans we use. Much more fundamental is demographics. You have to have homogeneity for society to be orderly and operate properly. Without that, you can forget about rights and liberties."

I said nothing because I hadn't really thought much about that. Was this right? I didn't hear such claims in college. People who talk like this are politically incorrect. This thinking leads to forbidden thoughts and tends toward the celebration of civic sins like racism, sexism, and xenophobia. So I had never really come to terms with it. I hadn't had to. But that also meant that I was caught off guard, intellectually unprepared to refute him or even know if it needed to be refuted.

And now we see the left saying basically the same thing as Francis said but with a different application. We need to have unity of values. There are words you must not say, thoughts you must not think, people you must not caricature, things you must believe and not believe, jokes you must not tell, and, implausibly, you must never ever appropriate someone else's culture because that would be like stealing (though every other form of stealing should be public policy). If a major writer or media commentator slips up slightly, the Twitter mob pounces hard and bombards the person with expressions of disgust. If they make enough noise, they can sometimes get the offending party fired for failing to conform.

Here is a counterclaim. Liberty and justice are not the outgrowth of homogeneity. Liberty is the solution to a seeming problem of heterogeneity, while justice is merely the realization of equal freedom. Liberty creates institutions like commercial settings, opportunities for trade and exchange, and settings for mutually beneficial trade and learning. It is precisely how liberty reconciles differences among people and creates wealth out of disagreement. That is the very source of its great magic.

This is not just my claim. It is literally the first great discovery of modernity and the core reason for the development of the liberal tradition. That society in all its inevitable and intractable diversity contains within itself the capacity for self-management is the foundational claim of freedom and the single most persistent theme of the liberal tradition. That both left and right have abandoned it is not a surprise. It is, however, disappointing that such a foundational point would be so forgotten.

Religious Toleration

Think back to the end of the religious wars. Enlightenment thinkers proposed that the solution to religious difference is not the burning of heretics and the imposition of an official creed. It was to allow people to believe whatever they wanted so long as they didn't hurt others. The system worked.

How many other ways would this idea of freedom work? Gradually, it came to be rolled out to affect speech, the press, and trade. Eventually it led to broad emancipation of slaves, and women, and everyone else. It created a new world, in which the power of the state was restrained and contained, and dismantled the old world of imposed hierarchy. The watchwords were tolerance and diversity. The rights that came to be enunciated were the right to own, associate, trade, and create.

But it took centuries to come to pass. Even following the Industrial Revolution, controversies over how much toleration society should exercise roiled European politics.

In 1790, Charles James Fox, the paragon of early 18th-century English liberalism, rose in Parliament to defend the rights of religious minorities. He referenced England's long history of burning heretics for daring to dissent from the existing religious opinion of the Crown, whatever the opinion happened to be. When he spoke, the Catholic Church was suppressed by law. He rose to speak in defense of the right of conscience:

> We should perceive no vice, evil, or detriment, had ever sprung from toleration. Persecution had always been a fertile source of much evil; perfidy, cruelty, and murder, had often been the consequence of intolerant principles.... It proceeded entirely on this grand fundamental error, that one man could better judge of the religious opinion of another than the man himself could. Upon this absurd principle, persecution might be consistent; but in this it resembled madness: the characteristic of which was acting consistently upon wrong principles.... Torture and death had been the auxiliaries of persecution; the grand engines used in support of one particular system of religious opinion, to the extermination of every other.

Eventually, his views won out. Even today, Fox's speech — which set the standard for liberal opinion — stands out as a great tribute to the great truth that society does not require unity even on such an important topic as religion. His point applies across the board, not only to religion but also to race, language, class, creed, and every other margin along which people want to slice and dice the human community.

From Fox to Mises

Gradually, over the following century and a half, and especially following the brutality of regimes that practiced identity politics of the left and right, the principle came into clearer focus. In 1927, Ludwig von Mises summarized it as follows:

> Liberalism demands tolerance as a matter of principle, not from opportunism. It demands toleration even of obviously nonsensical teachings, absurd forms of heterodoxy, and childishly silly superstitions. It

demands toleration for doctrines and opinions that it deems detrimental and ruinous to society and even for movements that it indefatigably combats. For what impels liberalism to demand and accord toleration is not consideration for the content of the doctrine to be tolerated, but the knowledge that only tolerance can create and preserve the condition of social peace without which humanity must relapse into the barbarism and penury of centuries long past.

In his postwar writing from 1957, he broadened the insight. Toleration is the essence of the liberal spirit because it is right and it works:

Those whom we may call the harmonists base their argument on Ricardo's law of association and on Malthus' principle of population. They do not, as some of their critics believe, assume that all men are biologically equal. They take fully into account the fact that there are innate biological differences among various groups of men as well as among individuals belonging to the same group. Ricardo's law has shown that cooperation under the principle of the division of labor is favorable to all participants. It is an advantage for every man to cooperate with other men, even if these others are in every respect — mental and bodily capacities and skills, diligence and moral worth — inferior.

Further:

In the philosophy of the antiharmonists, the various schools of nationalism and racism, two different lines of reasoning must be distinguished. One is the doctrine of the irreconcilable antagonism prevailing among various groups, such as nations or races.... The second dogma of the nationalist and racist philosophies is considered by its supporters a logical conclusion derived from their first dogma. As they see it, human conditions involve forever irreconcilable conflicts, first among the various groups fighting one another, later, after the final victory of the master group, between the latter and the enslaved rest of mankind. Hence this supreme elite group must always be ready to fight, first to crush the rival groups, then to quell rebellions of the slaves. The state of perpetual preparedness for war enjoins upon it the necessity of organizing society after the pattern of an army.

Mill and Eccentricity

Liberalism has long distinguished itself for being the champion of difference — and the right of individuals to be different. John Stuart Mill said that it is the eccentric, not the conformist, who moves society forward:

> In this age, the mere example of nonconformity, the mere refusal to bend the knee to custom, is itself a service. Precisely because the tyranny of opinion is such as to make eccentricity a reproach, it is desirable, in order to break through that tyranny, that people should be eccentric. Eccentricity has always abounded when and where strength of character has abounded; and the amount of eccentricity in a society has generally been proportional to the amount of genius, mental vigour, and moral courage which it contained. That so few now dare to be eccentric, marks the chief danger of the time.

You don't have to know this history of thought or the liberal theory as articulated by Fox, Mises, and Mill. Visit the bustling commercial district of any major American city and observe the crazy quilt of ethnicity, language, religion, race, and culture, where people are around buying, selling, and associating according to their own lights. Why is there not chaos? Why is there coexistence? Because the presence of commercial freedom allows everyone to pursue his or her own self-interest in a way that also benefits others.

Here is the beauty of the invisible hand at work.

The claim that liberty is preconditioned on the sameness of the population is to wish away the very problem that liberty is much adept at solving. After all, what is the problem that social thinkers are trying to solve? They seek to provide a setting in which people thrive as individuals even as the entire group is granted an opportunity for a better life. Differences among people are solved by freedom. This was an insight that changed the world for the better.

In fact, if you have a small tribe of the same race, language, religion, and cultural norms, the question of liberty does not have to be raised at all. Group coordination happens because of personal knowledge, verbal communication, and shared expectations of others' similar needs, and it usually features a single leader. The trouble is that a homogeneous and isolated tribal unit managed from the top will always be poor — mostly living hand to mouth, as small tribes in the Amazon do today — because the tribal model doesn't permit the expansion of the division of labor. It can work under some rarified conditions. But for the most part, life under imposed homogeneity eventually defaults to what Thomas Hobbes said of the state of nature: nasty, brutish, and short.

The Drive to Integrate

Liberty, on the other hand, rewards ever more integration of people of all kinds. It becomes profitable for everyone to do so. You are free to feel bigotry, racism, and loathing of all other religious views, different lifestyles, and so on. But when it comes to improving your life, you prefer dealing with the Jewish doctor to having a heart attack, grabbing lunch at the Moroccan restaurant, hiring the Mexican immigrant to tile your bathroom, listening to your favorite African-American pop band, and so on. And guess what? Gradually under these conditions, the primitive and tribalist ethos begins to subside.

This is precisely why any regime that seeks to enforce homogeneity must necessarily turn against the market and toward force. Recall that the Nazi Party at first only encouraged peaceful boycotts of Jewish businesses, protest signs in front of stores, and so on, and laid out explicit instructions that no one be hurt. That didn't work. The Nuremberg Laws were desperate measures to address the "problem" that the market wouldn't work to exclude people.

There is another insight that makes the whole claim about homogeneity a bit silly. As it turns out, no one is the same. And you know this. Think of a friend who shares your religion, race, language, and sex, but has different values. There is always the possibility for conflict because no two people are alike. Your friendships survive despite this because you value your friendships more than being enemies. Expand that model to the whole of the social order and you begin to understand how and why differences lead not to conflict, disorder, and acrimony but rather to friendship, prosperity, and enlightenment.

All this talk of doing away with diversity is a shibboleth. There is no pure race, no truly orthodox religion, no one language without variation, no final unity between any two people in thought, word, or deed. No one acts or thinks as a group or collective. There is no collective credit and no collective guilt. The social world will be, always and forever, a constellation of difference. We need the best possible social system for dealing with and making something beautiful come of it. Seeking unity would now achieve what it always has achieved: destruction and the enslavement or removal of some people and the emergence of a despotic class of rulers selected from among the winners of the great struggle.

The New Realization

To understand the awesome power of heterogeneity is to adopt a different outlook on society itself. It is to embrace the core liberal claim: society doesn't need top-down management, because it contains within itself the capacity for its own management. You come to be enraptured by Frédéric Bastiat's emphasis on harmony as the means by which we live better lives.

In contrast, the mental posture that homogeneity is a necessary condition leads to a series of strange obsessions over unending conflicts in society. You begin to exaggerate them in your mind. It seems like you are surrounded by a plethora of intractable wars. There is a war between blacks and whites, men and women, gays and straights, Christianity and Islam, the abled and disabled, our nation and their nation, and so on. This is the very mindset that the left and right have in common.

And guess what? If you build a large state, these conflicts do indeed appear to be more real than they are, simply because the state pits people against each other. You begin to hate that group because its members didn't vote for your candidate, it gets more of the tax loot, it favors various forms of imposition on your liberty. Thanks to this interventionist state, you feel as if you are surrounded by enemies and lose track of the possibility for human understanding.

Freedom and Difference

Let's return to the original claim by Mr. Francis, now widely shared and promoted by the alt-right and its sympathizers. It turns out that this is nothing new. The opponents of liberty have been barking up this tree for some 200 years, just as the left has done since Marx first fused Hegel with materialist socialist theory. While these people think in terms of homogeneous collectives, liberalism advanced the idea of individual rights and the capacity of people to organize themselves despite diversity, learning to gain value from each other through trade.

"You have to have homogeneity for society to be orderly and operate properly," Francis said. This claim amounts to a rejection of liberalism itself. So let's correct this. You have to have liberty to deal with the inescapable reality of heterogeneity. It's the longing for sameness that leads to conflict, despotism, and impoverished human lives.

7

Power and the Main
Threat to Liberty

W illiam Gillis's review of my last book Right-Wing Collectivism is complimentary but critical on many points and mainly on one central point to which he continually returns. He believes that my focus on state power has blinded me to other forms of power, and therefore to the urgency of a more comprehensive anarchism.

"If the book as a whole were a little stronger Right-Wing Collectivism would have stood as a wonderful counterbalance to the focuses of leftist antifascists," he writes. Instead, he says: "Tucker's focus on the state creates its own kind of myopia. If the left fails to really grapple with how anti-market fascism ultimately is, Tucker fails to really grapple with the problem of nationalism outside of formal statist contexts."

And it's not just nationalism, in the author's view; my supposed myopia extends to a huge range of social power: corporate, familial, gender, religion, and so on. I neglect these and therefore default back to anti-statism and therefore market economics as the solution to all life problems.

Stirner vs. Rothbard

This is why he regrets my literary rally for liberalism (classically understood) as an alternative to fascism. The only alternative is anarchism, in his view, which he sees as a comprehensive and complete opposition to all forms of power, not just state power, on grounds that power always diminishes the human person's full potential, attacks core rights, and blunts the capacity for humanity to rise to new levels of universal fulfillment.

You can gather from this statement that my critic's view of anarchism is of a different school from mine, more Max Stirner than Albert Jay Nock, more

Mikhail Bakunin than Murray Rothbard. In more colloquial terms, Gillis is the very archetype of the left anarchism whereas he would regard me (and I disagree) as a rightist, which is why he wrote such a detailed critique.

Let me concede a point here: it is possible for libertarians to oversimplify social and political dynamics into a clean binary of the state vs. the individual, as if to suggest that there is only one problematic form of power and no other. Being steeped in libertarian literature, you can come away with this impression. But actually, it's not the case that any major thinker in this tradition (not even Rothbard) ever wrote anything like: "The only power in this world that should concern us as human beings is state power." I've searched writings of hundreds of years and failed to find a statement like this. The focus on the state in this line of thinking is limited to political thought: here the libertarian concern is to reduce the state to the point of elimination if technically possible. Still, with a single-minded focus on the evil of state power — my book is probably an example — a broader rendering of the anti-statist perspective is common, as if the libertarian mind ought not concern itself with any other injustice.

I'm pretty sure that at some point in my own intellectual development, I fell into this tendency. It is unsubtle and, ultimately, unsustainable in light of real human experience. The state is always the main enemy of course but this is because it is the ultimate institutionalization, entrenchment, and monopolization of power as a means of human control. It is the main enemy because it is the single worst expression of the fundamental evil, which is power itself. (I'm going to avoid plunging into the pit of a pedantic discussion of definitions of power, exploitation, and aggression, because — how to put this? — it's too boring and such discussions never really solve anything.)

Forms of Power

At the same time, it's true that power can take other forms. There are bad, even horrible, bosses. There are abusive parents. There are manipulative and psychologically violent preachers of religious doctrine. There are terrible relationships in which one spouse lords it over another. These abuses can be instantiated in cultural habits, institutionalized in cultural values, practiced as an extension of widely accepted religious postulates, and so on. Indeed, there's so much trouble in the world, as Bob Marley said. There is nothing "unlibertarian" about conceding this and fighting against all bad things in the name of the emancipation of the human spirit.

Libertarians should not feel a threat to their worldview by granting all of this. It's also true that problematic kinds of power are not limited to coercive forms; there are many ways to control others and ruin their lives. Would you rather have a planter stolen off your porch or be unjustly smeared all over the internet as a pedophile? The former path involves coercion against your ownership rights; the latter path, though purely voluntary, represents the destruction of all your hopes and dreams about the only life you have.

And why is it not a problem for liberalism to recognize this? It is the goal of liberalism to diminish human suffering and increase opportunities for happiness, a condition which is linked to the right to choose, act, speak, and live in peace. There are many threats to that end, not all of which are brought about by the state. I like the formulation of F.A. Hayek: what we favor is a society of peace in which violence and the threat of violence is minimized as much as possible. That's as good a summary of liberal ambition as any I've heard (it's better than question-begging formulations that fit on laptop stickers).

Anarchism In All Things?

It is a concern for these factors that leads William Gillis to declare: "It is not enough just to free the market from the state, we must work to ensure that values of cosmopolitanism and compassion dominate the whole of humanity.... The state is bad, but it is only the apex predator in a vast ecosystem of power dynamics in our society."

My problem with the comprehensive anarchism of this variety is that it can be even more unsubtle and reckless than a reductionist and brutalist view of liberty. The brutalist ignores the general problem of man's inhumanity to man, as well as the liberal ethos of commercial life, to think only on one specific instance, namely state power over the individual will to act, while the Stirnerite view is so promiscuous in its critique of power relationships that it loses all practical meaning, and, even more dangerously, prepares the ground for the political demand to seek redress in ways that actually enhance state power at the expense of practical liberty.

If every form of human relationship is masking some form of exploitation, you can be tempted by the illiberal conviction that nothing works, nothing is beautiful, no kinds of human relationships are truly mutually beneficial. Society cannot manage itself. All hierarchies, all disparities in authority, all fundamental inequalities that persist over time cry out to be ended. And if so, we face a much bigger problem than merely keeping the state in its place. We need radical social reconstruction. The only real fix, in this case, is to deploy massive force in the form of state power — even if you imagine that you will eventually reduce and eliminate the state power (and this dream, no surprise, turns out to be unrealizable in practice).

The Problem of Bosses

A solid example concerns the relationship between the employer and the employee. An anarchism of the sort imagined by my critic would have all labor-related contracts based on equal power, such that no one is begging for a job or holding onto a job due to lack of other options. The entire world should operate like the most ideal peer-to-peer structure, so that hierarchies are flattened and everyone is equal.

To be sure, I wrote an entire book on the peer-to-peer economy that celebrated the possibility of radical disintermediation. Perhaps this is where we are headed technologically. At the same time, we need to keep in mind that the primary problem of mediation within current economic structures is due to force, namely the cartelization of banking, securities regulation, and the need to establish trust relationships that facilitate trade. To the extent such intermediating emerges from voluntary choice, they deserve defense, not condemnation. And, sorry, this is true even when voluntary choices involve "hierarchies," "authorities," and so on.

The problem of the bad boss is an example of an instance of exploitation that seems to be baked into the institutional relationship of capital and labor but which might actually trace to state intervention that grants employers disproportionate power over workers. Health insurance and mandated benefits are a great example. They were legislatively established in the name of workers' rights but what they actually do is create worker dependencies.

Many people today report that they would gladly leave their jobs and get work elsewhere, but they fear the loss of health care. Employers today know this and think of themselves holding this reality over workers' heads. This leads workers to put up with bad working conditions, humiliating relationships, and lower salaries than they should. This is the reality within our unfree labor markets. What began as programs to empower workers have actually done the opposite — a typical instance of a government intervention that realizes the opposite of its stated purpose.

Many Depredations of the State

This entire analysis requires a clear-headed focus on the remarkable poison that the state introduces into human relationships. A superficial look would say with the Marxian tradition that bosses are inherently exploitative. A deeper look shows that the exploitation is due not to the labor contract as such — the labor contract in a free market should be as mutually rewarding as any other exchange — but to government programs that mandate terms and conditions that the market itself would not likely include. The same kind of critique can be made of all kinds of "corporate power." Regulatory interventions in financial markets, industrial structure, intellectual property, and confiscatory taxation all conspire to reduce competition and infuse incumbent market players with privilege they would not otherwise enjoy.

An anti-statist libertarianism is uniquely prepared to see these factors, whereas a promiscuous anarchist is so quick merely to condemn all instances of power that the underlying causes and effects evaporate from consciousness, and, over time, prepare the way for too great a tolerance for state intervention. Consider the case of John Stuart Mill, whose libertarianism was solid until he introduced a generalized principle against all "harm," regardless of whether this harm was an actual physical imposition against person and property. This harm principle prepared the way for his eventual warming up to socialist policies, flipping his early allegiance to liberalism in favor of its opposite.

We've seen this same tendency occurring within libertarian circles in the last ten years. As the alt-right rose within its ranks (or invaded them, depending on your of view), the mirror image of the brutalist outlook has come to be called the "libertarian left," which is distinguished by the same vagaries that led to the apostasy of John Stuart Mill. And this is precisely why traditional liberalism has been so focussed not on perfecting the world, and inveighing against all known injustice, but rather observing, containing, and restraining the biggest known problem of all, which is the state itself.

Tradeoff Between Society and State

To erect a wall between society and the state occupied the energies of liberals from the high Middle Ages through modern times. This is why Albert Jay Nock called his book "Our Enemy, the State." To contain it is a gigantic job, to say the least. This agenda led to the Magna Carta, the Bill of Rights, the principles of religious freedom, free speech, women's rights, the anti-slavery cause, trial by jury, international law, and so on. These are hard-won victories. To muddle the liberal idea with a generalized opposition to "a vast ecosystem of power dynamics" is to evade the most obvious and destructive enemy of all and, ultimately, to endanger the institutional foundation of the realizable free society itself.

"The state is just one expression of power," says my critic, to which I answer that it is the most institutionalized, most monopolized, most destructive, most murderous, most capable of committing terrible crimes on its own but also covering up and backing so many other forms of power in society. That is why it is the focus of our energies. If we fail to focus, we create other problems.

Try to end "corporate power," the "patriarchy," psychological abuse, and all existing "harm" that you perceive in society and you could end up building the power and authority of the most harmful institution of all.

Cosmopolitanism

Permit me a final departure on the topic of cosmopolitanism, which my critic makes part of his credo. I understand why. A point shared among fascists of all stripes is that the natural state of human society is tribal segregation. They believe political structures should affirm and back this impulse. But the historical trajectory of the marketplace has been different. It has brought together people in commercial exchange regardless of race, religion, language, and geography. And this is the very origin of large cities in the world, the integration of peoples and the reduction of tribal loyalties, much to the chagrin of fascists and nationalists of all sorts. No amount of moral cajoling is going to prevent people from trading for their mutual betterment, which is why the fascists ultimately default to state power to achieve their tribalist aims.

Cosmopolitanism does indeed describe the ethos of the marketplace, which is precisely why Ludwig von Mises invoked the term in his 1929 book *Liberalism*. My concern here: the word works as a descriptor but not as a moral imperative. I see no reason to look down on people who cling to rural life, prefer to be around their religious tribe, and even (shudder!) like to speak with people of their own language and race. This can come from a decent place in the human heart and doesn't necessarily reflect a fascistic political impulse. Peaceful trade does drive the world toward integration, this is true, but inner loyalties also tend toward preserving differences among people. To condemn this in whole strikes me as intolerant.

Nor do we need to overlook the complex relationship between tribe and cultural and demographic diffusion. In a free society, everyone can develop different forms of attachment: one pattern in commercial life, one pattern in domestic life, one pattern regarding faith and family. There is no real threat here to liberalism. In fact, I don't know why this should be so complicated: the rule is that anything peaceful goes. No amount of moral cajoling will succeed in forcing people to give up attachments of the human heart. The consistent defender of freedom needs to have the wherewithal to stand up for the rights of all forms of peaceful preference, even that which contradicts his or her preferred aesthetic.

Perfectionism

Liberalism (and there is a liberal anarchism, and I consider myself to be an adherent) does not seek a perfect society but merely an adaptable one that can improve on the margin through experimentation and evolution in the right direction. Until the state is contained and out of the way, society cannot evolve, which is another reason to prioritize and focus.

Franz Oppenheimer, Albert Jay Nock, and Frank Chodorov postulated a trade off between state power and social power — and by "social power" they meant not exploitation but rather that the locus of decision making should rest with voluntary institutions outside the state. Legalized plunder vs. property rights and human choice. This is the essential binary. I believe this to be true. Liberalism — whether of the classical or anarchist variety — has always affirmed this.

It used to be a cliche to observe that libertarianism is neither left nor right. I don't hear that much anymore, so it needs to be restated. Mostly it needs to be understood. Left and right emerged in the 19th century as a revolt against liberalism. They each favored different forms of statism to push back against the progress liberty was making possible. It remains the same today.

The beauty of the liberal program is that it seeks to protect society against socialism and fascism, war and segregation, poverty and apartheid, cartelization and stagnation, and therefore to establish the best chance for the flourishing of the good life on earth.

Given all the threats we face today, from the left and right, the focus on opposing statism of all sorts holds out the best hope of protecting human rights and liberties against the main and primary threat, today and always, and thereby creating the best possible social template for the realization of the dreams we share for universal peace and prosperity.

8

To Lift Your Spirits, Fill Your
Head with Economics

Have you been feeling down? Here's my suggestion. Throw yourself into economics: news, theory, podcasts, articles, anything. It's an enormous source of joy.

Here's my thinking.

It's been a grueling political season. Yes, there's probably never been a time when that sentence wasn't true. But it seems like these times are worse, simply because the President's opinions are so frequent, frenetic, and fickle, and everyone responds in kind. It's a huge industry that lives off your attention span, your sense of civic obligation, and the perception that really important things are happening.

It's true this industry generates a kind of nonstop prattle that seems vaguely important. Get roped into this sector and you end up being buffeted this way and that by an information stream that may or may not have anything to do with the actual functioning of the world. What's more, there is literally nothing you can do about it either way, which is why political obsessions end up making people feel powerless and generally depressed.

Unplug from Politics

Fortunately, we are no longer stuck with a single news path. We have infinite websites we can go to, podcasts to download, books to read or listen on audio, movies we can watch, commentators and Twitter accounts we can follow. It takes some effort to move from one path to another. You have to change your habits and preferences. But it matters. The information that you elect to push into your brain affects your emotional outlook on the world.

Let's say you just push politics aside. What are you missing? Far less than you believe. From this year alone, I would estimate that 90% of political news

43

is not really related to anything that actually affects your life and impacts on any real decisions you need to make.

Trump's amazing call for a trade war is an example. It sounded terrifying but, as the weeks have progressed, it turns out that there have been so many exceptions and clarifications that the threat seems more like fiction than reality (at least we can hope so). Meanwhile, he now has fodder for campaign speeches for years. No one needs to check the reality because, in politics, the illusions are what matter.

Look, I'm speaking from experience here. After college, and my first job reporting from the Senate Press Gallery, I generally dropped politics out of disgust and went back to my first love of economics, technology, and the history of ideas. And so it remained for a very long time until the last few years, during which time I was drawn back in. It wasn't an entire waste: I read deeply in the history of political doctrine to find the roots of the rise of identitarianism on the left and right. I learned and shared my discoveries far and wide.

But this turn started a dangerous and addictive habit of following the ups and downs of appointments, Congressional leadership, speeches and blather from podiums, commentators on highly politicized news networks, YouTube debates, and so on. Once you start doing all of this, you are actually crowding out real information that actually matters.

Rediscover Reality

So what's the path to breaking the habit? How can you get back in touch with reality without losing track of the exciting pace of life? The answer is economics, and I would include here the business news, financial markets, and technology news (technology used to be called the "practical arts").

If economics has a defining characteristic it is that it is rooted in the existing realities of life. It reflects what Thomas Sowell calls a constrained vision of the possible. This is why Peter Boettke has emphasized (in his wonderful book) that economics is a special kind of social science. It is not unhinged. It is bound by the possible.

The beginning of economic wisdom is becoming aware of the ubiquity of scarcity, and the concomitant consciousness of human choice as the desideratum of life.

Which is to say: we cannot have it all, so there have to be systems in place that allocate, apportion, and create new wealth in order that human needs can be met. Economics is the study of how precisely that comes to happen in the world. In this way, economics is inherently disciplined and intellectually constrained. That comes as a relief in times when wild-eyed and often malicious daydreamers from the left and right are relentlessly pushing their visions for how the world should work, regardless of how it actually does work.

You don't need a book of high theory to discover how intellectually liberating economics can be. You can follow the business pages. You can watch technologies come and go. You can see companies rise and fall. You can observe nations growing richer and poorer. The subject of economics can be explored through the business news. This draws you into economic theory as the explanatory template to come to understand cause and effect in the social world.

To put it more simply, economics deals with reality as it affects everyday life. Dealing with reality has brought the discipline no shortage of grief through the years. Economists (good ones, anyway) are forever telling government officials about the actual effects of their policies.

- Restricting imports is not going to boost productivity.
- Spending above your means is dangerous because it will have to be paid for in some way, some day.
- Controlling prices creates artificial shortages and surpluses that delay market clearing.
- Regulation doesn't make products and services better or safer; it only diminishes competition and short circuits consumer control.
- Manipulating the money supply doesn't generate wealth; it distorts signaling and creates booms, busts, and inflation.

Not Dismal

All of that is bad news for politicians. But contrary to Thomas Carlyle, economics is not the dismal science. It is about the logic of wealth creation, opportunity, and a better life for all. And by the way, when Carlyle made that crack, he was speaking about how the English economists of the time believed that slavery could be abolished completely and humankind would flourish as never before. He found the very prospect to be outrageous and grim. The economists were right: the world can be liberated.

It's more than that actually. The realities of economics are a uniting force in the world. Everyone deals with them. Everyone struggles for a better life, no matter your "politics." In fact, Ludwig von Mises was searching around for a title for his book that came to be called "Human Action." It was a good choice but the title he initially preferred (but the publisher rejected) was pretty wonderful: "Mankind In Search of a Better Life."

That's it exactly!

Now, you might say that the business news is not really economics, certainly not rigorous theory. And that's right. But at least the topic is interesting and truly matters. So I've switched my news sources. I find myself listening mostly to my Google home assistant for news in the morning. I used to keep the defaults on National Public Radio because that's what smart people do, or so we are told. But then I learned: there are literally hundreds of choices about what you can listen to.

In this case, I've reset my audible news flow entirely, drawing mainly from The Economist, APM Marketplace and Morning Report, Blockchain Daily, TechCrunch, the Wall Street Journal, and so on. In web reading, I stick with these main sources, including and especially AIER. For deeper reading, few resources are as powerfully compelling at Dierdre McCloskey's trilogy on the bourgeoisie. Also, it is surprising just how compelling Adam Smith's Wealth of Nations is even today. If liberal commercial society has to have a bible, we could do far worse.

This is not to disparage other alternatives to politics. Music, religion, literature, movies, nature, the gym, and so on, these are all fabulous. But how about the tactical truth about how we actually live? Economics is lovely because it unlocks the great mysteries of the material world: why we thrive, why we experience progress, how we can build prosperity and peace, the path toward making the best out of our limited time in this world, and leave something better for the next generation. Knowing and contemplating these things is indeed a source of immense joy.

9

Liberalism Is Not
Profoundly Wretched

You might think Enlightenment liberalism, or classical liberalism, did some good for the world. It gave us political consciousness of individual rights, eroded slavery, ended religious wars, brought free trade, and encouraged humanity to embrace trade and creativity over war, violence, and authoritarianism. The story of liberalism is about universal human ennoblement.

That's my view, but hardly my own: even Karl Marx lavished praise on liberal capitalism for breaking up the old feudal order of tribe, hierarchy, and dynastic power. In fact, the most sweeping attacks on liberalism have generally come from the Hegelian right (think of The Concept of the Political by the Nazi jurist Carl Schmitt).

So it is startling to read Ryan Cooper, writing in *The Week*, who offers the world an amazing screed against a political outlook that hasn't come under fire in a long time. He writes that classical liberalism "profoundly wretched the historical record" and has "caused stupendous social carnage." He establishes this in an 800-word column filled with personal invective, selective history, and caricature while leaving out anything resembling a fair description of the idea at the core.

It's the New Thing

Why the attack? Cooper begins by observing that "conservatism" as a term doesn't have the best reputation these days. "President Trump is not exactly a good brand for people wanting to distinguish themselves as deep thinkers;" that is true enough. The meaning of the term itself — a postwar invention that has always lacked real substance — has ebbed and flowed and tumbled into absurdity, as one can easily observe by attending the annual event of the "Conservative Political Action Conference," where Trump was cheered to the rafters.

So, yes, the moniker classical liberal is being bandied about as a solid alternative. It's unfamiliar. It has a beautiful history. The idea of liberalism itself stretches back half a millennium, and is embodied in the ideals of many great thinkers over many countries — from Thomas Aquinas to Murray Rothbard and thousands of others in between. And this, Cooper theorizes, is why star intellectuals like Jordan Peterson self-identify as classical liberals (though plenty of his critics on the left call him a fascist, in complete defiance of his writings against both left and right).

Definition, Not Contradiction

And so Cooper goes on the attack. He begins with the general claim that liberalism is about "self-regulating markets," which he smacks down as absurd because "property, contracts, corporations, stock exchanges, currency, and so on — all the bedrock institutions of capitalism are underpinned and maintained by government laws, or are direct creations of government."

This is strange. The claim of liberalism is precisely that government ought to stick to maintaining such bedrock institutions and nothing else, as we learn, for example, from the Declaration of Independence. That is not a contradiction; it is a definition of what liberalism has long believed is the sole function of government: punishing force and fraud only. Moreover, he is not even correct that government creates property, contracts, currency and so on; the historical record shows precisely the opposite. But you don't even need a big book to reveal this: ask yourself in general whether, in your experience, government is more adept at securing or violating your personal property rights.

Liberalism's Crimes?

Next we come to his list of liberalism's supposed crimes: the enclosure movement, vagrancy laws, punitive workhouses, imperial crusades, violence against foreign peoples. But this is an odd list: liberalism spoke out against political violence of all sorts and including all the things he lists. It couldn't make the world a perfect place but it could improve it by beating back government (and putting up barriers to public authority) when possible. It's almost like he doesn't have Wikipedia.

But Cooper claims that when liberalism faced a choice between freedom and human life, "classical liberals tended to prioritize the former," which is a calumny since the whole point of liberalism is to favor freedom as the best foundation of life. It reveals so much about his own world view that he wants to drive a wedge between the two.

So that the reader doesn't have a chance to think about these strange claims that liberalism bears responsibility for the opposite, he immediately turns to a personal smear of liberal hero John Locke (1632-1704), observing that he invested in companies that had commercial interests in the slave trade. And it's true that more than 300 years later, we might all wish he had been more scrupulous, just as we might wish moral and spiritual perfection on the whole of human history.

But the slave trade had a grim and poisoning effect on commerce for centuries, which is precisely why liberalism opposed it so passionately. One might think that Locke would get some credit for ferociously opposing slavery a century and a half before it was finally opposed in Britain. "The natural liberty of man is to be free from any superior power on earth, and not to be under the will or legislative authority of man," he wrote, "a liberty to follow my own will in all things, where the rule prescribes not; and not to be subject to the inconstant, uncertain, unknown, arbitrary will of another man."

Sins and Contradictions

But this does raise the question: what can we say about liberal thinkers of the past who engage in inconsistent writings or actions? Let's consider Thomas Aquinas (1225-1274) for example. He had this beautiful liberal statement (especially considering the time) about the role of government. It is not designed to suppress all vices but only the "grievous" ones like "murder, theft and such like." That's a tremendous view, but it also happens to be in tension with his statements elsewhere that it is morally permissible for the Church to burn heretics.

This was the 13th century. Four hundred years later, the notion of burning heretics had fallen out of favor in most nations and eventually was seen as barbaric. The same happened with religious wars, indentured servitude, the king's divine right, slavery, women's subjection, forced segregation, mercantilism, travel restrictions, forced marriage, censorship, cruel punishments and torture, and so on. These are the triumphs of liberalism over many centuries and many countries.

(I'm going to bypass Cooper's passing claim that markets caused the Great Depression simply because 85 years of literature refuting that canard should be enough.)

What It Really Means

Let's finally gain some clarity about what we mean when we say liberalism. Cooper sums it up as "self regulating markets" but that's both misleading and too narrow. Liberalism believes that society manages itself better than any top-down authority can. That includes the commercial life of a nation. But it also pertains to civil liberties, international relations, migrations, family and cultural life, and religion.

And what does classical liberalism oppose? Managed economies, imperialism, ethnic cleansing, war, arbitrary rule, dictatorship, authoritarianism, and every action of government that goes beyond what is absolutely necessary, if any government is necessary at all. That the meaning of the term changed in the US in the first half of the 20th century is one of the most tragic language distortions on record.

Liberalism simply observed that things go better with freedom — not perfectly, not always, not toward creating utopia, but generally much better than any kind of imposition from above ever can. And it's not just about generating prosperity; it's about a political order of human rights and dignity for all. This is not wretched. It is beautiful.

10

This Is How David Hume
Would Interpret Peter Rabbit

T he classic story of Peter Rabbit is ultimately a tale about property rights: where they come from, how they are enforced, and the consequences of their violation. Here is the core of what makes the film remake of this story so wonderful. It challenges us to think carefully about the topic, and, as a bonus, offers up a Humean-Misesian view of property (an improvement over John Locke [1632-1704]) and its meaning in our lives.

I'll get to that in a bit but first things first. The movie is astonishingly beautiful, charming, hilarious (in a mature, not a kid-pandering, mode), and delightful in every way. It strikes me as a perfect integration of a classic story, extended to a full motion picture, plus mind-blowing CGI technology (omg the wonderful birds at the beginning and throughout), plus a subtle wit. It shows great deference to the original story while giving us a modern rendering that will convince even those who are squeamish about such projects that this was exactly what had to be done.

Bravo to this film! It enters into the annals of my own mind as one of my top favorite films in the last ten years.

#boycottpeterrabbit

However, not everyone agrees. Beatrix Potter's biographer, Matthew Dennison, has condemned the movie, saying with certainty that she would have objected to the extension of the plot and the turns it takes. I don't know how he can presume to know that. In fact, you can't really know how the mind of a person who has passed from this life would or would not have responded to contemporary events or retellings of stories that have become part of the cultural framework.

Also, like all good movies, this one has attracted the usual parade of pearl-clutching protestors. Allergy sufferers have objected to how the movie belittles their plight. Others have objected to the presence of guns in the films, the supposed glorification of bullying, the supposed violence in general (ever seen the Road Runner and Wile E. Coyote?), and, of course, the supposed sexism and racism of the film. You can follow all the high dudgeon at #boycottpeterrabbit.

These protesting people have become caricatures of themselves.

Who Owns the Garden?

In the original story, Peter Rabbit is warned not to go into Mr. McGregor's garden in search of food. Peter does so anyway. Mr. McGregor has to chase Peter out of his garden. Peter barely escapes but loses his shoes and pretty blue jacket, which end up on a scarecrow. Peter returns home to face the consequence of his disobedience. His mother figures that losing his jacket is punishment enough, and so gives him tea and puts him to bed.

The lesson here as regards property rights is pretty straightforward. You might want something that is not yours but violating the rights of another, even if the person is a bit villainous like Mr. McGregor, is imprudent and leads to very bad results. The point is that it is better to recognize and comply with existing property rules. There are other and better ways to get fed.

The retelling takes the story to a second generation. The original Mr. McGregor dies in pursuit of Peter and his siblings. Upon realizing their good fortune, the rabbits spread the word, and all the animals come to ravage the garden and live in the very nice estate. A distant cousin in the McGregor line shows up to reclaim the house and garden and faces an epic struggle against nature, in which both sides do very bad things to each other.

The struggle here is to find a way toward mutual coexistence. They have to put aside their antagonisms and find a way toward peace. The story is morally complex because it doesn't take the easy path of assigning roles of angel and devil to the main protagonists; there are shades of gray here just as there are in life.

Locke and Hume

You could say that the original version of the story takes a pure Lockean view of property rights. The land is justly titled to Mr. McGregor, and this ownership is reinforced by his working of the land. He cultivates the land and grows the vegetables so he is justly entitled to dispose of the products of his work as he wishes, while driving out interlopers. He has mixed his labor and therefore owns the product of his labor of his own land. Here is a clean application of the Lockean idea.

The new movie adds an interesting complication. The animals have a theory that they were the first owners of the land. It is Mr. McGregor, not they, who are the interlopers. Therefore they should be entitled to whatever is on the land, regardless of who worked the land to make the product. In other words, the initial Lockean conditions never applied, in the animals' view, because this land was never justly titled to Mr. McGregor simply because the land was not previously unowned. He is the thief. He should give back the land.

This is indeed a wrinkle. You could announce that the animals are wrong, but there is still the problem of enforcement. That is the practical reality. There are no agents of the state who can show up and sort out this mess. It has to be negotiated by the stakeholders operating within the arena of conflict.

As I watched the animals theorize along these lines, I was initially a bit befuddled. Don't they have a point, according to strict Lockean principles? They and not Mr. McGregor were the initial homesteaders of the land. How does Lockean theory deal with this?

I wanted to put the film on pause and think about it a bit but the action continued quickly, requiring that I put such thoughts on hold. Only later did I come to a full realization of the trouble with the animals' property theory: in reality animals are not rational in the way people are nor can they communicate this way. In the movie, they have a point; in reality, they could never make such a point. They can't actually speak!

But before we jump too far down this rabbit hole, consider another implication of the film. If someone's claimed property rights prove essentially unenforceable, in what sense do they actually exist in any operational sense?

Property Must Be Enforceable

Consider an example. Let's say that every time you put a planter on your porch, it is taken from you by the next morning. You do this every day and every day it is stolen. You can fulminate about your property rights but clearly they are not being recognized. In practical reality, you are not the effective owner in any sense.

What is happening here? Your just claims in the Lockean framework are running headlong into the practical realities emphasized by David Hume (1711-1776): the social context here is not prepared to recognize your claims. What is necessary in the Humean framework is the social assent necessary to make your property claims realizable and operationally authentic.

In Hume's view, this isn't really about some external dispenser of justice; it is all about the organic development of norms within society. As Hume writes, property rights emerged "by a convention enter'd into by all the members of the society to bestow stability on the possession of those external goods, and leave every one in the peaceable enjoyment of what he may acquire by his fortune and industry." There's no more to it than that. There is no great judge to stand outside the system to resolve conflict.

The rabbits and the animals clearly reject the Humean convention. Therefore, Mr. McGregor has a problem. He needs a technology that would protect his rights claims against invasion. Until he can do so, there is no practical sense in which he can really say: this house and garden are my own.

I was struck by watching how closely this accords with the social theory of Ludwig von Mises from his 1922 book Socialism. In his view, the enforcement of rights claim — by the owner himself or by contract with another — is the crucial stage in which private property becomes socially and economically relevant. No amount of theorizing and moralizing can overcome the practical problem that you have no "rights" if the society around you fails to recognize them as such.

Enforcement Technology

Thus does Mr. McGregor set out on his quest firmly to establish his ownership claims. He uses traps, guns, security fences, electric shocks, and, eventually, explosives. In each case, the rabbits continually outwit him. Meanwhile, he is falling in love with his next-door neighbor, cleverly named Beatrix, who loves rabbits and draws pictures of them. So McGregor has to pretend that he actually loves the rabbits, leading to some hilarious scenes of duplicity in the effort to secure his garden.

All parties involved in this unending dispute eventually find ways to resolve the conflict. This involves taking responsibility for causing unnecessary conflict that leads to destruction suffered by everyone. Both Mr. McGregor and the animals admit their moral culpability and we have the basis for a new property-rights arrangement that meets the demands of social peace while accommodating the moral sensibilities and practical needs of every stakeholder.

This is the realization of the Humean/Misesian world view in one film, and constitutes a subtle correction to the overly simplified view of property advanced by the Lockean framework. No, I don't think the filmmakers intended such a philosophical advance, but that's just fine. It is what the film in fact achieves on its own.

All that Aside

Even if you leave aside all philosophical considerations, this is a wonderful, fun, and hilarious movie. Every few minutes, something happens that is delightful, from the melodiously singing birds (who eventually turn to rap to get across their message) to the fishing frog who jumps into the water to get away from the rain. I've only seen it once but I was left with the desire to see Peter Rabbit another dozen times. Here is the proof: even the best of classic stories can be improved.

What Is a Price?

The large drop in financials of all sorts — both conventional and crypto — have people wondering what went wrong. What could have triggered this stunning selloff? What has spooked the markets? When there are no obvious answers, and there really aren't this time around, it tempts people to believe that markets themselves are broken. Surely prices should behave more rationally and predictably. There is no justification for prices to swing this much.

I'm here to argue a difficult truth. So long as markets are in charge, there is no such thing as a right, just, moral, rational, or stable price. There is only one basis for a price: a point of agreement between buyer and seller, decided upon by the judgments of the human mind as an extension of subjective human desires. This is true even with programmed trading, since it is humans that must do the programming.

It's a given that every buyer wants to pay nothing and every seller wants to be rich on one trade. Neither can get his or her way. Finding a point where both parties can benefit from the trade, giving up less than he or she is getting, is the whole point of markets. Prices we propose and accept today reflect information about completed trades from the past corrected in light of what we expect in the future.

The price reflects human judgments, and can, therefore, be said to be a carrier of information about what people believe about their current and expected needs. When we speak of a market price, known by anyone with an interest, we can regard it as an institution that conveys knowing about desires weighed against the availability of the thing desired.

That is a hugely important piece of information to which society has access. It permits efficient use of resources and builds an economic system that serves everyone. "We must look at the price system as such a mechanism for communicating information if we want to understand its real function," writes F.A. Hayek.

Maybe you read this and thought: no kidding. Everyone knows that. Not so. We can look at the writings of the ancient philosophers and find that they didn't really understand it. Aristotle articulated the prevailing view that the right price is one in which value is equal on both sides of the trade. But this equivalence standard doesn't make sense. If you are getting exactly what you are getting, there is no point to the trade. This equivalence theory is actually pernicious because it treats markets as pointless exercises, stuff moving here and there and changing hands for no particular reason.

As modern finance grew more sophisticated in the late Middle Ages, new theorists got involved in trying to theorize about prices. In times when moral theology was the queen of sciences, intellectuals like St. Thomas Aquinas postulated that a price needs to reflect the needs of justice. In his writings, there is some ambiguity, so that the just price was not necessarily the same as the market price (a mistake corrected over the centuries). This is a deeply dangerous view that gives rise to regulators, moralists, and ecclesiastical nobility who stand in constant judgment over what people are themselves deciding.

Centuries later, new theories of price emerged. Maybe the market price embodies the labor that it takes to produce the good or service in question. This view became the prevailing view in the classical period, and eventually gave rise to the Marxian position that workers — because they are the real value creators — were not getting their fair share of value out of the capitalist system. Indeed, they are being exploited.

This theory doesn't hold up, however. I can spend the rest of the week making sand castles and work harder than I ever have in my life. That work alone does not cause the products of my labor to thereby become valuable. A buyer doesn't care in the slightest bit how much labor time or sweat went into making a product. It is either valued or not. A billion-dollar idea can occur to you in one minute or take years to emerge. What matters is not the time you spent but the resulting idea.

A related theory says that prices reflected not only labor costs but all the costs of production. The higher the costs, the higher the price. This slipshod view finds some basis in empirical reality. It is harder to make a Maserati than a Honda Civic, so surely this is why the fancy car is so much more expensive. In fact, this reverses cause and effect. The reason the producer of Maseratis is willing to expend the resources necessary to make them is precisely because markets have shown to value the results. It's price that determines the costs that producers are willing to bear, and not the reverse.

In more modern times, there are all kinds of rule-of-thumb theories concerning financial markets. Stocks are said to be overvalued or undervalued based on underlying values of the issuing companies. You should look at assets, product development, consumer sales, debt loads, and prospects for the future. Combining all these factors can give you a rough idea of whether a stock is priced too high or too low.

This theory is great except when it is not. As we've seen this year in conventional financials, everything has fallen, suggesting that everything was overvalued. Those who predicted the selloff will tell you that they had a perfect understanding of where we were and where we were headed. They will throw out their models and claim to have special insight. But one thing we should have learned over the last fifty years is that no model can predict perfectly, else we would have found it by now, everyone would be using it, and no one would ever lose money.

Every technical model falters on the same grounds: the future is uncertain. No computer is able to overcome the terrible reality that seeing into the future is always a matter of seeing through the glass darkly, as St. Paul said.

There is a constant temptation to deconstruct a price into its constituent parts, and posit those as the real basis of price. This is especially true with cryptocurrencies. Bitcoin has shown itself to be a poor performer as a means of exchange; it is too slow and too expensive when it attempts to scale. Nor has it been a reliable store of value. How can a high price be justified? Well, in this case, the source of its value might be as a final settlement layer of the blockchain. What's the value of that? That is for the market to discover; it might be low or it might be much higher. We just do not know.

The value of crypto is determined by its use value to the human community, and the price represents an estimate of how that value translates into real trades. Finding the right price is a discovery process.

Let's return to the initial contention drawn from the work of Carl Menger. A price is a point of agreement. No more, no less. It cannot be deconstructed. It cannot be understood apart from human choice. It has no moral component to it at all. It is not about equality, justice, labor, or cost. It is just a price. Every price in a market is the right price, right now. Whatever the price is in an hour, day, week, or year, is also the right price.

Does that sound scary? Maybe. The only thing scarier is a world without prices at all. Think about every experiment in controlling or abolishing them. The results are never good. The purpose of prices is to reveal truth insofar as it can be known at all, however imperfectly. Prices provide us tremendous insight into data we need to know about the world around us, helping us to navigate an otherwise chaotic world.

12

The Economics of Autarky

The idea of autarky is that economic production should be restricted to the geography of the nation-state insofar as it is possible. It's an idea that has deeply influenced the current president of the United States, as he has made clear since at least the beginning of the presidential campaign in 2015. People were mostly in denial, ignoring his many statements to this effect, but daily tweets (for example, demanding that Apple bring all production home, and celebrating tariffs as wonderful for a nation) plus bad-faith negotiations with trading partners are causing the reality finally to set in.

It's time we understand what this notion of autarky is all about, simply because it seems to be making a big comeback in today's world, as surprising as that sounds in a time when global supply chains are more interwoven than ever. It's a lesson that no idea, no matter how often it has been refuted in theory and practice, is so fully beaten down that it cannot come back from the dead under the right conditions.

It Begins With List

The idea of national autarky in its modern form traces to the German economist Friedrich List and his 1841 book *The National System of Political Economy*. List came to the idea under the influence of Friedrich Wilhelm Joseph Schelling, who was Georg Friedrich Hegel's roommate in college. List moved to Pennsylvania in 1825 and worked as a journalist with a great deal of influence, pushing what he regarded as an update of the economic views of Alexander Hamilton.

The root here is Hegelian philosophy and its longing for a strong state to swamp individual decision-making. It is not so much economic as political and philosophical: history must drive toward centralized power under great men and their intellectual advisors. Economic forces must be restricted to the bounds of the nation-state, because those bounds are the limits of the jurisdiction of the powers that be. Trade outside the borders, in this case, represents a kind of treason against state power.

List articulated a core principle that "the interest of individuals" must be "subordinated to those of the nation," and that must be expressed most clearly in its policy toward trade. His crucial point was the rejection of the very idea of freedom that had given birth to the modern world and its replacement by a new idea of national management of economic life, requiring, in the first instance, a policy of autarky.

The idea of autarky stands in complete opposition to the theory of free trade. In Adam Smith's rendering, the fundamental basis of wealth creation is the expansion of the division of labor. The broader this expansion — whether outside a family, outside city walls, or beyond a nation's borders — the greater opportunity exists to build a prosperous society. This is the view that came to dominate in the 19th century, despite the push by autarkists. They didn't win the debate. By the late 19th century, economic nationalism was widely seen as a reactionary and defunct doctrine, so much so that even small tariffs were repealed and states found other ways to raise money for themselves.

The Great Depression

The problem for free traders is that no matter how many times they win the day, the idea of autarky is always lurking out there. It usually begins in the simple desire of domestic producers to be protected from cheaper foreign products. Then it mutates gradually based on simple economic errors. In what sense is it ever a benefit to a nation for any producer to make things abroad and bring them in? Doesn't that cost jobs? Doesn't that just drain the national wealth?

So in 1930, following the great stock market crash of 1929, Congress massively raised tariffs in the mistaken notion that this would help the economy recover. The Smoot-Hawley Tariff Act drove the economy into a deeper pit. As always, this action plus the deepening economic crisis bolstered anti-liberal opinion all over the world.

In 1933, none other than John Maynard Keynes reversed his lifelong warmth toward the free trade idea and made a case for autarky as a model. As usual, his rhetoric was evocative:

> I sympathise, therefore, with those who would minimise, rather than with those who would maximise, economic entanglement between nations. Ideas, knowledge, art, hospitality, travel — these are the things which should of their nature be international. But let goods be homespun whenever it is reasonably and conveniently possible;

and, above all, let finance be primarily national. Yet, at the same time, those who seek to disembarrass a country of its entanglements should be very slow and wary. It should not be a matter of tearing up roots but of slowly training a plant to grow in a different direction.

Can you imagine what a gigantic transformation of the old trading relationships this would be? It doesn't matter if it would take place slowly, as he recommends, or quickly. The results would be the same: to shrink rather than expand the division of labor, and hence prosperity along with it.

Why would Keynes go this direction? Because he had come to believe in a new form of macroeconomic planning that would supplant the old, laissez-faire model. If government and its intellectual leaders are going to be dedicated to economic planning, they have to control the resources. The extent of control is limited by the range of the jurisdiction. It then becomes crucial that both commerce and finance live only within the bounds of the nation-state. That is to say, autarky serves the purposes of economic planning.

This is why, for example, the same essay is effusive with praise of any nation that has left the old model of the free market:

> But today one country after another abandons these presumptions. Russia is still alone in her particular experiment, but no longer alone in her abandonment of the old presumptions. Italy, Ireland, Germany have cast their eyes, or are casting them, towards new modes of political economy. Many more countries after them will soon be seeking, one by one, after new economic gods. Even countries such as Great Britain and the United States, though conforming in the main to the old model, are striving, under the surface, after a new economic plan. We do not know what will be the outcome. We are — all of us, I expect — about to make many mistakes. No one can tell which of the new systems will prove itself best.

Now, the case of Russia is egregious. Stalin had gained full control by 1929. By the time Keynes published his essay, the Ukrainian famine was full on. By a year later, 6 to 7 million people had died of starvation or intentional killing. Some "experiment." Mussolini was the dictator of Italy. As for Germany, in 1933, the Nazi Party was mostly in control of the country. It was pushing its own policy of national autarky called Lebensraum. Two years later, Triumph of the Will appeared in cinemas as the Nuremberg Laws went into full effect.

Mises Weighs In

What role did autarky play in this? It was a primary economic goal of the National Socialists. Mises later wrote in his 1944 book Omnipotent Government as follows:

> The international division of labor is a more efficient system of production than is the economic autarky of every nation. The same amount of labor and of material factors of production yields a higher output. This surplus production benefits everyone concerned. Protectionism and autarky always result in shifting production from the centers where conditions are more favorable — i.e., from where the output for the same amount of physical input is higher — to centers where they are less favorable. The more productive resources remain unused while the less productive are utilized. The effect is a general drop in the productivity of human effort, and thereby a lowering of the standard of living all over the world.
>
> The economic consequences of protectionist policies and of the trend toward autarky are the same for all countries…. Germany does not aim at autarky because it is eager to wage war. It aims at war because it wants autarky — because it wants to live in economic self-sufficiency.

Mises could not have been clearer and more resounding in his conclusion:

> Our civilization is based on the international division of labor. It cannot survive under autarky. The United States and Canada would suffer less than other countries but even with them economic insulation would result in a tremendous drop in prosperity. Europe, whether itself united or divided, would be doomed in a world where each country was economically self-sufficient.

And following the Second World War, Mises's view prevailed. The drive toward free trade became a consensus for most of the world. The views of the Right Hegelians, List, Keynes, and the others were swept aside with the General Agreement on Tariffs and Trade and a trend extending over many decades toward ever freer trade. It was never perfect, and it all required too much state management and too many treaties, but it was happening. It was largely unquestioned, and the world grew incredibly prosperous as a result.

But we live in times when the notion of autarky as a productive force for a nation has made a wicked comeback, for the same reason it has always ascended. It is not about economic flourishing. It is about political control by the centralized nation-state, the well-being of the citizen be damned. Every tariff (a tax against the citizens), every non-tariff barrier (rising prices paid by citizens), exchange control, and regulatory demand for at-home production means a reduction in wealth and opportunity for everyone. Contrary to claims, autarky (for a nation, city, family, or individual) is not a plan for prosperity but for impoverishment.

13

What Anthony Bourdain
Taught Me About Economics

Many factors contribute to making a society prosperous. There is hard work, creativity, commercial intuition, entrepreneurship, the division of labor, frugality, saving, solid property relationships, complex production structures, access to a trading infrastructure, and so much more.

Among all of these, and other factors unnamed, which is absolutely essential? Which among them will doom a society to poverty in its absence? These are enormously complex questions that cry out for more than good theory; answering them accurately depends on real-world examples.

The Haitian Problem

Haiti is an excellent case in point. The World Bank says that "Haiti remains the poorest country in the Americas." "More than 6 million out of 10.4 million Haitians (59%) were living below the national poverty line of US$2.41 per day and over 2.5 million (24%) were living below the national extreme poverty line of US$1.23 per day."

What has gone wrong? When Anthony Bourdain set out to make a show in Haiti — which ends up being one of his most spectacular shows — he didn't seek an overt answer to this question. The lens through which he discovered the functioning of daily life was the same throughout his amazing career: food. Not fancy food. The food that real people prepare and eat in their daily lives. This kept his vision attached to the tactile, real, practical, authentic.

As Bourdain himself says at the outset, with the focus on food and cooking, we can see what it is that drives daily life among the Haitian multitudes. And what we find is surprising in so many ways. He takes viewers to Port-au-Prince, Haiti. Through this micro lens, we gain more insight than we would have if the program were entirely focused on economic issues. Such an episode on economics would have featured dull interviews with treasury officials and IMF experts and lots of talk about trade balances and other macroeconomic aggregates that miss the point entirely.

Unintended Consequences

In a scene early in the show set in this giant city after the earthquake, Bourdain and his crew stop to eat some local food from a vendor. He discusses its ingredients and samples some items. Crowds of hungry people begin to gather. They are doing more than gawking at the camera crews. They are waiting in the hope of getting something to eat.

Bourdain thinks of a way to do something nice for everyone. Realizing that in this one sitting, he is eating a quantity of food that would last most Haitians three days, he buys out the remaining food from the vendor and gives it away to locals.

Nice gesture! Except that something goes wrong. Once the word spreads about the free food — word-of-mouth in Haiti is faster than Snapchat — people start pouring in. Lines form and get long. Disorder ensues. Some people step forward to keep order. They bring belts and start hitting. The entire scene becomes very unpleasant for everyone — and the viewer gets the sense that it is worse than we are shown.

Bourdain correctly draws the lesson that the solutions to the problem of poverty here are more complex than it would appear at first glance. Good intentions go awry. They were thinking with their hearts instead of their heads, and ended up causing more pain than was originally there in the first place. From this event forward, he begins to approach the problems of this country with a bit more sophistication.

A Normal Place

The rest of the show takes us through shantytowns, markets, art shows, festivals, and parades — and interviews all kinds of people who know the lay of the land. This is not a show designed to tug at your heartstrings in the conventional sort of way. Yes, there is obvious human suffering, but the overall impression I got was not that. Instead, I came away with a sense that Haiti is a very normal place not unlike all places we know from experience, but with one major difference: it is very poor.

By the time the show was made, the glamour of the post-earthquake onslaught of American visitors seeking to help had vanished. One who remains is actor Sean Penn. Although he's known as a Hollywood lefty, he's actually lived there, chugging up and down the hills of a shantytown, unshaven and disheveled, being what he calls a "functionary" and getting stuff for people who need it. He had no easy answers, and he had sharp words for American donors who think that dumping money into new projects is going to help anyone.

The people of Haiti in the documentary conform to what every visitor says about them. They are wonderfully friendly, talented, enterprising, happy, and full of hope. Like most people, they hate their government. Actually, they hate their government more than most Americans hate theirs. There is a real sense of us-versus-them alive in Haiti, so much so that when the presidential palace collapsed in an earthquake, crowds gathered outside to cheer and cheer! It was the one saving grace of an otherwise terrible storm.

With all these enterprising, hard-working, and creative people, millions of them, what could possibly be wrong with the place? Well, for one thing, the earthquake destroyed most homes. If this had been the US, this earthquake would not have caused the same level of damage. This led many outsiders to think that somehow the absence of building codes was the core of the problem, and hence the solution is more imposition of government control.

But the reality shows that this building-code notion is some sort of joke. The very idea that a government could somehow go around beating up people who provide shelter for themselves while failing to obey the central plan is simply laughable. Coercion of this sort would bring about no positive results and lead only to vast corruption, violence, and homelessness.

Absence of Wealth

The core of the problem has nothing to do with a lack of regulations. The problem is the absence of wealth. It is obviously true that people prefer safer places to live, but the question is: what is the cost, and is this economically viable? The answer is that it is not viable, not in Haiti, not with this population that is barely getting by at all.

Where is the wealth? There is plenty of trade, plenty of doing, plenty of exchange and money changing hands. Why does the place remain desperately poor? If the market economists are correct that trade and commerce are the key to wealth, and there is plenty of both here, why is wealth not happening?

One can easily see how people can get confused, because the answer is not obvious until you have some economic understanding. A random visitor might easily conclude that Haiti is poor because somehow the wealth is being hogged by its northern neighbor, the United States. If we weren't devouring so much of the world's stock of wealth, it could be distributed more evenly and encompass Haiti too. Or another theory might be that the handful of international companies, or even aid workers, are somehow stealing all the money and denying it to the people.

These are not stupid theories. They are just theories — neither confirmed nor refuted by facts alone. They are only shown to be wrong once you realize a central insight of economics. It is this: trade and commerce are necessary conditions for the accumulation of wealth, but they are not sufficient conditions. Also necessary is that precious institution of capital.

Capital is the Key

What is capital? Capital is a thing (or service) that is produced not for consumption but for further production. The existence of capital industries implies several stages of production, or up to thousands upon thousands of steps in a long structure of production. Capital is the institution that gives rise to business-to-business trading, an extended workforce, firms, factories, ever more specialization, and generally the production of all kinds of things that by themselves cannot be useful in final consumption but rather are useful for the production of other things.

Capital is not so much defined as a particular good — most things have many varieties of uses — but rather a purpose of a good. Its purpose is extended over a long period of time with the goal of providing for final consumption. Capital is employed in a long structure of production that can last a month, a year, 10 years, or 50 years. The investment at the earliest (highest) stages has to take place long before the payoff circles around following final consumption.

As Hayek emphasized in The Pure Theory of Capital, another defining mark of capital is that it is a non-permanent resource that must nonetheless be maintained over time in order to provide a continuing stream of income. That means that the owner must be able to count on being able to hire workers, replace parts, provide for security, and generally maintain operations throughout an extended period of production.

In a developed economy, the vast majority of productive activities consist in participation in these capital-goods sectors and not in final-consumption-goods sectors. And why is that? Because the test of the value of all capital goods is conducted at the level of final consumption. The final consumer is the master of the richest capitalist.

Many people (I've been among them) rail against the term capitalism because it implies that freedom is all about privileging the owners of capital. But there is a sense in which capitalism is the perfect term for a developed economy: the development, accumulation, and sophistication of the capital-goods sector is the characteristic feature that makes it different from an undeveloped economy.

Live for the Day

Capitalism did in fact arise at a specific time in history and this was the beginning of the mass democratization of wealth. Rising wealth is always characterized by such extended orders of production. These are nearly absent in Haiti. Most all people are engaged in day-to-day commercial activities. They live for the day. They trade for the day. They plan for the day. Their time horizons are necessarily short, and their economic structures reflect that.

It is for this reason that all the toil and trading and busyness in Haiti feels like pedaling a stationary bicycle. You are working very hard and getting better and better at what you are doing, but you are not actually moving forward.

Now, this is interesting to me because anyone can easily miss this point just by looking around Haiti where you see people working and producing like crazy, and yet the people never seem to get their footing. Without an understanding of economics, it is nearly impossible to see the unseen: the capital that is absent that would otherwise permit economic growth. And this is the very reason for the persistence of poverty, which, after all, is the natural condition of mankind. It takes something heroic, something special, something historically unique, to dig out of it.

Now to the question of why the absence of capital.

The answer has to do with the regime. It is a well-known fact that any accumulation of wealth in Haiti makes you a target, if not of the population in general (which has grown suspicious of wealth, and probably for good reason), then certainly of the government. The regime, no matter who is in charge, is like a voracious dog on the loose, seeking to devour any private wealth that happens to emerge.

This creates something even worse than the problem of "regime uncertainty." The regime is certain: it is certain to steal anything it can, whenever it can, always and forever. So why don't people vote out the bad guys and vote in the good guys? Well, those of us in the United States who have a bit of experience with democracy know the answer: there are no good guys. The system itself is owned by the state and rooted in evil. Change is always illusory, a fiction designed for public consumption.

Looting and Pillaging

This is an interesting case of a peculiar way in which government is keeping prosperity at bay. It is not wrecking the country through an intense enforcement of taxation and regulation or nationalization. One gets the sense that most people never have any face time with a government official and never deal with paperwork or bureaucracy really. The state strikes only when there is something to loot. And loot it does: predictably and consistently. And that alone is enough to guarantee a permanent state of poverty.

Now, to be sure, there are plenty of Americans who are firmly convinced that we would all be better off if we grew our own food, bought only locally, kept firms small, eschewed modern conveniences like home appliances, went back to using only natural products, expropriated wealthy savers, harassed the capitalistic class until it felt itself unwelcome and vanished. This paradise has a name, and it is Haiti.

Bourdain didn't set out to teach the world about economics. But if you follow him closely, and reflect on his discoveries in distant lands and unfamiliar cultures, you discover great truths about prosperity, poverty, and wealth, through the daily lives of real people. Despite his intentions, he was a great teacher, mainly because he was a great explorer.

14

Would You Eat this Abandoned Chicken Stick?

Sitting at the airport bar, I was speaking lazily to the person next to me. I was feeling hungry but not willing to pay high airport prices for food. Plus I just wanted a small snack — such as that yummy-looking chicken stick on the plate in front of my new friend. The bar patron wasn't touching it. I nearly asked if I could eat, but thought again: that would be sort of tacky.

Seems like we should pay for our own food. Right? Maybe.

Suddenly he said he was late for a flight, paid his tab, and left the bar chair in a hurry. I'm sitting there next to this abandoned chicken stick. It was eight inches from my hand. I could have reached out and eaten it in less than five seconds. No one would have seen me, probably.

Something stopped me. I had to think about property rights, ownership, Lockean principles, a world with chaotic ownership claims, which led me to consider exactly who owned this chicken or whether perhaps it was like the Wild West, property waiting to be homesteaded.

Ask the Crowd

What would you do? I went to Twitter to find out. The famed free-market journalist John Stossel was very quick with an answer: "I would eat it." That's decisive!

Casey Head said: "Not morally wrong, but possibly a little gross." But it didn't look gross at all. It had never been touched.

Mike Karst said: "Just social pressure. Take it." Maybe that's right.

Tray Strawn said: "Mark Twain's character in the 'Million Pound Banknote' waited to grab a half-eaten pear on the street until no one was looking. But someone else nabbed it. Moral: take it. Now!"

Indeed! The street orphans of the late Victorian period lived off the trash of others. This wasn't disgusting. It was glorious. What a remarkable moment in history when there was enough left over from the abundance of production to feed vast amounts of people who made no money and produced no food at all. We take this for granted now, but this was actually evidence of a very high state of humanity.

Others began to speculate about the issue that had initially struck me: ownership. The bar patron paid for it but then abandoned it. Is it now up for grabs? What if the guy found out that his plane was delayed and came back to find I had eaten his chicken. Could he then demand a payment from me, as the victim of a tort?

If the chicken really is abandoned by the owner, perhaps the rights then revert to the bar itself. In that case, I would have to ask permission from the bartender. I wonder what he would say? Whatever he says, I would have to comply — provided that this is correct.

Another colleague suggested it would be wrong to take the chicken from a stranger's plate but that if I had temporarily become casual friends, that makes matters entirely different. In this case, I would be perfectly justified in picking it up and eating it. It's hard to know what kind of theory of property rights that view rests on. The friendship/communication theory of shared ownership rights?

In the back of my mind was Adam Smith's Theory of Moral Sentiments. He addressed these cases in which it seems right to do wrong:

> "The situations which call forth the noblest exertions of self-command, by imposing the necessity of violating sometimes the property, and sometimes the life of our neighbour, always tend to diminish, and too often to extinguish altogether, that sacred regard to both, which is the foundation of justice and humanity."
>
> I absolutely do not want to extinguish property, life, justice, or humanity. But it's hard to see why reaching over eight inches and munching a chicken stick would do that.

In the Trash

As I was thinking through all these considerations, a server swept in, picked up the plate, and vanished into the kitchen, probably throwing the chicken straight into the trash. Talk about waste. And why? All because I had some strange scrupulosity, emanating from I do not know where, that prevented me from choosing the far more efficient solution. I went for morals (or manners? Or social convention?) over efficiency.

As it turns out, this is the fate of vast amounts of perfectly good food. As much as a third of all food produced ends up in the trash, according to a new study: "30% of daily calories available for consumption, one-quarter of daily food (by weight) available for consumption, and 7% of annual cropland acreage."

It's one thing if this is all done voluntarily. But it is not. Vast waste is imposed by government regulations. A friend was recently trying to get grocery store bakeries to donate food for a social hour following a church service. She constantly ran into the same reason that it is not possible: regulations prohibit stores from allowing people to consume food after it cannot be sold.

Well, it's not technically prohibited. It's just that five guidelines from the federal government, plus countless and endless restrictions at the state and local levels, make it extremely difficult for stores to set up formal programs with nonprofits such as churches to do what otherwise seems perfectly reasonable: be generous with the leftovers.

What an amazing bounty surrounds us, so much so that we regulate its consumption to the point that we allow massive quantities to be thrown away, and then complain that there is too much trash.

Reflecting on our abundance, I feel a sense of deep gratitude for what capitalism has achieved. For more than 150,000 years, the daily plight of all of humanity was struggling to get food for today and tomorrow, and maybe even figuring out some way to prepare for the future. That defined the whole of life.

Birth of Plenty

Today? Our main problem is that we have too much. For example: at lunch today, I had access to piles of barbecued spiced sausage, roasted peppers, coleslaw, and bread. The great moral discipline I faced was not to eat too much. My goodness, what a luxury! I get why the 18th-century nobility had their visages painted to make them look as fat as possible: only the rich in those days could get fat. If you've got it, flaunt it. Today, it is the opposite: only the very rich can be beautifully thin.

None of it would have happened without the invention of the great technology that enabled us to stop stealing from each other and instead start to create wealth. That technology is the enforcement of private property norms over scarce goods. Such a technology does not create perfect rules applicable in all times and all places, much less provide us a perfect ethical template for all human interaction with the material world. Instead it creates a norm that rules out such silliness as socialism, which fantasizes about the impossible idea of collective ownership of scarce goods.

Ambiguities will also be with us. Can you sample from the olive bar? Can you stand at the magazine rack for an hour and read? Can you stay in the theater and watch a second film? Can you take the extra soap and shampoo from the hotel room? Some of these questions are governed by contract, some by cultural norms, and some solutions are left ambiguous for a reason.

Back to the chicken. I could have eaten it without violating anyone's rights, so far as I can tell. But doing so would bump into an idea that forms the basis of social order, the very distinction between what is mine and what is thine. And keep in mind that this norm thrives most (or only) in an environment in which we are not desperate. In famine and war, such norms become more flexible. Sitting at the airport bar, I had the luxury to be scrupulous ... and remain hungry, awaiting my chance to beg the flight attendant to give me an extra bag of salted almonds.

Let me ask you again: would you eat the chicken stick?

15

The Death of Karl Lagerfeld, and Clothing

The death of Karl Lagerfeld of Chanel (and so many other brands) was foreshadowed by an impending sense of doom in the world of fashion and clothing.

Lagerfeld's mind and imagination were pure magic. He took on brands with no reputation and cachet and turned them to gold. He recaptured, redefined, and forged a new and aspirational path. His every flash of virtuosic insight concerned the marketing of elegance. He did it with an uncanny sense of making the past live in better ways than it ever had. In this way, he made the world a more beautiful place to live.

(Also, so far as I know, he was the last surviving high-end designer to personally sport a high detachable collar, which tells you how much he knew that no one else seemed to know.)

Lagerfeld's Secret

Think of all the old brands that have died the death. His, in contrast, came to new life. His insight was that an old brand is a moat that no newcomer can cross. The trick is to market it. Owning it roots you. Wearing it immortalizes you. Flashing the brand gives you an edge over everyone else.

With this message, he tapped into the driving force that has given fashion its life for 500 years: one's desire to send a social signal that you occupy an ever-higher station in life. Which is to say: you are valuable.

Because of this insight, and his incredible gift of applying it, the very name Lagerfeld itself is immortal.

The Last of His Kind?

Two weeks before the news of his death, Business of Fashion announced the death of clothing:

> The apparel industry seems to have no solution to the dwindling dollars Americans devote to their closets. Many upstarts promising to revolutionize the industry drift away with barely a whimper. Who needs fashion these days when you can express yourself through social media? Why buy that pricey new dress when you could fund a weekend getaway instead?
>
> Apparel has simply lost its appeal. And there doesn't seem to be a savior in sight. As a result, more and more apparel companies — from big-name department stores to trendy online startups — are folding.

There are economic factors. Contrary to the article, that Americans are spending ever less of their household budgets on clothing reflects a dramatic fall in clothing prices due to labor outsourcing, online competition, and the rise of large retailers and their ability to produce knockoffs at a fraction of the price of exclusive brands. There's more going on than merely a change of taste.

That said, the change of taste is strikingly obvious. I just attended a 2,500-person event, and I and one other person were the only two who wore a tie for the entire week. Perhaps two other people wore anything like a suit or sportcoat. Everyone else was wearing the modern uniform, which I would describe (without trying to sound disparaging) as a random assembly of loose-fitting cotton items that cover your body.

True, this was a casual event. But the same is true in professional life. People don't dress up. The less they dress up, the more they reflect the sense of the moment. Tech billionaires wear sneakers, sweats, and tees. It's not quite grunge wear; it's whatever wear. There is this presumption that clothing doesn't matter in the slightest. I've seen lecturers on stage at professional events sitting on stools dangling their bare feet, something that would have been a career killer just 15 years ago.

A Case for Slobbery?

I've heard all the defenses. If you are smart and killing it as an entrepreneur, your value is in what you do. It's your mind, not your clothing. You don't have to prove anything with what you wear. It's what you do that matters.

It sounds vaguely plausible except one's suspicions should be aroused given that this flips the narrative of half a millennium.

In the Middle Ages, you could immediately discern the difference between the rulers, the aristocracy, the merchants, the farmers, the workers, the slaves, by their dress alone. Crossing over, getting outside your born-that-way station in life was not only culturally verboten; it was often illegal (recall the sumptuary laws). Such was life before the dawn of modernity.

Capitalism eventually made that untenable. People could aspire. They could move. They could change professions. They could succeed on their own merits. In one lifetime, they could leap up the ladder of social success. They could literally go from rags to riches, which is to say that they were permitted to dress in ever-higher-class ways. The social-class signaling systems were bound up with what you wore. The opportunity to look as awesome as Louis XIV was now available to everyone — provided they had the success to show it.

This system of ascending social class marked by fashion was a driving force of the industry from the late 16th century until very recently. Take a look at the meritocrats of the Gilded Age with their high hats, high collars, and spats, their canes and watch fobs, their bright-white shirts and suits with tails. The point was to adorn yourself in the highest possible way, anything to send the sought-after sign that you have made it. No factory-floor manager could get away with this, and certainly not just any laborer. You had to be truly awesome to look this way.

In the 20th century, with the spread of the democratic ethos, this approach came to be seen as excessively ostentatious or just downright gauche. The getups were dialed back, but the class structure of clothing still survived even until the 1990s.

The Flipping

In the 21st century, however, the relationship between class and clothing began to break down because of the mass availability of clothing. Today — and I've tested this — I can spend $100 at Walmart and look as good from a slight distance as what would have required me to spend $2,500 at Burberry 20 years ago.

If such pretense is available to absolutely everyone, it's no longer special. It took someone to pull the trigger to blow it all up. That person was Steve Jobs. Riffing off his extreme minimalism and adding an overlay of pure tackiness was Mark Zuckerberg. If these awesome, super rich, super successful dudes can eschew the push for sartorial escalation, so can everyone else. Thus came clothing nihilism. The only true faux pas was believing in faux pas at all.

Somehow in this mix, Lagerfeld survived. Does his death entrench the death of clothing? Is this the new permanent condition of humankind? Allow me to demur. I predict that the opposite could happen. We could all wake up tomorrow and wonder what we were thinking. Just as people look back at leisure suits, big bells, and wide ties with horror, the same will happen to the typical outfits of the well-to-do today. What were we thinking?

Honoring Others

Here's why this will happen. People completely misunderstand the more serious and robust reason for fashion and for the aspiration to dress above your station of birth. It's not only about leading others to believe you are awesome. It is also, and especially, about letting others know that you think they are awesome enough to deserve your best.

When you dress well, you are honoring the occasion, your hosts, the venue, the profession, the setting, the other guests at dinner, your family, your coworkers, and so on. You are sending a signal: I think so highly of you that I went out of my way to honor you with trying to improve how I look. And here's the thing: it truly does work.

I've never boarded a flight without being thanked for dressing up. Wearing a suit to anything, anytime, gains you countless numbers of special little favors from others, and why? It's a way for others to thank you for honoring them. You feel it too: when guests come to your house for a party, who among them would you say is especially grateful for the invitation? It's a pretty good guess that the answer is connected to how well they dress.

The point is incredibly obvious once you make it. It's so obvious that it will soon be rediscovered. On that glorious day, we will see that we can use the gift of capitalism — universal access to the tools to live amazingly well — as a method by which we come to honor each other's presence in the world by dressing up and caring once again.

This will be accompanied by a new dawning realization: dressing like a slob is a selfish act that fails others and finally fails yourself. Just look at Zuckerberg: do you think he cares about anything but himself, really? His clothing choice makes the point. And it's not working for him anymore.

The death of the brilliant Karl Lagerfeld does not mean the certain and forever death of elegance. His death might shock us all into a new sensibility that helps us all see what he saw: if we want the world to be beautiful, we have to make it so.

16

They Fight Economics But Economics Always Wins

This year began with an audacious attempt to restore American industrial manufacturing by force of political will. The means toward that end were taxes on imports and a forced disruption of global supply chains supposedly to put America First.

Among the results: factory closings, collapsed sales of American-made motorcycles, falling financials, double-digit increases in steel prices laying waste to corporate profits, higher prices and reduced incomes for American consumers, loss of export markets, higher (yes, higher) trade deficits, and a loss of regime stability so that global confidence in the US has taken a hit.

Whoops.

This was not supposed to happen. But it did. And why? Because economics. Someone has to pay these tariffs, and it is not foreigners. Those costs add up and negatively affect profits, which triggers production slowdowns, price increases, and lower sales. It's not all at once. It takes place at the margin. But over time, in a highly competitive global marketplace, you live or die by small margins. Defying these forces is expensive and pointless: policy makers have to acquiesce to reality at some point, and then they are left with nothing but wasted time and resources.

Another example concerns the protests for a $15 minimum wage, as if wages are set solely by an act of will rather than supply and demand. All around the country, we saw labor strikes, inevitably accompanied by loving media coverage. How did that work out? Today, you walk into a McDonald's just about anywhere in the country and place your order through a kiosk that works 24/7 and receives $0 in wages. It's an expensive machine but brings a revenue bounceback. Those protesting workers presumably found other work.

Whoops.

And that's the truly interesting thing about economics. It's the discipline that seeks not to control but understand. And what does it understand? Two things. On the happy side, it seeks a greater appreciation for how freedom — the seeming chaos of the market — outwits all intellectual pretense to unleash the full potential of the human mind. On the heavier side, it demonstrates the profound limits on the human imagination by elucidating the rock-hard limits of the political (violent) means of controlling the world.

This has been the role of economics for hundreds of years. It's the science that says to the prince: your power is limited by forces outside of your control. In every country since the High Middle Ages, it has been this way. In so doing, economics has shot down exchange controls, price floors and ceilings, high taxes, protectionism, producer subsidies, cartels, and every act of government that messes with the price system and market process.

The Boettke Way

AIER contributor Peter Boettke quotes David Prychitko to sum up the idea: "Economics puts parameters on people's utopias." That is the theme of his wonderful book Living Economics, 450 pages of wisdom concerning economics and its place in the world of learning and living. "The teachings of the principles of economics should inform as much on what not to do, perhaps even more than providing a guide to public action."

For this reason, economists just keep bursting people's bubbles. Don't control prices. Don't socialize medicine. Don't raise taxes. Don't inflate the money supply. Don't put up trade barriers. Don't go to war. Every generation for the past 500 years has seen the battle waged between those who want to use the power of the state to fit some daydream on the one hand and the economists who have seen the futility in this manipulation and warn against it on the other.

For Boettke, the phrase "living economics" means two things: (1) economics is part of life whether we recognize it or not, and (2) economics is a living discipline, rooted in universal principles but always changing in nuance and application.

Professor Boettke's purpose is to provide a guided tour through the profession as it is now and to say how he would like to see it changed. He does this by first explaining what got him interested in the science.

When the market is allowed to work, beauty and growth results. Humanity flourishes.

It turns out that he remembers the gas lines of the 1970s and recalls being amazed to discover that they were wholly manufactured by Washington policy. It was the price control on oil combined with inflationary pressures from bad monetary policy. Contrary to what the media mavens and politicians were saying at the time, it had nothing to do with producer greed, secret price manipulation, or financial speculation.

That's what did it for him. He realized that economics is woven into every aspect of our lives. It is inescapable. When the market is allowed to work, beauty and growth result. Humanity flourishes. When markets are truncated and hobbled, people suffer.

Then he realized how little public understanding there is of economics. And he realized that he could play a role in changing this. Since then, he has. His students are now teaching other students in six different Ph.D.-granting institutions, among dozens of other institutions.

Boettke reflects on the decision to make economics his vocation. Economics as a reality in our world will exist whether there are people around to study and explain it or not. As a discipline, it was very late in developing. And it came about precisely to elucidate the way the world works in order to prevent kings and other big shots from using force to interfere with its mechanisms.

As Boettke puts it, "We do not need to understand economics in order to experience the benefits of freedom of exchange and production. But we may very well need to understand economics in order to sustain and maintain the institutional framework that enables us to realize the benefits that flow from freedom of exchange and production."

What follows this beginning material is a plunge straight into the core of what economics teaches. Boettke chooses a very engaging path. He tells the story through a series of intellectual biographies of the economists he most admires. We read about his teacher Hans Sennholz, about Ludwig von Mises, F.A. Hayek, and Murray Rothbard — his chapter on Rothbard being particularly celebratory. He covers James Buchanan and Gordon Tullock. Perhaps the most interesting sections are the ones that find "Austrianness" in unusual places — in the work of Kenneth Boulding, for example.

In contrast to most books on economics, this book is very warm and humane. He goes all out to describe economics as the science of human choice in the real world. The prose matches his intellectual sense. We are spared the usual academic pomp and the absurdities of trying to cram people and their spontaneous decisions into mechanical models. He never talks down to his readers; this reader found no showing off, no strutting around, no defensiveness or bickering. The prose and line of thinking are open and generous.

It's no surprise that the Austrian school is at the core of the narrative. And it informs the whole of his worldview, accounts for why he is able to write about real-world problems, and explains the failure of planning in such lucid terms.

At the same time, Boettke cautions: "The main thing that makes someone an Austrian is not the willingness to identify one's work with that label, but the substantive propositions in economics that an economist identifies with." With this in mind, he shows that Austrian ideas are much more widespread than one might suppose.

A book like this will provide anyone vast insight into what economics has to offer the world of ideas. It is an excellent overview about what is great and what is awful in the profession today. But even when he criticizes, there is no anger; instead, there is conviction that openness and frankness is the best path to finding truth. I can't think of a better book for an economics major to have on hand when the lecture content begins to depart from reality.

Boettke has managed to make economists themselves re-excited about what they do. He will do the same for you, and help you appreciate the creativity, courage, and sheer adventure associated with this grand craft that elucidates the workings of our world like no other. His book is a guide to help politicians and other people to stop fighting the losing battle against economics and start seeing economics as the beautiful science of human possibility.

Moreover, if you take Boettke seriously, you realize something even more spectacular: economics makes it impossible that powerful people can finally rule the world.

17

The Reason We Love The Nutcracker

Many people in the holiday season will experience the joy of attending a local performance of "The Nutcracker" ballet by Pyotr Ilyich Tchaikovsky. It's the most implausible American tradition imaginable, an import from fin-de-siècle Russia straight to your hometown. It's living proof of the capacity of music and the art of dance to leap the bounds of time and space and delight us forever.

Perhaps some viewer's own children will perform in it, and that's part of the appeal. But there's more. Some reports suggest that this one ballet accounts for 40 percent of the annual revenue for professional companies. It's no wonder why: The music is brilliant, elegant, and vaguely familiar to everyone (it is out of copyright and therefore featured in countless ads).

It's also the big-city favorite. Andrew Litton, New York City Ballet's music director, in an interview admits how much he loves the piece. "I'm actually in love with the whole two hours," he told the New York Times of this season's sold-out performances." "I'm only conducting seven of the performances, but the seventh will feel just as great as the first."

It's true: the melodies are filled with magic, fantasy, mystery, love, strange sounds you never otherwise hear, and unrelenting spectacle. And no matter how "classical" old-world ballet is, it never ceases to amaze us to watch this highly specialized combination of athleticism and art in action.

The Beautiful Epoch

What theatergoers don't entirely realize is that they are watching something even more wonderful than what they see. In this one ballet, we gain a picture of a prosperous world that emerged in the late nineteenth century, was shortly shattered by war and revolution, and then was nearly killed off by the political and ideological experimentation of the twentieth century.

Think of it: This ballet debuted in 1892. The generation of Russians living in St. Petersburg that saw it for the first time were experiencing a level of prosperity never before seen in history. It was the same all over Europe, of which Russia was considered a part.

This was a time of the full maturation of the Industrial Revolution. Income was growing dramatically. Lives were longer. Infant mortality was plummeting. The middle class could live in security and in comfortable homes, and the practical arts—electricity, lighting, telephones, universal medicine, indoor plumbing—were in a boom phase.

We see hints of all these themes in the opening scenes of "The Nutcracker." We are in a home with a beautifully lit tree, and several generations of an extended family are celebrating the great season with abundant gifts. Gifts, that great symbol of abundance! There was enough not only for oneself but also for others, and the more elaborate the gift, the more it illustrated the existence of prosperity and confidence in the future of prosperity.

Soldier of Peace

Consider the person of the nutcracker himself. He is a soldier but not a killer, not a person destined for being maimed and killed or slaughtering others. A soldier in those days was a symbol of the nation, a protector and a well-dressed person of discipline and dignity who made the peace possible. He was an extension of regular society, someone performing a light duty deserving of extra respect.

The gift of the nutcracker first breaks and the child cries, but then a magician arrives to put it back together again, and it grows and grows until it becomes real and then a true love. You can make any symbol you want to out of this little man, but it is not a stretch to see it as a symbol of the economic life of this nation and many other nations at the time. There was no limit to prosperity, no limit to growth, no end to the magic that could come to the world. Something that broke could be fixed and grow to new life.

Love of Prosperity

This was a world that loved globalism and celebrated cross-cultural exchange. It was an age before the creation of passports, and traveling the world and seeing it all was first becoming possible for many people. You could ride on ships and not die of scurvy. Trains could take people from place to place in safety. Goods crossed borders as never before, and multicultural chic invaded arts and literature of all sorts. And hence in the ballet, we see not only the famed sugar plum fairies but also Arabian coffee dancers, Chinese tea dancers,

Danish shepherdesses, and of course Russian candy cane dancers along with a beautiful array of fantasy figures.

Here is a vision of a time and a place. It was not just Russia. In "The Nutcracker" we gain a vision of an emerging global ethos. I first realized that the late nineteenth century was really different following a binge reading of several plays by Oscar Wilde, several novels by Mark Twain, a biography of Lord Acton, an essay on capital by William Graham Sumner, and a few Victorian Gothic thrillers. A theme began to emerge that has haunted me ever since.

What do all of these works have in common? It wouldn't seem like much. But once you see it, it is not possible to read this literature the same way. The key is this: None of these writers, and this goes for Tchaikovsky himself, could have imagined the horror that was unleashed by World War I. The killing fields—38 million ended up dead, wounded, or missing—were inconceivable. The concept of a "total war" that did not exclude the civilian population but rather made everyone part of the army was not in their field of vision.

Peace Wrecked

Many historians describe World War I as a calamity that no one in particular intended. It was a result of states pushing out the boundaries of their belligerence and power, a consequence of leaders who imagined that the more they pushed, the more they could create a globe of justice, freedom, and peace. But look at the reality of the mess they made. It was not only the direct carnage. It was the ghastly possibilities this war opened up. It inaugurated a century of central planning, statism, socialism, and war.

How could they have known? Nothing like this had ever happened. And so this late-nineteenth-century generation was innocent and delightfully so. To this generation, the injustices they intended to purge from the world were slavery, remnants of the bondage of women, the perpetuation of feuds and duels, the despotism of the monarchical class, debtors' prisons, and the like. What they could not imagine was the much vaster injustice that was just around the historical corner: mass use of poison gas, universal enslavement of the wartime draft, famine as a war tactic, the gulag, the Holocaust, mass incineration at Hiroshima and Nagasaki.

This is a particularly interesting fact given Russian history. What are the institutional features of the Nutcracker ballet? Faith, property, family, security. Following Russia's disastrous involvement in World War I—resulting in horrible death and economic ruin—there was a revolution in 1917, one designed to overthrow despots and replace them with something completely new. The party that took control ruled under the pretext of ideological communism. And of what did that consist? Opposition to faith, property, family, and the very bourgeois life that is so celebrated in this ballet.

If you look at the demographic data following the October 1917 revolution, you see calamity. Income fell by half. Life expectancy became static and fell. It was the total wreckage, exactly what you would expect if you tried to get rid of property and attack the voluntary society at its core. A full 70 years of communist rule in Russia gutted the country of the life and joy that this ballet puts on display. None of us were there. But those who were there tell stories of terrible things. It was a wholesale looting of all the progress that Russia had experienced until that point in its history.

Age of Innocence

What's beautiful about "The Nutcracker" is that we see none of it. This ballet was created in that great time of innocence when all the world foresaw a beautiful future of unstoppable and unending peace, prosperity, and justice.

Here's what else moves me about this ballet. Fully formed and just as wonderful as ever, it has leapt over the century of statism, the century of bloodshed and mass murder by states, and is presented to us right now in our hometown. We can sit in our lovely arts centers and drink it all in, and smile wide smiles for two solid hours. We can share in this vision of that generation we never knew. We can dream that dream too.

I would never say that the time in which this ballet came to be was a naive time. No. It was a time of clarity when the artists, inventors, intellectuals, and even statesmen saw what was right and true, what was possible and what the human imagination can make real.

The themes of "The Nutcracker"—a culture of free association, gift giving, personal and material growth, dancing and dreaming—can and should be our future. We need not repeat the blunders of the past, the wars and horrors; rather, we can make a new world with a new theme as joyful as the melodies that have enraptured millions in this holiday season.

Work

18

Labor Markets Work When They Are Free

L ast month, business pundits were stoking fears that rising wages would lead to inflation. It was classic fake economics. Contrary to crude Keynesian hydraulics, inflation is a monetary problem, not a cost-push problem. In the world of financial punditry, the news cycle changes fast, so we wake up today to find yet another and seemingly contradictory concern.

This month, the concern is different and perhaps more justified. There's growing frustration that despite low unemployment and high corporate profits, wages still aren't rising as one might expect them to. The theory here is that the monopsony power of corporations is suppressing labor competition. Workers can't seem to get their wages bid up.

Alan Krueger and Eric Posner make the argument:

> It turns out that many corporations possess bargaining power over their workers, not just over their consumers. Their workers accept low wages and substandard working conditions because few alternative job opportunities exist for them or because switching jobs is costly. In other words, in the labor market, effectively a small number of employers are competing for their labor.

There's nothing particularly wrong with the claim as such. It's true that it makes absolutely no sense at all why 70% of Americans should hate their jobs. Why not bail and get one you like? We do this with products constantly, changing apps, restaurants, and consumer products constantly. Why don't we do this with jobs?

Where these economists go wrong (fake economics) is in the assignment of blame. For them, it is about the absence of effective antitrust regulations, the presence of noncompete clauses, and certain failing features inherent in the labor market itself. All of this, say our authors, can be fixed by more government regulation and management of both corporations and labor. Only government, in their view, can give us the competition we need.

Think of their theory as an extension of the Marxian canard that markets give inordinate power to capital over labor, because of the tendency of corporations to extract surplus value from the labor contract. Theirs is a softer version that assigns blame in slightly different ways but the conclusion is the same: outside-the-means that rely on coercion are necessary to balance out the power between capital and labor.

Job Lock

This entire theory is strangely detached from the on-the-ground reality of people's working lives today. Non-compete clauses can be annoying but workers can also push back on them, so long as they are willing to walk away from a new position. I've done this several times; such clauses are easily removed. In the panoply of concerns that keep workers locked into jobs in which they are unhappy or underpaid, these are a trivial concern.

The real question is why so many workers feel locked into their positions and are unable to make their talents in a way that bids up their market value. In other words, the question is: what is it that makes the market seem to fail? The best place to look is to discover non-market considerations in work, hiring, and firing that grant employers disproportionate power in the wage negotiation process.

The leading cause of job lock is unbearably obvious: health care. In the decades following World War II, its provision came to be attached to the workplace, through a series of tax changes, mandates, and corporate expectations. Every change in health care regulation (until very recently) has tended to cement this relationship. Obamacare did terrible damage by making affordable independent health care (that actually functions in real life) far more difficult to get. What this means for workers is that many hold on to jobs solely to stay on their health plans.

Yes, all this was done in the name of worker rights. The result has been the opposite. It has not empowered workers; it has employed employers. It has tied workers to jobs they do not like at wages that are beneath their market worth. This criticism of company-provided health care is widely recognized by economists of all stripes. In fact, part of the purpose of Obamacare was to break this pattern by creating a large marketplace in which workers could actually shop. But the system was so over regulated, packed with mandates, and disabling the capacity for insurers to administer economic rational systems, it made the problem of health-care job-lock far worse.

And it's not only about the job a worker currently has. It's about the time, cost, and frustration about getting a new job. You need quite a lot of savings to tell the boss goodbye. You need to have two months of living expenses. It is quite difficult to get another full-time position with the full benefits you have left. If you are holding out for that kind of job, you could be waiting many months, simply because employers are extremely reluctant to hire because it is so costly and so difficult to fire. As a result, people decided to stay and suffer.

I'm sure you know a dozen people in this situation. Maybe you are. What this really amounts to are millions of small tragedies, all due to factors that have nothing to do with the market as such. It is possible that employers in a free market would offer health care, but the history shows that the practice only began as a workaround during wartime. It was a way to pay people without violating wage controls.

Besides health care, take a look at the pay stubs. The very high payroll tax is costly to administer and tends to rope workers into their position. With that tax, you have social security, unemployment insurance, and funding for Medicare. Most Americans pay more in payroll taxes than in income taxes. This entire system ties people to their existing jobs, and all the pre-committed wages that go to various tax strategies for retirement all worsen the situation. No longer do people think of their workplace as a way to get paid in exchange for adding value; thanks to endless government interventions, a workplace has become a kind of safe harbor from the wiles of life itself, providing health, legal protection, and end-of-life care. Why would anyone voluntarily leave? Once you are in, you stay. It feels like security.

It's the same with firing. Employers have to worry about endless concerns over legal liabilities, and take out insurance packages as protections against lawsuits. Maybe that sounds pro-worker. It is not. Remember that the harder it is to fire people, the more reluctant to hire people a firm becomes. It hurts everyone in the long run. And the expense of new hires can be overwhelming, sometimes as much as one third of the total package going to non-wage benefits. And speaking of benefits, the incredible cruft of regulations concerning working hours, vacation time, maternity leave, protection against discrimination, and all the rest, contribute even more to the problem.

But here is what is remarkable. In the entire article by Posner and Krueger, there was not one mention of any of these real-world factors that actually do cause capital to have more power over labor than would otherwise be the case in a real free market. Not one mention of any of these very obvious points.

Instead, they take us in the exact opposite direction of suggesting even more control over the workplace.

Yes, I'm suggesting a series of dramatic changes to the way employment works. No more payroll tax. No more withholding. No more health-care mandates. No more mandates of any kind. And no more policing of either hiring or firing by the state. In other words, free the market. Economic exchange is about equal power between negotiators, which only means that the same rules should apply to everyone. The more we mess with the freedom of contract, the more we privilege one party over another, with sometimes unpredictable results.

19

Swift vs. Sweep: The Eternal Battle

It's barely the beginning of daybreak at the New England manor home of the American Institute for Economic Research. I'm awakened by a flutter, scrape, and a jumble of bird chirps, coming from somewhere vaguely over there.

Back to sleep. A few minutes later, it repeats itself. The birds don't have a song. It's more of a quick and exultant announcement that comes and goes in a few seconds before resting again for a random bit of time before starting over again.

Where are they? Outside? In the attic?

On the first day, it was charming. Less so on the second and third. By the fourth day, it was on the verge of being intolerable so I reported the disturbance to the caretakers of the home. A few hours later, following a careful investigation, the diagnosis was presented to me with great elan: "The fireplace in your room has a problem with chimney swifts."

The Fix

Somehow it seemed like the right problem for this house to have. It was built in the old English manor Cotswold style, a huge stone house built as an extension of the original property constructed in the interwar years from financial resources accumulated as far back as the Gilded Age. That's America's version of what was called late Victorian in England, a time when chimney cleaning became a huge and wonderful industry with its own culture, economic impact, and sartorial style.

My immediate hope was that someone would hire a chimney sweep and that he would arrive in top hat and suit, carrying a brush on a stick, and that he would look like a character from the musical Oliver or Mary Poppins. Please let it be so!

The maintenance masters, however, had other plans. The eternal battle between sweep and swift would take place with modern technology. There is a machine with a high-pitched tone designed to drive the birds away. It was installed. So far it seems like the birds absolutely love it. Maybe there is hope for a chimney sweep after all. More likely, I'm guessing, a fire will be lit in the fireplace and that will be the end of the problem.

The Meaning of the Sweep

Still, the entire incident got me thinking about the industry of chimney sweeping and its place in history. Why do images of sweeps figure so large in our cultural imaginations?

It didn't take long to discover a rich and amazing history.

Chimney sweeps are associated with three great things: wealth, good luck, and sartorial elegance. There is a reason for all three.

Great Innovations

First, wealth. Chimneys were themselves excellent innovations over the open fires that shelters had in feudal times. The appearance of the fireplace and the technology for moving the smoke out of the room itself suggested an uptick in wealth, making its appearance in Europe around the 12th century (a time when other innovations such as the ribbed ceiling, the wine press, liquor distillation, and glass mirror gave us early glimpses of modernity).

As people moved to the city to pursue new opportunities, houses began to be built closer together, each abode having its own fireplace, forming neighborhoods with beautiful skylines of chimneys. By the 18th century, England and Germany (the most prosperous of the Industrial Revolution), had large industries devoted to the cleaning of these chimneys.

To be sure, the necessity of cleaning them involves a storied history of child labor here. As everyone knows, the largest cities had large orphan populations, and their ubiquitous presence became a source of pathos among reformers of all sorts. But what is not often noted is that in past centuries, these people might not have been around at all, simply because they would not have been able to travel, find shelter, or live off the food and clothing that other people threw away. That was never possible before in history!

What the eye saw — and many writers documented it — was thousands of poor orphans living in the streets or finding protection under business-men who gave them food and shelter in exchange for work such as chimney sweeping. What the eye does not see is what would have been the poverty and early death for these very people in previous ages. What look like signs of poverty are actually signs of rising wealth.

When you look at the details, and the sad lives of children who did this work, condemned by William Blake in his 18th-century poem, it does indeed look indefensibly grim. Children as young as 6 were dropped into tiny tunnels filled with soot, shimmying down naked while carrying a brush, scraping up their elbows and knees, and falling down the other side into the fireplace. The goal was to do this 5 to 6 times per day, marketing their services by shouting "soot-oh sweep!" all over town, in exchange for which the orphans received food and shelter. Sometimes they got stuck. Sometimes they died in service of the people.

So, yes, of course we are all against this. And yet the efforts to ban the practice, which were spectacularly unsuccessful from the earliest attempt in 1788, lacked that one critical thing: a better option. Where were these orphan sweeps going to go if they lost their jobs? They didn't have homes, parents, or income. They would have lived on the streets and be exposed to even worse dangers. The do-gooders and their pieties were never able to generate a good answer to that critical question.

Good Luck!

Second, luck. One story, which is probably apocryphal, is that a chimney sweep in the late Middle Ages in England pushed the King out of the way of a runaway horse and carriage. The King then declared that henceforth, sweeps should be considered a source of good luck. Another story is that a sweep fell from a roof and got his pant leg caught on a rain gutter. A hand from inside a window reached to save him. It was the hand of a person who would later turn out to be his bride. This is why (did you know this?) it is considered lucky to have a chimney sweep at your wedding.

Top Hats

Third, sartorial style. This story again involves a 12th-century English king saved by a chimney sweep, who calmed a scared horse. The King not only declared sweeps to be lucky but also declared that they should be permitted to dress as nobles. In later centuries, the permission to dress up was embodied in top hats and tails.

In the 18th and 19th centuries, this was a glorious mark of pride, which also helped recruit boys into the profession. My goodness, you can dress like a king, or at least like Prince Albert, who was responsible for popularizing the top hat.

In these times, clothing marked your class, birth, and station. It took centuries for capitalism to break down these class barriers, to get to the point where we are today when anyone can wear anything. Back in the day, to be permissioned to dress like the upper class was glorious. The chimney sweepers gained this privilege.

The Past and Future

There's something about the physical experience of a spot like Cotswold Cottage at the American Institute for Economic Research that connects you to the deep past, in all its tribulations and struggle for progress, but also points to a brilliant future. Sometimes we need experiences like this to cause reflection of where we've been and where we are going in the forward motion of time, all while experiencing the truly permanent things, like the never-ending battle between the swifts and the sweeps.

We'll win this one.

20

Should You Quit Your Job?

There is something absolutely beautiful about a tight labor market. It seems to shift decision-making from the boss to the employee. The jobs report is better than we've seen since the 2008 financial crisis, and perhaps in decades, and wages are on the rise. It's a matter of supply and demand. Employers now are begging for talent, and ready to pay to keep it. That gives workers more confidence that they can leave one job for another.

One of the great socialist lies about capitalism is that capital owners have all the power, while the workers live in servitude and exploitation. Tight labor markets provide evidence all around us that this is not true. Anyone can leave a job when it seems to be in his or her interest.

That said, there are features of socialism embedded in worklife that tend to lock people in jobs, no matter how unhappy they might be. The hiring process is bureaucratized and expensive because of payroll taxes and regulations — now more than ever. Business-provided health insurance also works as a job lock.

How many people do you know who hate their jobs but stay on just to cling to that coveted health-insurance card? I can think of dozens of cases personally. This is the great irony of employer-provided insurance. It was supposed to grant new rights to employees. It does the opposite by making workers afraid to walk away. The result is an imbalance of power that favors employers.

At Some Point

But when employment is high and the private sector is hiring, we reach the threshold at which the benefits of quitting outweigh the risks and costs. The Wall Street Journal reports that "Labor Department data show that 3.4 million Americans quit their jobs in April, near a 2001 peak and twice the 1.7 million who were laid off from jobs in April." It's the fastest rate of quitting in 17 years (though still below the rate in the 1970s).

What do you get for quitting? People who switched jobs in May of this year are getting a 30 percent increase in pay over those who stayed in their jobs over the past 12 months. Employees might be switching to more highly capitalized companies that can afford to pay more. It might also be the case that existing employers have mispriced certain labor inputs and employees just get fed up with being undervalued and move on.

It's a very common feature of professional life that bosses and institutions come to take the in-house talent for granted, limiting wage increases and presuming they will be there forever. Sometimes workers have to disrupt their own lives to see their value as employees realized in the market. The more they do this, the more employers have the incentive to treat workers better, if only to retain them.

Here is another reason why tight labor markets are so wonderful. They are a teaching moment for everyone about what life might be like if we had a real free market in labor.

The Way It's Supposed to Work

In a real free market, labor and capital have equal "power," if you want to call it that. They simply make a deal like any other. I will provide you services in exchange for which you give me money. If at any point this doesn't benefit both parties, either party can bail on the deal. The right of the employer to fire is the other side of the coin of the right of the employee to leave the job. They go together. Servitude is forbidden on either side of the exchange.

This is why restrictions on firing are so insidious. They bind one side of the deal in ways that are contrary to the voluntarism of the market economy. We rarely hear politicians speak of restrictions on the right to quit. Those are taken for granted (with the one big exception of the military, which from the ancient world to the present presumes that the worker is in a position of servitude and cannot quit without facing serious repercussions).

Hobbled Labor Markets

Sadly, we don't have a free market. The employment contract is saddled with an ever-increasing amount of interventions that add cost, paperwork, documentation requirements, mandated benefits, and detailed reporting requirements. If you have taken a new job with a big company lately, you know this. There is no ending to the signing you have to do, all handled by the human resources department, a division of a business that was unknown in the days of laissez-faire.

Restrictions on the right to fire only work to discourage business from hiring. These take many forms. Litigation for discrimination (of hundreds of different kinds) is always a risk. Employers still must pay into a fund for unemployment benefits. It's a given that a fired employee is going to be bitter, but when that bitterness is weaponized by law, the damage to a company can be devastating. Here we have another case of unintended consequences: all these restrictions are supposed to help workers, but they only end in making employers risk-averse in the hiring process.

More recently, the enhanced enforcement by the government of citizenship rules has imposed another layer of burdens on employers and employees alike. It wasn't too long ago that many businesses could find ways to use undocumented workers, which benefited workers, businesses, and consumers. These days are coming to an end, creating higher compliance costs, higher demands on wages, and less consumer service. Farming and construction are especially suffering. The workforce in the US has become a papers-please environment.

It's not just about immigration. It's everything about your personal identity. It wasn't that long ago that a certain amount of slippage in labor law was part of national life. I had no problem getting jobs when I was 11 and 12 years old, and getting a high-responsibility job in department store maintenance at the age of 14. Today that would be essentially unthinkable unless you worked for a family business. This is truly tragic for young people, and for everyone. In fact, I would consider restrictions on work of this sort to be a violation of human rights.

Top of the Market?

One thing you notice by looking at long-term trends in job switching is that it becomes highest at the height of the economic boom. The recession hits and once again people cling to their existing jobs like life itself. This is another tragic aspect of recessions: people get stuck in jobs they don't like.

It doesn't have to be this way. Imagine a world in which an employment contract worked like any other exchange in the market economy: two parties make a deal, and that's the end of it. That would require an end to the payroll tax, anti-discrimination law, employer-provided health care, and every kind of mandated benefit, along with an end to all restrictions on work, including age laws and coercion against the hiring of immigrant workers.

Ending on a note from my own experience here: I've never known a person who was worse off for quitting. My entire professional life has shown me the opposite. If you are thinking about quitting, now is the time.

If we freed the market, tight labor markets would be the norm. The beautiful and empowering act of quitting (and moving on to something better) would be an expected feature of professional life.

21

How a New Definition of Personality Wrecked a Generation (or Two)

M y father wrote his dissertation in the 1980s, when the Myers-Briggs Type Indicator was in full vogue. His topic required him to administer thousands of tests to students in music school and assess them based on their choice of focus.

He turned up some significant results that contributed to the ethos of the time: your personality is baked into who you are and is probably secretly determining many of your choices in life. Your job is to discover your personality and then find the right role for yourself in life so that you can find happiness without doing violence to your true self. (Remember how they wrote "never change" in your yearbook?)

In the course of my father's study, he administered the full test to me probably 6 times or so, and each time I grew more frustrated with the whole process. I grew tired of having to discover my inner self. What was I supposed to do with this information anyway? Merely acquiesce and be happy with that? Basically, yes. You have an operating system in you; let it operate. That was the message of this whole enterprise. Discover who you are and be content.

I never liked that attitude. I wanted to know something different. What traits should I cultivate and adopt to make me into the person I ought to be? I don't mean ought in a moral sense. I mean it in a professional or life-success sort of way. What do successful people do and what kinds of behaviors, values, and attitudes do they have that have made them successful? That was a far more interesting question to me.

What Is Personality?

So these tests always made me uncomfortable, and not only for that reason.

I always had that sense that the whole apparatus was built on a tautology. Are you reserved and shy in a crowd? Yes. You are an introvert. What's an introvert? A person who is reserved and shy in a crowd. You can continue this tautology to a huge range of complexity, further defining, slicing, dicing, and reassembling traits to build dozens or thousands of variants.

This week I picked up a book published in 1939. It is Building Your Personality, by Hattie Marie Marsh. It opens with this sentence: "This book is based upon the idea that personality is ever changing and that each individual can, by her own directed efforts, shape and change her personality to a great extent."

It doesn't deny "natural" and biological inclinations. But it observes that if they are there, they probably can't be changed. Instead, the book argues, you should focus on what you can change. If you fail to do that, you have failed to realize your potential. Reading along, you come to realize that the author is working from a completely different sense of personality than anything we know today. It is truly a different term.

"Many people think that their personalities are so well established before birth that little can be done. This is far from the truth." The author gives an example of a person who has talent for playing the piano but if she never tries to play or doesn't practice, she will never be good at it. Further, "a person may have inherited a quick temper, but by early training he may be taught to control it."

The entire project of this book from 1939 is about achievement in life as the basis of personal happiness. "Contrary to the teachings of some psychics, palmists, phrenologists, and astrologers, personality is not miraculously given, and it can be transformed." Thus does the book reject from the outside the view that "blondes are flighty" or that "a long line in the center of the palm denotes great intelligence." So too many people are drawn to "zodiacal signs." Why are people drawn to the theory that personality is a given part of your constitution? "Many accept these beliefs because such acceptance relieves them of any responsibility for self-improvement."

Wow. Yes. Indeed.

Thus does the book proceed to focus on behavior and good choices. It explains how to project your voice, how to speak with good grammar and pronunciation, how to breathe properly and have a good posture, what to wear to various events, how to groom yourself, how to set a table and deal with a finger bowl, how to interact at a cocktail party and introduce people and be introduced, and so on. Most all of the book is directed toward cultivating a personality that will bring you personal success.

"As a rule, the road to personal betterment and achievement is hidden behind things people do not like to do. Those who are too lazy to perform these tasks never find the road. They never blame themselves, but complain about 'fate' and 'never getting a break.'"

Don't we know it!

In the 21st century, this is a shocking way to approach the whole problem of personality. It contradicts everything I was taught, and it contradicts pretty much everything most anyone under the age of 30 today thinks. This is now the generation of Myers-Briggs: you are who you are and it is contrary to nature, even violent to the human spirit, to break outside the personality type you have been given by birth. In other words, your job is not to aspire but to acquiesce.

Amazing.

This 1939 book, which went through five printings and two editions, now seems completely foreign. We just don't think this way anymore. It strikes me as very possible that, without entirely knowing what we were doing, that in the course of a few decades, we replaced a view of the human project that was inspired by human choice, personal ambition, and individual achievement with a completely different view that insists that aspiration is utterly pointless and probably even dangerous. We've replaced a sense of personal responsibility with a sense of the fate of destiny that is baked into the unique way we are made: our true selves.

The Personality Industry

To get a sense of how this happened, I downloaded the very interesting book The Personality Brokers, by Merve Emre, which provides a history of the Myers-Briggs test. In 1939, the idea of testing for personality was not common. They existed, yes, but were seen as inventories to guide direction for personal improvement. By the late 1950s, the test as self definition had swept through management circles, and tests were everywhere in government and high-end corporate culture. They were seen as the answer to how people could be placed, and place themselves, in a role that would lead to great happiness. What began to develop was a culture of deference to what is innate rather than a culture of aspiration to what anyone can become.

Myers-Briggs was the most popular but it spawned a massive industry that flooded the world with personality tests, not with the goal of inspiring people to get better but with the ambition of pigeonholing everyone in a way that will maximize personal satisfaction. And now the corporate world is swimming in confusion about why young workers are so unadaptable, spoiled, undisciplined, and unambitious. It's really no mystery: we told them that this is the right way to be: be only yourself and nothing more.

As the author told NPR, "I think it really shifts you away from that language of accomplishment toward a language of the self.… I think that can be an incredibly comforting fantasy… I think it can make you feel like you don't have to take responsibility for changing."

That's precisely what my 1939 book said of any theory that says you can't create your own personality. We once knew this, but the fashion for personality science changed that view, gradually and imperceptibly, and without our knowing it. We replaced one practice of life management with a different view entirely, one that has worked to disable individual volition and encourage a fatalistic and feudalistic outlook on the life project.

Merve Emre writes about how people are smart enough to very quickly learn how to game the tests to produce whatever result is desired on the part of the testers. I know this feature well. My father gave me these tests at a young age. I got better at taking them, answering all the questions according to my perceptions concerning what kind of person I was supposed to be.

My father was confused as to why every test I took produced a different result. Where is the true me? It turns out that the true me, and the true everyone, is to become something better than you are. We once knew this. This is what it meant to build a personality. We were better off for it.

None of which is to say that curiosity about our innate personality features will go away. For those who are curious, they maybe find enough satisfaction in the surprisingly insightful medieval theory of four temperaments. It is probably no more less scientific than what we came to embrace in the 1950s. And they are broad enough to very clearly give plenty of room for personal improvement.

How Technology Bolsters Your Right to Work, Choose, and Earn

I t's hard to remember how hard it was to look for work — or leave your current job — before technology changed everything.

Consider what LinkedIn does for you. It allows you to have your own identity apart from your current employer, as if you own your labor. You gather your own network and keep it as you move from job to job.

You can job hunt without seeming to betray your boss. You can be available for job offers too, even if you don't think of yourself as being on the market. When you change jobs, you can add that to your profile with a few clicks and have that change announced to your network. Otherwise everything is the same. You are faced with a daily variety of choice among employers competing to hire you for your skills. Or you can very easily go solo, choosing to gig and contract as your own personal business.

This is emancipation. This gives you freedom of choice.

Maybe that doesn't impress you too much. We take it all for granted. But actually social media platforms have changed everything about the right to work. Before you had the ability to make a public profile page that people could follow, moving jobs was fraught with risk. You had to send in your resume, but you could not use your current employer as a reference or let your coworkers know you were in the market. You were stuck looking through help-wanted ads or getting news of open offers from a word-of-mouth network.

It was hard to make or take calls about possible new positions from the office because you didn't have a cell phone. You had to scramble on nights and weekends. You dressed for a job interview — everything depended on the interview because there was no way for people to post testimonials about you — and everyone at the office would get suspicious. When you left your job, or got fired, much of the capital you developed in your last job you had to forgo. You had to start over entirely. The prospect alone was enough to discourage you from even looking for a new position.

Technological limitations and government interventions hobbled labor market adjustments. It could not clear as a market should.

Then Came the Internet

We think of internet commerce as eBay or Amazon, or perhaps Craigslist, but it is the job marketplace that has made the massive difference in our lives. Anyone can recommend you for a position by sharing a link to your professional profile. You can stay on the market at all times, posting on your profile without raising suspicions or being seen as a betrayer. Your resume is before the world at all times. If disaster should strike after a fallout with the boss, you have a network to tap instantly to provide a bridge to the future.

And it's not just you. Every participant in the global market can upload a work history and resume, catalog skills, gather endorsements, post personal testimonies, and so on. What it means is truly striking. LinkedIn, then, takes that crucial step toward a real market for labor. Then add to that the remarkable power of ride sharing, task rabbiting, remote working, digital nomadism, and gigging in general.

The information economy has liberated those who do the work from servile dependency on any single capital-controlling employer. We didn't need Karl Marx to invent a new political order to do that; we just needed a better software infrastructure.

As I've pointed out, one of the terrible consequences of government intervention in the workplace is how it has chained workers to their jobs. The American corporate structure after WWII was modeled on the European welfare state except with the benefits provided privately through mandates. The results have been terrible for the American worker. Health care benefits, complicated tax accounting, and all sorts of mandates have caused the labor market to be far less fluid than it was a century ago.

Now, thanks to digital entrepreneurship, we are starting to see what competition for labor looks like. You can go to a site like Indeed.com and see postings for your skills right in your town or anywhere you want to move. Or you can post a job availability. Every industry has a micro version of the same. You can advertise too.

The contribution this makes toward better placement is incalculable. It might be one of the factors driving the low unemployment numbers, though I've never seen anyone give software the credit.

What Determines Wages

It should be obvious that market competition is good for workers because it makes their value more clear and enables them to charge the right price for their work. In economic theory, over the long term, in a free market, workers earn what they contribute to the profitability of the firm (a theory that comes from Knut Wicksell).

In real market conditions, however, what determines the wage is more immediately influenced by the worker's next-best wage option in the market. You are paid enough to keep you there because the pay is better than you can get elsewhere. But that supposes you are always on the market as a worker. The more you know about your market worth, the better off you are.

I wrote Alexander Tabarrok about this aspect of wage determination. My question: in economic theory, wages equal marginal product, but in practice it seems like the wage is determined more by the opportunity cost of the current job. His answer is brilliant:

> I don't think your thinking is wrong, it's more like this is the process by which the economic theory turns out to be approximately true. Consider the following. In economics we teach that profits tend toward zero (normal). If you talk to a business person, however, they will say what are you talking about — what I am always thinking about is maximizing my profits, getting them bigger, that's what a successful business person does! Quite so but the net result of everyone trying to increase profits is that profits are driven down!
>
> In the case of wages, I agree that the simple model that we teach doesn't really fit the facts that well. In the simple model it's often identical workers producing identical products and there is one wage given by the market for all the workers and the manager hires until the point where w=mp. In the more common situation, the workers are all different, the employer isn't hiring more than one for the same position and the wage is negotiated not given.
>
> Still, each employer has to evaluate the worker and the job and each employer has to say, do I want the worker or not, and over time workers with w>mp get let go and everyone wants to hire when w<mp so wages get pushed up. But it's a messy process. Not as clean as in the model. And also the perspective of the employer is not the perspective of the economist. We might say w=mp is more a product of human action than human design! FYI, note that this also means there is more room for discrimination, for example, than in the simple model.

What this "messy process" means in practice is that you have to differentiate yourself, offering labor as a unique individual rather than as part of a labor pool. To do that, in a world in which millions are competing for your job, you need a tool. The digital world has provided us with just that. It is wonderful and brilliant, and ever more valuable in a tight labor market such as we have now.

All of which is to say, if you have not beefed up your online profile as a worker, or consider leaving the grind of a corporate job for a market-based gig, today might be the time to get to work on it. The market is doing everything possible to enhance your dignity as a worker and make it possible for you to earn your economic worth.

Here again, software (not ideology, not politics) has proven to be the friend of the worker, making dreams come true that would not have been possible in ages past.

23

How To Become Talented

I have a beef with the phrase "natural talent." Not that such a thing doesn't exist. But anyone we consider to be truly talented — in music, sports, literature, finance, medicine, you name it — has had to work like crazy to develop that talent into a stable skill.

This is true of the concert violinist as well as the rock star, the Shakespearean actor or the Hollywood movie star, the Olympic skater or the professional football player. They are all highly accomplished but nothing like that kind of talent comes naturally. You might not like the performance or even the industry but let's not deny that rising to the top is anything but natural.

Sometimes we use the phrase "natural talent" in a way that disparages or denies the crucial reality that every skill we have requires cultivation, meaning hard work, unrelenting practice, and plenty of failures and correction along the way. All this requires a conscious choice to displace every evidence of failure with overwhelming virtuosity. Getting there requires discipline that extends from a deep and passionate desire to do what it takes to achieve excellence.

By the time the talent reaches our eyes and ears, the hard work is done. We see only the finished product. In our attempt to discern the difference between their level of awesome and ourselves, we reach for the easiest answer: the person must have been born this way. It just comes naturally.

It's nonsense. And this is precisely what is uniquely valuable about a new series on Amazon Prime. In conversations with people who have seen The Marvelous Mrs. Maisel, it fascinates me how people take different messages away from the first season. Some people think it is about a woman finding a place in a man's world. Others see it as a drama about family life. I see it as an allegory about turning a minor talent into greatness based entirely on the desire to achieve.

A young married woman with two kids is trying to coach her husband on realizing his dream to be a comic. In the course of this, she discovers her own talent. Once he bumps up against his limits, she tries her own stand-up routine and is a great success. This eventually dooms a marriage that is already on the rocks. The woman then needs a career and decides that comedy can be it.

There's a problem. She has thus far relied mostly on liquor and spontaneity to carry the day. It works. It works again. But then it doesn't. And it doesn't again. Now she has a problem. She has to figure out a way to codify her spontaneous genius and realize it every single night and do it without liquor.

The initial attempts were disastrous. She becomes imitative and inauthentic and then falls flat. She does not immediately have an automatic intuition about what made her initially successful. So she has to reverse engineer it, find that core ability, build on it, package it in a way that is consistently good, while maintaining her originality.

In this long endeavor, filled with many failed attempts at the microphone, she has a coach who helps her, just as every great performer has a coach. So too with every violinist, every pop star, every ballerina, and so on. Excellence requires this. But no coach can cause excellence to happen. It is always and everywhere up to the volition of the performer to figure it out, complete with nonstop failure. This is true of the beginning pianist all the way through the top-of-the game performer in any industry.

What's beautiful about this show is that we get to watch it emerge in real time. We cheer for Mrs. Maisel and suffer with her when she fails. And we can all learn from her process, no matter our profession.

As a person who is honored to be called on to speak often, I've come to marvel at stand-up comedy. The best of it is highly intellectual but the humor part is the part that is difficult to master. The timing. The attitude. The conversational authenticity that seems spontaneous but is actually extremely well-rehearsed.

To achieve Louis C.K. levels of genius requires years and a vast amount of private study time. The goal, in the end, is to come across like a natural. When you finally achieve it, being called a "natural talent" might be the highest compliment simply because very few can ever imagine the hard work that goes into becoming that person.

The great merit of the show is how it shows that the realization of virtuosity comes from only one place: the individual will. The coach can't do it. The boss can't do it. The politician can't do it. The central planner certainly can't do it. A society that encourages and rewards excellence is built bit by bit, one dedicated human mind at a time.

24

Mistakes People Make When They Are Fired

The labor contract in a market economy should be based on mutual benefit. The freedom to quit and the freedom to fire are the mechanisms that keep that exchange relationship working. Getting fired is not always a tragedy. Ideally, we live and learn and move on.

Moreover, it's not always about incompetence. I've never known a productive, ambitious, skilled employee who was not fired from at least one job. Sometimes great employees are disruptive, and the legacy structure fights back. Steve Jobs is a famous case; he was fired from his own company in 1985, returning later to lead Apple to greatness.

That said, people are rarely prepared. For this reason, people who get fired from jobs tend to make the same mistakes when the announcement is made. This is because the experience is new, and nothing in our education has prepared us for what to do (actually, our education prepares us for virtually no real-world employment situations). So we get the bad news, panic, and make the situation worse.

Getting fired has happened to me, and it will probably happen to you at some point in your career. It seems like one of the great traumas in life. However, we all have the tendency to wildly exaggerate the implications and then spend far too much time dwelling on them rather than seeing the experience as a challenge and opportunity.

First, realize that not every job is the right fit. Value creation has to run in both directions: from you to the employer and back again. This exchange relationship needs to continue daily. If there is a mismatch, it makes no sense to continue the deal. In firing you, no one is trying to harm you any more than you are trying to harm a jewelry store by declining to buy its product. They are merely declining to continue the exchange in the relationship, which is their human right. You want no job in which you are not seen as a net value creator. If it is not working, you need to know that.

If your company decides you are no longer the right fit, it does no good to languish in denial, thinking, for example, that someone is going to call you to beg you to come back. It's not going to happen, even if it should. That period of your life is over, and a new period is beginning. Process that as fast as possible.

Second, do not lash out in anger. This would be a huge mistake. You need to bridge from your current job to the next one. Your exit needs to be gracious, with expressions of genuine gratitude for the confidence your firm showed you. Express this in every way you can — leaving aside every bit of revenge fantasy — with as much sincerity as you can muster. You can be certain that the place will collapse without you, but let that be their problem, not yours.

You will be glad you made this choice to behave like a mature and decent person. Your employer will be impressed, for one thing, and then might be delighted to give you the best-possible recommendation for your next job. Never be tempted by the idea that this is not important.

Within weeks or months, you will get the question of how your previous employment relationship ended. You will need to explain. It's almost a guarantee that your next employer will contact your previous one. You want that conversation to go well. If you leave your employer with a sense that you are a decent, even magnanimous, person, that is all the better for you.

And keep in mind too that the relationships you have built will pay reputational returns for many years, even decades. It's not just about the paycheck of the moment. It's about building a network of respect and admiration for your intelligence, character, and discipline. There's no better time to show this than when the bad news is delivered.

Third, you should realize right away that you have a serious problem: cash flow. For whatever reason, people forget this, having taken the income stream for granted. Then they are shocked after two weeks to find that it has stopped. It sneaks up extremely fast. You need to get busy right away finding a way to plug the hard leak in your personal finances.

There is a corporate convention to give you two weeks of income and perhaps a month of health care. Getting another source for health care coverage is a bear these days, and it is made worse without income to actually pay for whatever you find. Perhaps you can do without for a while, but you are taking some risks.

This extremely short time frame is coupled with the reality of the job marketplace: it will take you six to eight weeks to seal your next gig. Then it could be as much as 30 days before your next paycheck arrives. This is the cruel reality, and it is mostly due to the government-imposed expense and risk of hiring. It doesn't have to be this way, and wouldn't be in a free market. But we don't live in that world.

So we have here a one- or two-month gap between jobs. If, during that time, you have maxed out your credit cards and done without any income stream from another source, this is a serious problem from which it could take you as much as a year to recover.

I have a friend who had an awesome job in D.C. and then landed on the wrong side of the temper of the new manager of the firm. She was suddenly without work. Being scrappy, she quickly realized that she now had two new jobs: finding another regular job and getting income in the door from any source. She became a dishwasher for the diner down the street, even as she perfected her LinkedIn profile. Awesome! So inspiring! Shortly, she landed another position better than the first one, and she is now ascending the corporate ladder. This is the way to do it.

Fourth, cast a wide net when looking for your next position. You have your heart set on a new institution because, perhaps, you have a friend there. You lean in hard and push for that position. It is where you imagine yourself. In fact, you are not in control, not solely in any case. You need to imagine yourself in a variety of new positions and institutions, and apply to them all, as soon as possible.

There is a practical element here. Your next employer needs to think that you are in demand and needs to start bidding for your services as soon as possible. From your own point of view, you need to be somewhat detached. You need to be in the position of walking away, and even perhaps (though this is tricky) play one institution off another. To be a free agent in the hiring process, you need options. But only you can create those.

Fifth, learn from your mistakes. We've all made them. The first time I was fired, it was because of insubordination. I promised some suit tailoring sooner than the company had guaranteed in the holiday season. I ended up doing the tailoring myself, which was a great experience, but it cost me my job. This was not an injustice. No boss will put up with insubordination on this level. I learned that, grew up, and killed it at my next job.

We all make errors. Figure out what yours were, learn from them, and apply those lessons in your next position. Leave the bitterness on the table and think of yourself as an asset that grows more valuable over time, mistakes and all.

Or perhaps there weren't errors. The relationship worked for a while and then stopped working. I've faced this situation on several occasions. There is nothing wrong with that. This can happen to any employment situation. For this reason, the smart employee imagines himself or herself always on the job market, perhaps not actively looking but keeping an eye out for possible options. This is not disloyal. It is about finding your highest value in the marketplace, and this benefits your present employer as much as it does you.

Everyone will get fired at some point in a career. Whether you turn this to the good in your life is up to you.

25

The Phenomenal Excellence of Bill Watrous

My heart just sank. I was curious what the mighty trombonist Bill Watrous was doing these days. He died July 2, 2018. This is the first I've heard about it. I met him only briefly, and implausibly, one night in a jazz club and was honored to play alongside him for a song or two. I was 17 years old. It was my life dream. Thinking back on it, I would say Watrous had a greater influence on my life than just about anyone else apart from my own mother and father.

How is it possible that a musician could have this kind of influence? It's because his level of excellence is beyond description. He made the trombone do things that no one even thought possible. Even now, you can tell your home assistant to play his music and you immediately enter into a realm of performance impossibility. Each time I think: maybe no one should ever have to play trombone besides him? It's a silly thought of course, but his level of distinction in his craft surpasses anything known on planet earth.

No Words

I'm just sitting here now listening, and I'm getting chills. It's distracting me from being able to write. The management of vibrato, the range extending probably two octaves (or more!) beyond normal standards, the razor-sharp articulation at breakneck speeds, the infinite creativity, the complexity of his use of modal scales, his seamless circular breathing techniques, the absence of anything resembling a misstep or mistake, and, above all else, his tender interpretations — it all combines to create a product that is otherworldly.

Here's some background on my wild infatuation with this artist. I was nearly born with a trombone in my hands, put there by my father, who remained a formidable player long after I gave up the craft. My second-grade show-and-tell was to play trombone for the class. When official band class finally got going five years later, I was already playing for the high school. By the time I was in high school, I was playing for the university jazz ensemble. Then I paid for my schooling by gigging around town.

All these years, from the age of 8 through 18, I only wanted to play like Bill Watrous. I listened incessantly. I spent countless hours transcribing his solos to musical staff paper. I ended up with hundreds of pages of transcriptions (just typing those words really makes me wonder why my childhood was so strange). I tried to mimic his sound, his technique, his musical demeanor.

I even saved up money to have a special instrument built that was exactly like his. As I recall, it was a Bach 16 with a pretty small bore but a larger bell than the factory normally made. I used his same mouthpiece. I put black tape on the upper section just like he did.

As for my skill, I was the classic case of a young kid who always had enormous potential. What I did not realize then — though my father constantly warned me — was that there comes a point when you can no longer live off your potential. You have to actually be good. I never crossed into that territory, mainly because I was lazy and too satisfied with my early fame, unaware that it would run out at some point.

The Nature of Genius

But back to Watrous. At some point, he was coming through town to play at a jazz club. I counted the days. Then I was tapped to bring my instrument because he liked to invite local players on the stage to play with him, as a way of encouraging young musicians. I was on stage for a song or two and played. It's a bit of blur to me now because my aesthetic intoxication was at an all-time high.

I do of course recall his absolute perfection. I also noticed that he had an eccentric personality, almost a bit detached from the reality around him, as if the whole of his person was poured only into his music and the sound he made. I think this might often be true with true geniuses. Others cannot access what makes them what they are. We can only listen, be inspired, be in awe.

There are people who come our way who reach this level of accomplishment that seems superhuman. My list includes Aristotle, Shakespeare, Josquin, Bach, Adam Smith, William Byrd, Mahler, Ludwig von Mises, and Watrous — talents that go beyond good and great to become forces of immortal achievement. There are more than a few of them around today. You encounter them at high-end concert venues: the perfect tenor, the amazing clarinetist, the impossibly brilliant violinist, and so on.

We should revere such people and protect them. And be careful about calling them natural talents. There is endless hard work built into every note they play. At the same time, there is something else in operation. There is a gift of some sort too but a gift that must absolutely be cultivated with discipline, drive, and unrelenting tenacity. They must give of themselves completely to art in order for that art to achieve transcendent levels of perfection. The rest of the world, before they become known for their achievements, considers them to be fanatics, obsessed, even freaky.

Immortalized

But look at this. Right now, Bill Watrous can be in my living room right now playing. Thanks to technology. Thanks to a commercial culture that gives us access. It's a miracle. We lived through hundreds of thousands of years of human experience without the ability to record and preserve genius. Now we have that ability. How rich this makes us! How much this beautifully improves our lives! Now every genius can be immortalized and forever contribute to the capital base of civilization.

Indulge me for one final paragraph on why I gave up the trombone. At the age of 19, I crossed that invisible line when I had to stop having potential and actually be good. I was playing at a club and got carried away on a solo cadenza. A shout came from the back of the bar: "Cut it with the bull****!" I did. I ended the song and sat down. Fellow band members assured me that he was just some drunk. But I knew the truth: he was right. I needed to move on in life. And move on I did.

Let me say this. I will never achieve anything remotely close to what Watrous did. But his music never stops inspiring me. It affects all my thinking, all my writing, all my daily routines, my aesthetic, and even my life aspirations. His talent produced the music that became the soundtrack to my life. He never knew that. None of us know who we influence and how.

We need geniuses among us. We need the freedom and tolerance to let them become what they need to be, for their sake and ours.

26

I, Tonya, and the
Malleability of Class

The film I, Tonya tells the story of Tonya Harding's rise and fall as an Olympic ice skater, her stunning talents, her grim private and family life, her wild fame followed by mass public derision, and her final banishment from the sport. Aside from being a fascinating story, it is a rare film for dealing directly with a topic that Americans talk about often but think about hardly any at all: class distinctions and the barriers they create to social and economic mobility.

In the world of ice skating, Tonya was widely seen as tacky, trashy, and a poor example of the ideal type of young woman that the guardians of the sport wanted to put on display. The film treats the problem head on. Tonya believed that judges routinely downgraded her for her demeanor, costumes, choice of music, and lack of the demure elegance they desired in women athletes. Still, she mastered the sport and became the first woman to perform the triple axel in national and international competitions in 1991. No one could deny her credit for that.

She succeeded in sports. She failed to ascend the social ladder. Part of the reason was her own terrible disadvantages. In the film version, the viewer is horrified at the abuse she endures from her mother and boyfriend, and mortified that she keeps getting tripped up by circumstances beyond her control. And yet we are also aware that she bears plenty of personal responsibility for her plight. She seethes with resentment, wallows in victimology, and repeatedly confirms every stereotype. It is a story of fantastic athletic success within a framework of terrible social failure.

Just how malleable is class? What is chosen by the person vs constructed by society? The counterintuitive casting of Margot Robbie as the leading woman flips the observation of Bernard Shaw's Pygmalion. Makeup, accents, demeanor, and temperament can bring anyone up or down the social ladder.

Class as a Concept

And so the movie helps us all confront this strange reality of class that few can define but everyone vaguely knows exists. In American English, we have no "upper class" or even "lower classes"; there is only middle class. We speak of upper and lower middle class. When a politician speaks of coming to the defense of the middle class, that means pretty much every person who can hear.

This interesting use of language is a mighty tribute to the extraordinary power of the American economic engine, that over 250 years it has managed to redefine the entire concept of social stratification. The old world was all about status; the New World provided opportunity for all. We expect people to take advantage of it. When they do not, there is something judgy about the American cultural ethos. We expect all people to rise to the occasion, to behave and think in a way that is up to the standards of their "betters" precisely because we don't believe that anyone is really better than anyone else.

This concept of class still has meaning in American life but defining it is elusive. It's not really about money, education, privilege of birth, or occupation. To be classy is something within the reach of anyone who wants to master the etiquette manual, dress the part, repair an awkward regional brogue, and otherwise play the part. We speak of people who "marry up" or "date down" so the concept of class is a living reality, even if economic opportunity and our love of merit above station has made it all very blurry.

Tonya's problem was not so much the perception that she was trashy but rather that she seemed unwilling to upgrade according to the professional expectation. She aspired to be an ice skater. All she had to do, in addition to learning to be the greatest skater in history, was to behave properly, be more sparing in her use of vulgarity, and stop flaunting her low-end class origins. Whenever she tried, however briefly, she failed, and thus came to embrace her difference with others as a badge of honor.

Class and Capitalism

It was Karl Marx who embedded our academic brains with the concept of class as it applies to economics. His notion was not the hazy sense of social status that we commonly think about. He wanted to tie the idea of class to strict categories. There were workers. There was capitalism. They were in conflict, forever facing a terrible reality in which the capital-owners would pillage what should have been justly owned by the workers because it is they who are the value creators. With this model in mind, he made history's worst prediction: that under capitalism, the workers would grow ever poorer and the capital owners would grow ever richer.

He made the prediction in 1848, just on the cusp of the most gigantic expansion in mass prosperity witnessed until that point in history. Over the following half century, we saw the poor grow rich, lifespans jump, infant mortality plummet, income rise and rise, and the old category of social station grow incredibly malleable. So much for the entrenched Marxian categories; we were moving into a new world of universal opportunity for everyone.

Threatened Position

The great irony of capitalism is not that it entrenched classes; the problem was that it fed resentment among the upper classes (excuse me, "upper middle classes") that too many people were entering their ranks and threatening their position. The revolt against it took many forms, some of them Marxian. More often, it was the opposite: entrenched elites did not appreciate the uppity ways of the new middle class, the longer lives of the previously poor, the expansion of the population of the previously marginalized.

World GDP per capita (1000-2000 CE)

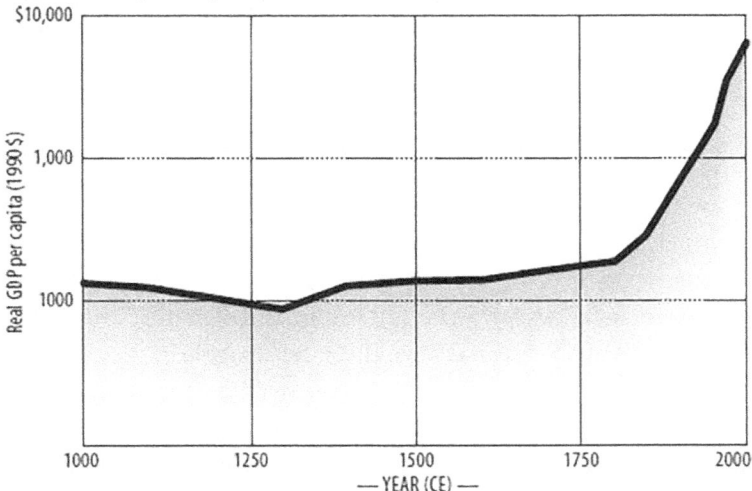

Source: J. Bradford DeLong, "Estimating World GDP, One Million B.C. - Present," Department of Economics, U.C. Berkeley, 1998.
Raw data at http://www.j-bradford-delong.net/TCEH/1998_Draft/World_GDP/Estimating_World_GDP.html accessed on July 20, 2014.

Having written an entire book on the resentment and revolt of the elites in these years, let me just focus on the strange rise of eugenics in the late 19th century. The literature of the time reflected a sense of panic that just about anyone could mate with anyone else to bear children and thus cause a degeneration in the overall quality of the national stock. This was a large part of the motivation for segregation, marriage licenses, labor restrictions, immigration controls, and compulsory schooling. The drive was not a longing for greater equality but to slow down the mixing of social classes and keeping the rich with a solid monopoly hold on power.

Does that shock you? It shouldn't. The attempt by the ruling classes to keep their inferiors in their place dates back to the Sumptuary Laws of Colonial New England, as Sarah Laskow explains:

> New England's Puritan colonies had many laws restricting how citizens—particularly women—could dress. "Sumptuary laws" like these weren't unique to that time or place; they had governed personal behavior as far back as ancient Rome. Usually sumptuary laws were enacted to control behavior in order to distinguish the high classes from the lower ones, though sometimes they were intended to keep wealthy-enough people from squandering all these resources on fashionable indulgences. Pirates' dramatic and colorful style of dressing was, for instance, a deliberate and brazen violation of these laws…
>
> The Massachusetts Bay Colony passed its first law limiting the excesses of dress in 1634, when it prohibited citizens from wearing "new fashions, or long hair, or anything of the like nature." That meant no silver or gold hatbands, girdles, or belts, and no cloth woven with gold thread or lace. It was also forbidden to create clothes with more than two slashes in the sleeves (a style meant to reveal one's rich and fancy undergarments). Anyone who wore such items would have to forfeit them if caught.

We don't have such laws anymore, but the ambition of the rich to distinguish themselves from everyone else has been the great struggle in the capitalist world in which classes kept getting mixed up. By the twentieth century, this took the form of ever more refinement in tastes of food, manner of behavior, music, and art. And today, you can see this tendency in operation at, for example, the Met Gala where the stars flaunted their edge by dressing Catholic as a way of tweaking the religion of the peasants and working classes.

Refinement in the Class Idea

Under capitalism, it is ever hard to define class by money, occupation, birth, or education, since the freest economies open opportunity to everyone. The impulse to separate "us" from "them" has to take other forms, ever more subtle, ever more refined, ever more easy to bridge. This is surely the most glorious thing about freedom itself; its replacement of an entrenched aristocracy with a new idea of meritocracy. Revealingly, the term only became popular in the late 19th century as it pertained to the civilian bureaucracy: it was not just reserved for the privileged but for everyone based on merit.

The cultural panic about class mixing never ends. We look at popular music, sports, or business and never stop being aghast that this tacky person or that uncouth person could possibly have become rich and famous. We make reality shows about these people, and laugh and laugh at them.

The whole endeavor is harmless, so long as it doesn't take a political form. What bothers us mostly about the case of Tonya Harding is the perception that her life disadvantages could have found expression in how she was judged in her talent, and also her own indefatigable refusal to step it up a bit to meet with the social and aesthetic demands of the sport. We sense the tragedy. In the end, we as Americans also know the hard truth: she bears most of the blame for her fate.

27

Bohemian Rhapsody Shows That Artists Should Care About Audiences

B ohemian Rhapsody, a biographical account of the lead singer of the band Queen, is one of the best films about a great musician that I've seen. I say this in defiance of some critics. The rap on the film is that it is too much about the music and the creative and performative genius of Freddie Mercury, and not enough about certain lifestyle issues for which he was notorious.

The opposite is true. The failing of most musician-centered movies is that there is not enough about the art itself. I'm thinking of Immortal Beloved (1994). If you wanted to see a movie about Ludwig van Beethoven as a musician, this was not it. You would think that his real passion was not his art but some secret unconsummated love. Even Amadeus, while better than most attempts, was disappointing in this respect.

It can be difficult to find actors who can provide a compelling recreation of musical greatness. But to bury the story of art in the muck of personal eccentricity is not a good way to honor genius. Bohemian Rhapsody is foremost a film about an amazing singer and a creative process that rocked the pop world through the 1970s and 1980s and left us with iconic songs that changed everything. The movie presents the creative process here realistically and with exciting drama.

Commerce and Art

Even better, this film has a lesson that pertains to the creation of great art in a commercial society. Queen was rewarded in every way for making music that people love. Yes, the same could be said of many top pop artists today. Maybe this doesn't sound like a radical proposition, but there is a tendency in high-end musical circles to believe that quality and popularity are mechanistically opposed to each other.

If you get famous and rich, you must have "sold out." If you borrow pop tropes for serious music, you have compromised your art. The tendency to believe that there must be a high wall between artistic integrity and commercial success stretches far back in history, and is with us still.

At the age of 16, I was sure I would become a lifetime professional musician, so I started hanging out at the school of music during as much spare time as I had. I began to notice a certain ethos alive in these circles. They didn't like audiences. They didn't like customers. They saw every demand that their art be deployed to please popular tastes to be a terrible imposition. They wanted to be exempt from economic forces at work. I could hardly stand it, so I changed my life plans and, in reaction, went into a field that celebrated commercial life (economics).

Sacred and Secular

The perception that commerce and art don't mix created a notorious case in the 16th century. Orlando di Lasso was a much-beloved composer of polyphonic Catholic Church music. Many of his masses and motets became standard performance repertoire in cathedrals all over Europe. The clerical class delighted in their pious sound and quality of inspiring prayer and soulful reflection.

Then one day, someone noted a certain familiarity to some of the melodic structures. Sure enough, they were identical to some folk music popular among the less-than-spiritual crowd. Some were drinking songs. Some had bawdy lyrics. His "Missa Entre vous Filles" was based on tunes that included lyrics that can't be printed here. Panic ensued and di Lasso's compositions were quickly banned.

This was not uncommon in the age of faith. There was a perception that music composed for a high-end purpose could never be tainted by musical forms coming from secular life. Two centuries later, with the rise of commercial culture, opportunities for composers to rely on ticket sales and sheet music sales increased. No longer was patronage the only option.

But even here, the perception that commerce would taint serious music persisted. And it persisted despite all evidence. G.F. Handel moved from Germany to Italy to England chasing commercial opportunities. He reused tropes from his Italian liturgical music for his English oratorios. And the themes of his oratorios finally settled on stories from Hebrew scriptures precisely because these stories experienced popular success in 18th-century England.

Some people might imagine that someone like J.S. Bach would be free from such grubby commercial dealings, but his hundreds of cantatas were written as a job obligation in exchange for wages. His famous Brandenburg Concertos were composed as demonstration projects when seeking a new gig. And just as with later composers like Johannes Brahms, he paid the bills through teaching far less than through performance. Other composers like Gioacchino Rossini and Giuseppe Verdi experienced wild popular success, while Richard Wagner became the subject of a cult of his own.

Keep in mind that all of this happened before the advent of musical copyright. Bach, Mozart, Brahms, and Beethoven all managed some degree of commercial success without using the law to maintain exclusive rights. They relied on teaching, concertizing, and marketing first-run access to their newest compositions. Once universal copyright came into being with the Berne Convention, there was a new complication: composers believed they could never borrow from contemporaries, whether low- or high-brow sources. But the result was new forms of "serious" music that stopped connecting with audiences completely (who listens to 12-tone rows to relax at home?).

Now to Queen

Queen distinguished itself for its focus on connecting to listeners in a special way, but the band achieved this not through mimicry but innovation. The movie recreates the moment when the band reluctantly decides to try its hand at disco forms. No one was truly happy about the idea until the bass player pushed out the affecting (and apparently eternal) riff from the opening of "Another One Bites the Dust." Probably a majority of the human race today can recognize the song just from the beat and the three-note pattern it covers. It's even used in CPR training so that people know how quickly to compress the chest.

As for the signature song of the band, the wildly weird and enormously popular "Bohemian Rhapsody," the piece redefined what could be popularly played on the radio. It evokes a strange seriousness with its operatic motifs, dire subject matter, and implausibly smooth transitions from one style to another. The band's producer completely ruled out its release as a single, based on conventions of the time. He was wrong. The song is considered one of the greatest in the history of pop, even achieving a number one status twice.

The movie tells the story behind the song and the band's ambitions to cross over into several genres. It remains a paradigmatic refutation of the idea that there are tall walls that separate serious art from commercial success. My impression is that these walls today are not nearly as high as they were several decades ago. (The Atlanta Symphony hosts pop artists, folk artists, known musicians from all genres, all in the same season as it presents Mahler's 7th to adoring audiences.)

The wonderful movie based on the life of Freddie Mercury and his band makes a great case that commerce can be and is a friend to art. It has always been so, but we are only now fully coming to terms with what this implies for the artistic endeavor generally.

28

In Praise of Expertise

It was a helpless feeling. I'm standing next to my pretty car that won't move because the clutch slipped (it was my fault entirely but the story is too embarrassing to tell). I had to get my car one half mile down the road to the dealership to get it fixed.

That meant getting it towed. It was a holiday. How is this going to happen?

Then I dialed Gordon's Towing. Gordon answered. I explained my problem. He said no problem. He was there in less than 10 minutes. He drove up in a huge flat-bed truck. What happened then confuses but impresses me mightly.

The Expert Arrives

He stepped off the truck and grunted a hello. I pointed out which car needed towing. He hopped back in the truck and got to work. He knew exactly where to position the truck. He released the back and down it rolled so that the edge of it was exactly 6 inches away from my front tires. How he got the distance right on the first try is beyond me.

His next step was to examine whether my tiny two-seater (an S2K) had a towing bar. It did not. He went to his truck and grabbed some kind of strap with two steel rings. He crawled under my car and somehow managed to hook a steel cord around it. He then noticed that my car was only about 5 inches above the ground and so fixed the ramp with two boards so that it would not scrape.

Within a few minutes, my car was being pulled up the ramp. His next step had something to do with strapping the two left-side tires with woolen holders (why not the right side?). The whole thing was accomplished so fast. He asked where it was going and I told him. Next thing you know, we arrived at the dealership and he knew exactly where to park it. He reversed the process, took a credit card payment for $85, and drove off to continue his purpose-driven life.

I stood there with my mouth open in astonishment at his skill, precision, speed, agility, and, above all else, his expertise. He said no more than 5 words to me. He was all business, and probably headed to the next person in need.

There I stood as the beneficiary of his lifetime of experience and achievement. He had no idea that day that I would be calling. He didn't know if anyone would be calling. But he was ready to swing into action on the ringing of his phone. He had never met me nor I him. He was in it for the money, but not that much, if you think about it. But his "selfish" desire for money was not inconsistent with the social service he provided me on that day.

There is no law in effect that private towing services have to exist, that there must be people like Gordon who can manage every situation. There is no central plan, no municipal authority mandating this, no intellectuals running the system from above.

Nothing compelled him to answer that phone. He could easily have declined. And yet it happened anyway, and my whole problem was solved in the blink of an eye. We exchanged services: he gave me an enormous gift of service and I gave him $85 and the problems in my life were suddenly diminished.

What would I have done without him? I now know I can depend on someone out there knowing vastly more about what I need to have done than I could know in years of study. There are probably other towing services, true. But that makes things all-the-more marvelous because there is competition for prices and quality.

Gordon and I inhabit completely different worlds. And yet we came together on this, as complete strangers, to make a mutually beneficial exchange between my need and his skill. I feel sure that I will never see him again. I'm quite sure that he developed no real interest in or appreciation for me as a person. It was pure economics, nothing more. And yet the job got done.

Communities of Enterprise

Had I been living in a state of isolation, I would have to possess a towing truck in addition to every other life skill from growing food, sewing clothing, building shelter, and everything else. It would not be possible. I would never leave the nature of nature. In civilization, I depend on others who can cultivate their own specialization and make their skills available on the market for purchase. We are all strong and competent together because our skills are widely dispersed,

Gordon too benefits from the division of labor, from the people who made his truck to the manufacturers of his towing cords to the phone service he uses to answer calls. In this one exchange, millions upon millions of people were involved in making it possible. Not only that but the technology that enabled him to perfect his skills stretches far back in time. The accumulation of all this knowledge that went into making this possible involves many centuries and many countries, involving billions of people.

Literally the whole of human society from time immemorial was involved in this one exchange, not directly but indirectly through vast amounts of human cooperation and gradual expansion of opportunities to specialize. Adam Smith noticed this phenomenon in the 18th century and concluded that the division of labor is essential for wealth creation; indeed it is the most fundamental factor in making prosperity possible.

The political and economic outlook undergirding the market order is often called individualism because of the central role of human volition in its unfolding. At the same time, this individualism creates a beautiful community of enterprise, one far more reliable, effective, and life-affirming than the false communities that politics assembles for us. We all need each other to live good and prosperous lives. It's the market that makes this possible. I began the day feeling helpless but discovered that, thanks to the market economy, I'm surrounded by experts who are ready to meet every need.

29

How To Secede from the Biology Wars

The government shutdown has put a fine point on what everyone now recognizes. The struggle for control of the institutions of the United States government has turned into a full tribal war. Us vs. Them. Pick a side, rally for your team, never believe anything the other team says, declare everything an emergency, pose as the victim when you don't get your way, fantasize about the final defeat of your enemies, and dream of the spoils that will come your way when history declares you the winner.

Polarization Worse Than You Think

You might say this is nothing new. Politics is always this way. It's one side vs. the other. True, but it is getting worse. The two parties now vote as a block, almost without exception. You think you are voting for the man or woman. Actually, you are voting for a D or an R. The enforcement of party discipline these days compares to the totalitarian regimes of the interwar period. As candidates, they only pretend to have particularized opinions; as elected politicos, they comply or else.

But there is an even more vicious twist to the current struggles that go beyond politics as usual. What began as conventional politics has mutated into a culture war which took what now appears to be an inevitable turn to become a demographic war. It's one group vs. another; at least this is what we are being told by the clerisy on a daily basis. We are being encouraged to think that there is no difference between politics and biology, same as with certain well-known nationalist movements in interwar Germany.

Diversity that Bites

An example comes from a mainstream podcast this morning that celebrates the new demographic composition of the House of Representatives. More women. More minorities. More religious diversity. More gender/sexual identities. Oh, how American is changing! Look at the glorious excitement this is generating! We are constantly lectured that this is the result of a mighty struggle. This breaks new ground. But it also raises the possibility of blowback from the old guard.

I want to be happy about a move to more inclusionary politics. But the next scene cuts to the Senate where the bad old ways still persist. And how do we know? Just look at them. Old. White. Men. These are the bad guys, the ones to overthrow, the powers that be, the people to blame for all existing problems. It's barely a subtext anymore. A Google trends analysis over the last 15 years reveals the point. The messaging is incessant and unrelenting: men possess toxicity by virtue of historical dominance; the patriarchy has ruled for too long and must be displaced; whites, well, you know the story.

Forget ideology. Forget philosophy. We are being told that all the core struggles of our time are basically biological. According to this theory, you are either born oppressed or oppressor. You can't change who you are. Your political obligations are thus dictated by birth.

I don't need to go into detail about this particular report because you have heard it all a thousand times already. The news media is so enraptured with this theory that they can barely see beyond it. Vox thinks nothing of writing analysis like the following: "The Democratic side of the chamber was filled with bright outfits — including some that offered their own underlying meanings [read: identity]. The Republican side had a lot of suits."

How boring are the members of the oppressor class, and how colorful and awesome are the newly liberated.

Identity-based analysis has become a very safe reflex for the entire information machine. It allows reporters and commentators to occupy what seems to be the moral high ground while avoiding questions about political bias. Who is against more diversity? It's the ultimate journalistic safe space but at what cost? The signaling is targeted and unmistakable, and hence fuels the next problem.

The Ferocity of the Other Side

On the other side of the aisle, we have the great struggle to make America great again but what does this mean? It means the wall. A wall on the southern border. To stop an invasion. It's an emergency. We are being invaded by them.

Let's leave it to the imagination to fill in the rest with the biological component. Basically, the implications are the opposite of the above, a flipped narrative about who is oppressed and who is the oppressor.

And it doesn't stop there. Look at what these foreign peoples are doing to us in trade. They owe us money. They've been robbing us for too long. They can take their economies and shove it. We are going our own way. This is especially true of that strange country called China, filled with oddballs who think differently from us and have been cleverly getting ever more powerful even as this great country is sinking into a pit of pathology. Someone is to blame. It's them. They are hurting us.

We've got to stop the robbery taking place, we are being told. Our place in history is slipping and we can't allow that. We must take back what is ours, with walls and barriers to both trade and migration, all led by a great man who embodies the heart of who we are.

All with this blowback, you find the cult of hyper-masclinity, again, embodied in the great leader. If the left thinks that the war on "patriarchy" is easily won, take a few moments to peruse a men's rights forum online. You won't believe what you see. And you can't dismiss this as a handful of lunatics. This is ferocious.

Here again, identity politics is primary. It's not just identity politics. It's biological politics. The once-sane right wing — that group that celebrated civility, tradition, and the rule of law — has taken the bait of the Left and reconstituted itself as a mirror image. Or maybe you think the causation runs the other way, that the right's excesses fueled those of the left. The left had to go biological in light of the existential threat posed by the weaponized biology of the right. The blame game can toggle between the two far back in history, and you can tell any story you want to tell. Whatever suits your interest, based on your biology.

Break It Up!

Here's the thing. I don't really care who started this war. It's a war that no one can win. I don't care whether the right is a response to the left or vice versa. This whole argument is starting to remind me of playground fights in the elementary school, before the teacher arrived to say: break it up and get back to doing what you should be doing.

The problem with American public life today is the dearth of people who are willing to play the role of the adult who happens upon a vicious playground fight. Someone needs to rise above this muck and model what it is like to be mature. This needs to happen because so many others are being caught up in tribal wars based on cockamamie theories of causation, spinning tales of victimization that are becoming so entrenched that they operate as a kind of brain cancer that eats away at the ability to be rational.

Resolutions

How can each of us do this? For the new year, I've made the following resolutions.

First, never play whataboutism. I'm sure it is true that there is someone worse than the existing president and there is someone who is worse than the person who seeks to depose the existing president. Because you can name someone worse doesn't make your hero a good person in the great struggle to write the next chapter of the human narrative. Fear of the other is not a sound basis for picking the leaders of the present.

Second, I'm not listening to any argument on any topic that relies on self-declared identity as a precondition for the points being made. You can always recognize such arguments. They begin with "as a fill in the blank," whereupon we are encouraged to believe the victim/authority based on identity alone. For now on, I will edit out that intro and respond only to rational points.

Third, I will no longer participate in the tired American habit of gathering demographic data about me or anyone. If I have the option, I will no longer voluntarily declare my gender, race, or religion. I will regard myself as a human being alone and expect others to do the same. I will not cough up answers that I know for sure will be used in someone's war against someone else.

This is a start, a way we can contribute to social peace. We can, where possible, decline to make matters worse. We need to make a decision that we will not allow any cause to draft us as a member of an army by virtue of biology or any other conditions that are baked into who we believe ourselves to be.

We need to do all this now before things get worse. History shows where this viciousness of demographic struggles and wars ends up. It is extremely ugly. No one wins. The politics of conflict must be replaced by the realization that human cooperation among all people is possible. Not only possible: it is essential for the building of life. It is up to all of us, in our own way, to secede from the demographic wars, as a contribution we can all make to ending the struggles that are dragging us down to become less than we are and can be.

30

Financial Freedom Means Learning to Love Uncertainty

There I was listening to a panel with the lead developers of the cryptocurrency Dash, a very successful project with a $4 billion market cap. Like many other assets in this space, it aspires to be a currency for the world.

I couldn't pass up the opportunity to ask a question that had long burned in my mind. What is it like for a company, in the course of four months, to go from a market capitalization of $4.2 billion up to $12 billion and back down to $4.4 billion?

This wild swing, which is pretty much typical in the cryptoasset sector now again valued at half a trillion, is precisely what happened to Dash between November 2017 and March 2018. Developer Chuck Williams's answer was interesting: stay calm, manage your risks, and recognize that uncertainty is a universal condition of life.

The panelist went on to observe that government control of money comes with the loss of control over many aspects of our life and, along with that, the illusory promise of security. Government will take care of everything. There are no serious risks that we need to focus on as a matter of life management. Everything is too big to fail. Trust the banks. Trust the government. Trust the bond-rating agencies. Everything will be fine.

He continued to point out that every real entrepreneur, operating in the real world, knows there are good days and bad days. You use the good days to prepare for the bad days. You use the bad days to get creative, debug the system, find new marketing paths, and prepare the ground for future successes.

Bitcoin Market Capitalization

When the successes arrive, you stay humble, you save, you conserve, you prepare. It's called risk management. You have to hedge. You look for patterns. You make informed guesses. You never stop innovating. This is the life of running a business.

The Illusion of Financial Security

Actually, it is the real way that all of life should be. But for average people, government has tried to create a different reality in exchange for which you give up control over your life and property. For most of the twentieth century, people have acquiesced to the bargain, that guarantee that the future is not about risk but about compliance. Again, everything will be fine…except when it is not.

What's happened with the advent of cryptoassets, now owned by vast numbers of young people but, in general, about 8% of the population, is that they have been plunged into a world with grand promise, huge risk, and unrelenting uncertainty of the future. Is it scary? Yes. One of the main complaints that people have against this sector is its volatility. Moreover, there is the serious question of which among these assets are going to die (most) and which are going to thrive. There is also the question of whether they will all be displaced by something else.

The truth is that no one knows the answers to these questions, all Twitter wars aside. We just don't know. This is not a problem without a solution. The solution is the market process, a main virtue of which is its capacity to gradually reveal the unknown through nonstop discovery. In fact, this is the main job of the market. Day by day, the market process is pulling back on the curtain that hides the future. No living human being knows what is behind that curtain, which is to say that uncertainty is a ubiquitous condition of life.

Uncertainty is also a mighty leveller. Microsoft and Apple face it daily. So does the lemonade stand managed by 10-year olds. No one can be sure whether the customer will show up, much less buy. Yes, highly capitalized companies can outlast losses better than others, but no one can survive losses over the long term. There is no security, even at the top. The smallest business and the largest one deal with this reality daily.

And this is precisely what makes merchantcraft so difficult. It also makes it exciting, inspiring, and a living tribute to the drama of life.

Theory and History

A book that entrenched this conception of time and uncertainty in my mind is Ludwig von Mises's 1956 masterwork Theory and History. It burned into my brain a map of the trajectory of time. What has happened before just now can be documented as a flow of facts. It is stable. It can be studied. It can be interpreted. Mostly it can be known. Mises calls all time that took place before just now as history.

He contrasts this with theory, which he argues is rooted in known truths about how the world works in all times and places. In his case, he focussed on the social sciences in particular, which have variously conflated these two topics. The empiricists are fine insofar as they are describing events, tracing causes and effects, and crunching numbers of known patterns from the past. But can we derive theory from these? Mises says not ultimately. Good economic theory is deduced from an understanding of the structure of human life itself.

What's important here is not Mises's controversial position on "praxeology" itself but the core conception of the great divide that exists between the past, the present, and the future. That divide marks what can be known from what is not known. St. Paul offered this beautiful metaphor concerning the human plight in the course of time. "For now we see through a glass, darkly," he says. "now I know in part; but then [in eternity] shall I know even as also I am known."

The State and Knowledge

It is the great presumption of public policy that some people with power, resources, and status can know what is true, and therefore what must be better. This is in contrast to the lowly actors in the marketplace who must deal daily with the problem of not knowing. To navigate life, to find profitable investment opportunities, to discover what it is that society needs now and what can wait, is the great challenge of material life. But the state takes a different route. It declares what is true, attempts to freeze the process of life, and then impose it as a matter of law.

To attempt to override uncertainty is the driving force of many government regulations in the financial marketplace. We have a Fed with the power to inflate unto infinity. They issue debt instruments with a guaranteed payout. They fix price, try to control interest rates, create systems to tame market swings and business cycles. These have been spectacularly unsuccessful because they represent a foundational attack on the structure of the flow of time itself.

There is another cost to this approach: exclusion. Only certain people are admitted to the club of investors and capital builders. The rest are pushed aside, not permitted to live the adventure and thrill of real life but instead doomed to either become a subject and live off the state's dole or accept a lower financial status. You can find out about these people by googling "unbanked." In my own city of Atlanta, some 40% of adults live without "an account at a bank or other financial institution and are considered to be outside the mainstream for one reason or another."

The advent of crypto has been a godsend for the unbanked and the financially excluded. It is available to everyone, very easily and quickly. It's an example of real democracy at work: inclusive and universally empowering. And yes, with it comes a look at reality. It is volatile. Its future is uncertain. And being an owner is filled with opportunity. This is what freedom feels like.

Incredibles 2 and the Power of Envy

Have you ever experienced personal and professional harm because someone resented you for your talents and achievements? Sadly, this is a huge fact of life for which few are prepared. From childhood forward, we believe that the key to a successful life is hard work, high skills, and solid performance. The rest is automated, we think. At some point, you come to learn that these virtues make you a target. You need to develop the emotional wherewithal to confront it.

There are now two movies in the Disney/Pixar series that deal with this important theme: The Incredibles (2004) and Incredibles 2 (2018). The second one is as solid as the first. Both distinguish themselves by dealing with a ubiquitous reality all around us — resentment causes vast personal and social carnage — that we only otherwise see treated in fiction (Ayn Rand's Atlas Shrugged) and nonfiction (Helmut Schoeck's Envy).

That's what gives these movies a special appeal.

Superhero Protection

The second film opens after many years in which the Incredible family, all with superhero skills, have been decommissioned by law. They are living normal lives in a protection program set up by the government. But now this program is coming to an end, and they must integrate into society more fully without ever using their special skills.

Why had society turned against them? It was a classic case of a mix-up of cause and effect. Every time they had done some heroic work against crime, people saw lots of damage plus the presence of superheroes. Because people are sometimes stupid, they concluded that the superheroes were the cause of the damage. This is not a crazy plot: think of how guns are constantly blamed for criminal behavior.

In addition, there is a subtext of envy going on here. Superheroes have special skills others do not have. Politicians, in particular, resent this and see their presence as some kind of threat to the political monopoly on protection services. So the political class seeks to tear them down. The Incredible family unit has to deal with this as teaching moments for their kids. In their own lives, they have to come to terms with the strange reality: they have been forced not to be incredible.

In this film, a marketing guy named Winston Deavor has an idea for a fix. He explains that the real reason that superheroes have been banned is public perception. The only real solution is to change perceptions. He suggests that they wear cameras to stream some heroic deed. This film can be shown on the news and everyone will rally around them. (Winston's character is voiced by Bob Odenkirk of Better Call Saul and Breaking Bad fame.)

But there is an interesting problem. Winston works with his sister, who is very smart but has a serious problem. She resents her brother for getting so much attention and garnering so much fame even though he only sells things whereas she makes technically ingenious products. She tries to drip poison in the ear of the wife of Mr. Incredible. Isn't she tired of living in his shadow? Isn't it wicked how much society values the man but not the woman even though she is just as talented if not more so?

His wife, known as Plastigirl, demurs, not really buying into the victim mindset, much to her credit. She senses something is amiss. Still, she goes along with the plot to film some heroic deed and show it to the public. The scheme works, and the public demands an end to the ban on superheroes. As it turns out, however, Winston's wife is rotten to the core and is secretly working on a metaplot to seek all power for herself. She is the biggest villain of all.

Telling you this is not a spoiler, because this theme is integral to the whole Incredibles genre. The bad guys become that way because they are driven by resentment against others who possess skills they don't have. They try to enlist others in their envious plots. The plot is always about gaining power over others, disabling and discrediting excellence in every way possible. It's an especially delightful twist that Incredibles 2 explores the gender wars through this lens, giving this film a special meaning in our times.

Dealing With Envy

The film also presents a path for dealing with the problem of envy. The lesson is to stop being shocked by it and recognize it as a reality. Indeed, any high-performing individual will necessarily confront this problem as a fact of life. Someone, somewhere, sometime will attempt to destroy you for your virtues.

Then you have two choices. You can acquiesce. That requires dumbing yourself down, putting your skills on hold, reducing yourself to their level, and declining to live a big and great life. Or you can push through and outsmart such people by being more excellent still, recognizing that the path forward is never easy. This requires far more of you than you ever anticipated. If you choose the second path, you have to be agile, you have to think for yourself, and you have to develop thick skin to deal with the smears, trolling, lies, and worse.

Both Incredibles films put on display this difficult choice. In both cases, the family begins by going along, presuming that society is not really prepared to absorb and use their special skills. But this choice leads to personal unhappiness, bureaucratization, and social decay, just as you would expect in any society that punishes achievement. Realizing this truth, the Incredibles must discover the fortitude to push through and say no to those who want to bury talent in a thicket of mediocracy.

Social media has put social and professional life on fast forward, so it is far more likely now that anyone of achievement in any area of life will experience the ghastly effects of envy, simply because the envious have more access to communication tools than ever before. Then you are faced with this precise decision: give up or press on.

The slogan "don't feed the trolls" is actually a pretty good rule, not only in digital media but in life generally. The path to personal progress is never easy; it is often a grueling slog, punctuated by unavoidable demoralization and temptation to accept defeat. To be incredible in life means refusing to give in and let the trolls win.

The reviews for both movies have been over-the-top fabulous. Yes, they are exciting movies. Yes, they are funny and dramatic. Yes, the computer animation is glorious. But these factors alone do not account for their popularity. The reason we love them is that the moral theme here is extremely rare in movies even though it is everywhere in life.

32

An Education in One Evening, Courtesy of Jordan Peterson

Jordan Peterson might be today's most influential public intellectual, having achieved that fame in only two years following a long career as an academic (with an impeccable record) and a practicing clinical psychologist. He burst onto the media scene with a hard stand against forced speech imposed by a law in Canada. Then he became a symbol of resistance against the wild excesses of postmodern identity politics.

The media have yet to figure this out, but their jeering attacks on him unleashed a lion.

Today he travels the country and the world, selling out theater venues like a rockstar, with tickets going for $60 to $300 each, along with hats and t-shirts snapped up in the lobby, plus a long line of people wanting pictures for their social profiles. He has just re-booked for another 50 appearances in addition to the 50 currently on the list, with the venues getting larger by the week.

Think of it: you can buy tickets to hear the thoughts of a quiet liberal intellectual on Stubhub!

It's all truly hard to believe or even imagine. For those of us who believe in ideas — at a time when free speech and free thought in academia are rare and when media culture reduces all ideas to angry sound bites and partisan politics — this is a hugely encouraging phenomenon. It means that serious thought is not dying; on the contrary, there is such a high demand for penetrating and profound ideas that regular people are willing to pay to get them.

A Singular Figure

It's perhaps true that Noam Chomsky could have filled up such a theater at the height of the Vietnam War. Maybe William F. Buckley could have done the same at one point in his career. But I'm not sure either one of these could have gone on tour and reliably filled thousands of seats with paying customers night after night for month after month. Ayn Rand is another possible case but I doubt her demographic draw would have been as vast and varied.

I'm trying to think of another living intellectual — a pure intellectual, not a comedian or sports star or musician or rabble-rousing political commentator — who can pack a house for 3,000 people paying this amount to see him. Maybe I've overlooked someone but I can't think of anyone.

And so you wonder what is really behind this remarkable rise of this man and his show. If you look it up, you will find no shortage of opinion pieces that suggest that the Peterson phenom is all about anger, resentment against modernity, some rebellious and maybe bigoted movement of reaction and authoritarianism.

The problem with these claims is that there is not a shred of evidence to back them up. They are easily and instantly refuted by the slightest exposure to the Peterson corpus whether on video or in print.

Appearance

Last night I attended a lecture in a venue outside of Hartford, Connecticut. The show seemed to have every seat filled: people from all walks of life but they mostly tilted in the young direction. The loudspeaker announced a no-video policy, otherwise our view would have been blocked by hundreds of iPhones held high for 90 minutes.

The announcer further said there would be no heckling of any sort allowed under any circumstances. The people cheered, I among them. I think we are all pretty well fed up with tribal wars being fought with screams, signs, and anger. We came to listen and learn. That's all.

The opener was Dave Rubin (who recently interviewed me). He skillfully warmed up the crowd with an introduction worthy of a beloved hero. The crowd cheered at every sentence. Dave knows why people are here. He knows what Peterson has meant to this generation. He knows that everyone there has watched the thousands of YouTubes and bought his mega-bestselling book 12 Rules.

Then Peterson came out on stage, and revealed an authentic sense of gratitude and appreciation for those who came just to hear him talk for 90 minutes. He had no magic opening to get people going. On the contrary, he seemed anxious to lower expectations. He began with some small observations about the tour and his book, the strange place in which he finds himself, and some fascinating anecdotes from his long career, spotted with some vignettes from political and economic history.

He is sometimes inadvertently funny, so sometimes the audience would laugh affectionately. This would make him laugh in turn, and then wonder out loud why people thought what he said was funny.

His humility is endearing, really a model. His absolute refusal to engage in any kind of manipulative demagoguery is a fantastic relief. He made it clear within the first ten minutes that if anyone had come for red meat, he or she will be deeply disappointed.

This is not a rally. It's not a cult. It's not a religion. It's not designed for any political purpose. It's not even about Jordan Peterson. This show is about serious ideas and nothing else. Its sole goal is to inspire deep thought about life, meaning, purpose, and all of our futures on this earth, which, as he kept reminding us, we will not leave alive.

Improvisation

A captivating aspect of listening to Peterson in any venue is merely to observe his uncommon erudition. His vocabulary is vast and effortlessly transferred from mind to voice, flowing from sentence to sentence with penetrating power that seems almost without limit, without a single utterance of "uh" or "hmmm." He is unveiling gradually, with a powerful inner fire, the contents of his mind as it pertains to the great topic of understanding and navigating ourselves and the world around us. It's not clear that he had a particular plan for what he would say that night but he might have; regardless, his speech is different every single time. It has an improvisatory feel. The entire package is nothing short of awe inspiring, and all the more so because Peterson himself is not particularly interested in his personal talent; for him, it is all about the insight and understanding. He is in awe of the opportunity to do what he does best: teach and counsel.

Hope

Once the speech got going, he chose to talk first about the things about the world that are not getting the headlines today. If you pick up the papers, you would think everything around us is collapsing. But if you look at the data, what you see is very different. Poverty is falling at a rate never seen in history. Many fatal diseases are being eradicated. War is less common than ever. Violence is falling. Technology has brought information to the masses. The standard of living the world over — even where it never before existed in any form — is rising at an amazing rate, with only one exception: where political totalitarianism keeps people down.

And here he began that real point. It's not enough to rattle off the phenomenal statistics about the improvement of the human condition. We must understand the why. His answer was clear as a bell: growing amounts of freedom are unleashing creativity within the structures of capitalistic institutions that are encouraging people to enter into networks of productivity, cooperation, and marvelous achievement.

And here I heard his clearest statement yet about his ideological commitments. He is a proponent of human freedom and human rights, a liberal in the classical sense, which is to say, a genuine liberal who believes in freedom of speech, association, and trade. That seems rather simple to observe but, apparently, not.

He has been a severe critic of the conventional left, and thereby been brutally treated by mainstream media, with countless interlocutors attempting to ferret out his inner malice. Incredibly, he has been smeared as having some kind of secret rightist agenda to pave the way for some kind of authoritarian (or racist, misogynist, or you name it) takeover; most absurdly, he has been accused, without the slightest bit of evidence, of carrying water for the alt-right.

Truth

That last claim is truly infuriating. If anything, he has done herculean work in drawing people away from both rightist and leftist versions of identitarian collectivism. People who worry about the rise of identitarian nationalism and racism as a reaction to the social-democratic left — I wrote a whole book on the topic — should be deeply grateful to him for explaining that there is a liberal alternative.

Here is a man who stood on stage and talked at length about the two types of poisonous totalitarianism that wrecked the 20th century, Communism and Nazism. He urged everyone to read two great books by authors who suffered deeply for their dissent against the regime: Solzhenitsyn's Gulag Archipelago and Frankl's Man's Search for Meaning. This is not extremist literature. These books serve to illustrate the moral core of what it means to live in truth and resist the lie even to the point of massive personal suffering.

At this point, he revealed so much about what is really driving him. He explained that his study of 20th century totalitarian bloodshed showed him that all modern cases of absolutist despotism were not really about bad men leading good people into Hell. These experiences were about the willingness of vast numbers of people around the leader and ruled by the leader to lie — or at least decline to tell the truth — because they lacked the conviction to speak truth, or were too lazy, or feared the consequences.

The lie, he said, is the reason for the loss of liberty and the good life. The reverse is also true. The key to building and maintaining freedom is to think and speak the truth even when confronting a world bent on ignoring and disparaging that truth.

At this point in his lecture, the audience entered into a new level of engagement. Rapt attention. Mouths wide open. No one checking their phones. Everyone still. And so it lasted for another full hour as Peterson's mind travelled through more history, philosophy, sociology, economics, and moral psychology.

As I thought about it later, it struck me that this 90-minute tour de force darn near amounted to an undergraduate liberal-arts education, with this one difference: students are simply not learning this material in today's regimented and agenda-driven educational institutions. It's not so much that Peterson is saying new and amazingly innovative things, though there is plenty of new insight here; it's that he is saying real and truly useful things that have emerged from a genuine search for truth.

Faith

He demonstrated what this search for truth looks like in his riff on religious faith, which somehow manages to be deeply respectful of the religious narratives without pushing an implausible piety that today's students would find tendentious and tedious. His now-famous commentary on Genesis struck me as truly creative, with an argument that the key to the Western faith is its conviction that humans are made in the image and likeness of God — with the spark of Divinity — and possessing of some features of the creative power that led to the invention of the world itself. If we lose that story, we risk the destruction of the deepest cultural foundation that undergirds our freedom, rights, and prosperity.

His point is not that students should be taught religious dogma. Rather, his point was that a real education should lead not to nihilism but a paradigm of meaning that informs the way we conduct our lives. It is not enough just to tear everything down and cause students to believe only in power as the one real thing, whether good or bad; educators and intellectuals have a duty to inspire the search for truth and to assist the discovery of the good in their own lives and the world around them.

He gave the following vivid illustration of the life of a post-graduation senior just entering the wiles of the workforce and regular life with all its confusions and challenges. Imagine a helicopter dropping a 22-year old in the middle of the ocean and the pilot yelling through a megaphone: "find your way to shore!"

This is the situation young people find themselves in today, which is precisely why Peterson's clarion call for heroic responsibility resonates so loudly.

Meaning

He finally turned to the issue of meaning in life, and the need for adventure, somewhat circling back to his list of modern achievements for human well being. The achievements came about because people dedicated themselves to an impossible idea. They took risks. They confronted their deepest fears. They overcame envy, bureaucracy, doubts, and smears. They stood for truth. And they very likely didn't get the credit. But they lived and are living lives of great adventure and meaning.

So should we all.

You might be wondering where politics fits into all of this. He mentioned the current US president only one time and in a mostly dismissive way that elicited sympathetic snickers from the audience. If any members of the mainstream press who have been smearing this man as nothing but a waterboy for the titanic shift in national and world politics are reading now, please know this. He made himself extremely clear: the key to a good life is not to be found within politics; it is to be found from within.

And you know what? The audience cheered. Cheered! What does this tell us about what is happening at these Peterson events? For one thing, it tells me that my initial impressions of him from two years ago were entirely wrong.

I'm embarrassed to admit that I thought he was just another political pundit on the make, a man who would exploit our angers to gather a cult around himself. I was dead wrong. My presumption reflected my personal exhaustion with this mode of public manipulation that always collapses into some kind of unseemly personality cult or financial racket.

That is not what Jordan Peterson is about. As he himself has gradually come to learn, his voice is in a long line of liberal intellectuals — even if he rises above most of them in history — who is there to urge people to turn toward peace, tolerance, personal heroism, and truth, in service of making the best possible use of our days on earth.

It Ends

Every great demagogue has a rehearsed and inspiring ending to his speech, something to give people a desire to do something wild and inspire devotion to the person who inspired them to do it. Peterson again defied expectations. He maintained the soft delivery style he used for the entire speech. He finished a final point about being a good person, living a great life, and getting along with others, and then he waited a few seconds and quietly said, "And that's all for now."

The audience rose in applause immediately, out of respect for this man but mainly out of appreciation for his message. As I waited to go backstage, I asked three young men why they had come to this event. The first one, a senior in college and a major in engineering, said very quickly: "I'm searching for meaning in life." His other two colleagues concurred. That was the beginning and end of it. They were thrilled to be here.

Politics promised to give us a meaningful life. It failed. Now we have to find it elsewhere. As the poet Virgil led Dante through Heaven, Purgatory, and Hell, Jordan Peterson is the tour guide of the modern world in its confrontation with our inner selves.

Government

33

Government Is Like a Bad Football Fan

I loved my dear father so much. A kind soul. A gentle man. Except on Sunday afternoons when the Dallas Cowboys were on television. He would sit in his recliner. Even from the kickoff, he would start yelling at the players.

"Run to the left! No, you dummy! Oh, see? He took you down because you weren't looking."

It happened nearly every play.

"Dumb Staubach, why are you running the ball so much? You need to pass against this defense!"

"Awww, dumb Dorsett, you did it again! You ran right into the iron defense instead of around it."

When his team made a touchdown, he would say: "That's the right way to do it! That's what I've been saying!"

This would go on for three hours. As a child, I started to develop abiding sympathy for the players. I hoped they couldn't hear my father yelling at them. After all, he wasn't playing the game. He would have died after one play. Instead, he was sitting on a comfortable chair. They, on the other hand, were getting beat up, crashed into, bashed, and exhausted, all while being yelled at by fans.

What's more, my father was only denouncing or praising them for things the players had already done. The players, on the other hand, had to make decisions about an uncertain future. They had skin in the game. He was just sitting there without having to bear any consequences at all for his lounge-chair coaching.

I sometimes wished some magical voice would appear and say, "Okay, Dr. Tucker, you are obviously very smart, to the point of high expertise. It's 4th and 10. Please call the next play and bear total responsibility for the results."

I wonder how he would have reacted. Most likely, he would have said, "No way. That's the coach's job, not mine."

Or maybe a voice would say, "Hey, why don't you try being a quarterback on the next play?"

The New Nafta

My mind raced back to those days when I saw the following report on the new trade negotiations with Mexico. Two leaders have reached an agreement on dozens if not hundreds or thousands of products — how and where they should be produced, what kinds of fees are applicable, what workers are to be paid, and so on. Here is the paragraph that struck me:

> Under the changes agreed to by Mexico and the United States, car companies would be required to manufacture at least 75 percent of an automobile's value in North America under the new rules, up from 62.5 percent, to qualify for Nafta's zero tariffs. They will also be required to use more local steel, aluminum and auto parts, and have 40 to 45 percent of the car made by workers earning at least $16 an hour, a boon to both the United States and Canada and a win for labor unions, which have been among Nafta's biggest critics.

Keep in mind that the people who are declaring all this aren't making cars, or steel, or aluminum, or auto parts. They aren't paying the workers either. They are on the sidelines, meeting in boardrooms, declaring what should be done with other people's businesses and property. Their decisions are ultimately a power game between them, and the specific results that emerge are basically arbitrary. Why 75 percent and not 78 percent? Why $16 and not $30? Why cars? There are so many questions.

Ultimately these people are in the same position as my father watching football. But of course there is one critical difference. They are granted the power to impose their decisions. As for the voice that came down and invited them to call the plays, they obey it and then tell people what to do. They enforce their decisions at the point of a gun.

The Fan From Hell

Government here is behaving like a pathological sports fan, a person with no real skill or skin in the game who pretends to know all and is empowered to enforce the decisions. My father had the humility to know it was not his job to either play or coach; he was just doing what fans do.

It's the same with music or book critics: they are neither singing nor writing but delighting themselves in having vast opinions about both.

Nothing wrong with that, even if it can be annoying. What's objectionable is when such people are given the power to actually dictate the results.

Think how much government does this. This tendency touches everything in life these days. That worker is underpaid. That lightbulb uses too much energy. You can't transfer that much money at once. That toilet tank uses too much water. That gasoline should include a healthy dose of corn in it. That milk is hereby banned because it is raw. You can't import or sell that many things from that country.

And so on for millions and billions of items, services, actions, and words. Government presumes the right to manage everything, even though it is not actually doing the things it is demanding control over. It is not paying workers in private firms. It is not making light bulbs. It is not trying to make a profit trying to persuade consumers to buy things.

Actually, government has no money of its own. It takes its money from people who create wealth. Then it presumes that it knows better how to do things than the people from whom it extracts the wealth.

Fans will be fans. Peanut galleries will always be with us. It's entertainment, and a major reason why we actually like sports, music, and books. Everyone is a critic. That's all fine. But let's not forget the profound difference between those who do and those who pretend to do, nor the difference between those whose wealth rests on creativity and human volition and those who bully others to get their way.

34

Political Division Is How We Grow Rich

Y ou are probably tired of reading about it. I am. Every day the pages of our favorite publications are filled with apocalyptic warnings of the grim consequences of intractable political differences. The anger out there is tearing us apart. Democracy is in danger, even dying. The old systems are broken. Unity of the past seems permanently gone. We can't count on leadership at all any more. Most of the public thinks the news is fake. The mainstream press thinks the president is fake. And there seems to be no end to it.

There is a competition among writers for the New York Times among who can write the most overblown, paranoid, frenzied, and dire warnings of impending doom, as if finding new levels of maniacal expressions make it all true. Among readers, the result has a name: outrage fatigue. You can only be mad, panicked, and hysterical about the state of the world for so long before you wonder whether this whole thing might be overblown.

After all, you look around and note that the economy seems to be undergoing impressive recovery. Incomes, profits, investment, jobs, finances — everything is rising. The commerce sector is positively giddy about two things in particular: tax cuts and deregulation. It turns out that lifting the boot off the neck of free enterprise, even just a bit, has unleashed pent-up energy.

It's hard to argue with that kind of success.I look outside the window and I see construction cranes, bustling businesses, happy workers and customers, start up companies, help wanted signs, and smiles all around. If this is what the collapse of democracy looks like, it must not be the worst fate.

Not even Jay-Z could come up with a compelling answer to Trump's observation that black unemployment is at historic lows. He tweeted the same regarding the women's marches: look at the job rate! Silence follows. It's a serious question: would you rather have political unity and poverty or political division and wealth? I'm pretty sure of the answer here.

It's time we question the value of political unity. By that I do not mean that it is good to fight with friends and family over politics. That kind of thing enacts a terrible personal price, as every last one of us knows. It also achieves little. There is very rarely a good reason to lose friends over political differences, if you can help it. A friend who demands that you agree with him or her on political values is probably missing the whole point of friendship in the first place.

When I praise disunity, I do not mean picking fights with friends. I mean the absence of political consensus leading to consolidation. Consider a time when there is seeming universal political togetherness. Think back to the Iraq War, which enjoyed 90% approval while President Bush's approval soared to its highest. War tends to do that but surely that should not be the model we seek, to be constantly at war in order to unite the population. The same was true in World Wars one and two. Wars suppress differences but during peacetime, differences emerge.

This is not a bad thing. It's a sign of the diminution of national emergency and the consolidation of power. A free society needs many centers of power, none of which achieve universal assent.

Nathan Rosenberg's classic work How the West Grew Rich demonstrates that diffuse power is not only a feature of the emergence of freedom; it is the cause of that freedom in history. The state, the locality, the church, the family, the merchants, the individuals, all have particular interests to advance. They usually involve gaining more power to game the social and economic system toward their own interests. If one interest prevails, freedom is in danger. When they all compete, with a sense of jealousy toward their own rights, the result is freedom and thereby prosperity. This was the history of the high Middle Ages and how it gradually came to lead to the Industrial Revolution. No one could get their stuff together well enough to prevent it, and that is precisely how and why it happened.

Impressed by this reality, the framers of the US Constitution attempted to build this separation of powers into the structure of government itself. The idea was to pit the branches against each other, as a check against any single interest prevailing. The unitary state, the single-purpose government with a god-like figure up top who embodies the soul of the nation, was never the American, nor medieval European, idea.

What's interesting about this thesis is that it turns our usual suppositions on their head. We tend to think that a successful society needs a unity purpose and therefore controlling force. How can we as a people achieve anything without that? The counterintuitive reality is that we only achieve success insofar as we have the absence of a unity purpose and single center of power.

Now let's think about the Trump presidency. *Fire and Fury* reports that Trump genuinely believed that once he won the election, he would benefit from the American tradition of recognizing his legitimacy as the leader of the country. Media commentators would instruct everyone to bury the hatchet, recognize the genius of democracy, and defer to the greatness of the new commander in chief. Oddly, this didn't happen. He was truly shocked by this.

The author reports that this is why, in the first months of his presidency, he never stopped reminding people that he won and by how much. Instead of universal acclaim, he faced the opposite. The opposing party claimed that the election outcome had been realized because of Russian manipulation and the media, maybe with the complicity of the Trump campaign itself. The mainstream media itself couldn't accept that someone like Trump could actually control the center of power. The intellectual classes have generally refused even to acknowledge the victory.

This is what has created the grim divisions we see today. It's total war every day: Trump vs. Media vs. Intellectuals vs. Everyman vs. his own party establishment vs. foreign leaders vs. you can fill in the blank. And this is the reality we are getting used to every single hour of our lives.

But let's try an experiment. Let's say that you just stop listening to the news. You stop reading political books. You turn off CNN, Fox, Breitbart, and HuffPo. It all shuts down. For a full year, you have heard none of it. But you look around and what do you see? You see a growing economy, a paycheck with less robbed from you by the government, an ever more vibrant commercial sector, and a world mostly fed up with all the squabbling and all for finding non-government methods of making the world a better place.

What I'm suggesting here is that the divisions between these various centers of political, cultural, and intellectual power are actually a good thing. I wouldn't want anyone to win the great debates of our time. The end of division itself might be the worst possible outcome because it would imply that some one power source is now in charge. We actually don't want anyone in charge. We want to recreate the conditions that made the West rich in the first place: tremendous diffusion of power and unending competition between all sectors of society.

So forgive me but I don't want to pick sides in the great battles of our times. I'm suspicious that the very existence of these struggles are the reason why life seems suddenly to be looking up again. Disunity. Division. Competition. This is precisely what we need in public affairs, precisely so that the rest of our lives can proceed in peace, prosperity, and harmony.

35

Deregulation Is an
Anti-Racist Policy

The American media loves few topics more than race and racism because it is something everyone can agree is wrong. Reporters are always on firm moral ground when ferreting out a racist and condemning him or her, based usually on offensive words, biases, or caricatures. This approach of policing words and thoughts trivializes the real damage of racialist ideology and its deep history of deploying the state to turn one group against another.

It so happens that the American regulatory state — affecting labor, housing, commercial zoning, medicine, and industrial structure — was born at a time when "scientific racism" had massively infected elite culture in academia and government. The time was the Progressive Era, but it was the wrong name.

It wasn't about progress. It was about using government power to slow down and redirect the vast material gains of the second half of the 19th century, a time when every sector of American economic life took a dramatic new turn. There was internal combustion, the commercial viability of steel, growing communications networks, electricity in homes and city streets, and flight. This was genuine progress, as driven by entrepreneurship and market forces.

The misnamed Progressives worried that it was too much, too fast, and the core of their concern was demographics, which is to say that they believed that there was too much race mixing and the wrong people were reproducing too fast and making too much money. Believing that they were following up on warnings by Charles Darwin that too much material progress was threatening the course of biological evolution, Progressive intellectuals and policy makers hatched plans for saving the white race in America from sure destruction.

A classic statement comes from The New Republic in 1916: "Imbecility breeds imbecility as certainly as white hens breed white chickens; and under laissez-faire imbecility is given full chance to breed, and does so in fact at a rate far superior to that of able stocks."

If that sounds shocking to you, even implausible that anyone would believe it, I would invite you to examine any mainstream academic writing on the topic between 1890 and 1935. What you will find is a hard-core racist presumption and an exterminationist policy agenda.

Consider this 1896 book published by the newly formed American Economic Association.

> "It is not in the conditions of life, but in race and heredity that we find the explanation of the fact to be observed in all parts of the globe, in all times and among all peoples, namely, the superiority of one race over another, and of the Aryan race over all…. The Aryan race is possessed of all the essential characteristics that make for success in the struggle for the higher life, in contrast with other races which lack in either one or the other of the determining qualities."

For this reason, there must be absolute racial segregation: "Intercourse with the white race must absolutely cease and race purity must be insisted upon in marriage as well as outside of it…. The presence of the colored population is a serious hindrance to the economic progress of the white race."

The book concludes that with the right segregationist and exclusionist measures, the black race can become extinct. Hence, the white race should "not hesitate to make war upon those races who prove themselves useless factors in the progress of mankind."

What were some of the measures adopted in policy to make such a war? Occupational licensing in law and medicine were driven by racialist concerns, including the earliest regulation of medical schools, which shut out blacks from the profession. Zoning laws in cities were designed to segregate and exclude. Marriage licenses had a specific eugenics intent of promoting procreation only among the "fit."

The earliest labor regulations implemented the idea of a minimum wage. It was widely supported by Progressive intellectuals precisely because it could be used as a tool to socially isolate and economically exclude undesirable persons. It's not hard to understand how this works. If you raise the bar high enough for people to enter the workforce, they are forced into unemployment and doomed to poverty.

This is precisely what the leading economist Frank Taussig pushed in his 1911 text Principles of Economics. Regretting that "we have not reached the stage where we can proceed to chloroform them once and for all," he suggested that the unfit "can be segregated, shut up in refuges and asylums, and prevented from propagating their kind." The minimum wage would be ideal: "The persons affected by such legislation would be those in the lowest economic and social group."

Royal Meeker, Woodrow Wilson's commissioner on labor, stated the intention clearly: "It is much better to enact a minimum-wage law even if it deprives these unfortunates of work." The famed British socialist Sydney Webb agreed, writing, "The unemployable, to put it bluntly, do not and cannot under any circumstances earn their keep. What we have to do with them is to see that as few as possible of them are produced."

The earliest experiments in wage regulation were "successful" in this sense: they did reduce employment among marginalized population groups. But that was just the beginning. If the driving purpose of economic life is to curate the population toward race supremacy, women must be steered away from commercial employment and toward full-time motherhood. This is why the earliest tests of maximum working hours legislation, and control of working hours generally, all specified that the legislation pertained exclusively to women.

Moving forward in time, the eugenic aspirations of the ruling class yielded more regulation of economic life. The immigration acts of the 1920s were constructed to exclude unfit populations such as Slavs, Jews, and Italians. The labor regulations of the 1930s had white supremacist intentions. The business regulation in cities zoned black and other minority-owned businesses into special districts. Even the anti-cabaret regulation of the 1940s, repealed only late last year in New York, was structured to prevent racial mixing.

You might think that with so many great scholars unearthing all of this unseemly history that people on the left would rethink their support of the regulation of economic life. They should. Further, they should embrace market-driven commercial life as the one form of economic organization that offers up the best-possible hope for the realization of peace between groups and ever-expanding circles of shared prosperity.

Markets breed integrated communities. Go to any large city with a heterogeneous population (New York, Miami, Atlanta) and you see it in the everyday business life of the city. Commerce is what breaks down prejudicial barriers and brings people together. Deregulation in every area — from labor to immigration to medical provision to land use to marriage regulation — is the best-possible anti-racism policy. This emancipationist agenda will go much farther to stamp out racism than policing politicians and their silly pronouncements.

36

Centrally Planned Security
Doesn't Work Either

The mainstream narrative on the shooting at the Florida school has been reduced to absurdity. It comes down to the claim that people have too much access to weapons in the United States, and this is due to the lobbying power of the National Rifle Association, which pays off politicians with money donated by gun manufacturers. Believing that this message is starting to stick, and fearing a consumer backlash, many large companies (United, Delta, Enterprise, and TrueCar) have pulled out of deals they had with the NRA. A casual observer would come to believe that the NRA is directly responsible for the murder of the school kids.

It's hard to know where to begin showing where this narrative goes wrong. It might as well be structured to evade all the real issues. Contrary to what many commentaries are implying, it is not enough merely to be outraged to cause one's brain to generate correct solutions to the problem of school violence. You have to look at facts.

Failure of Public Authority

As it turns out, the shooting is the perfect illustration of the failure of public authority and law enforcement. What's more, this scenario is an ever-more predictable feature of these kinds of calamities. Last year in the Las Vegas shooting, as details gradually unfolded, what we discovered was that police and public security authorities were extremely cautious about their own safety at the expense of the lives of those they are expected to protect. The situation in Florida is proving to be eerily similar.

As it turns out, more than a week after the shooting, we are now getting reports of what really happened. Fully four sheriff deputies waited outside the school while the shooting was going on, refusing even to go inside. They had been tasked with protecting the school, counter any violence that might appear within this "gun-free zone." What happened instead is deeply disturbing. Instead of protecting the kids, they protected themselves. Their level of caution for their own safety created astonishing confusion.

Many emergency medical workers had no idea where the suspect was for at least 30 minutes after the gunfire erupted, and the authorities struggled to identify him for another 15 minutes…. For as long as 45 minutes after the shooting stopped, some students were still cowering behind locked doors, unsure if the person banging on their door was a police officer or the gunman, according to students.

Donald Trump has been a champion of "first responders" and the police generally. But this was just too much for him. Referring to one deputy who refused to act, and has since resigned his job, Trump said: "He trained his whole life. When it came time to get in there and do something, he didn't have the courage or something happened, but he certainly did a poor job."

The Problem of Training

What's especially troubling about this behavior is that it doesn't appear to be too much of an anomaly. Many security professionals in public institutions are trained to protect their own interests in such cases, and most anyone with experience with violent situations such as this can tell you. That's not to say that there are not heroic and brave cops, men and women who risk their lives to keep us safe. The problem is that the tendency to hide and pass the buck is very common, and baked into the training they all receive from the first day to the last. As one excellent account of this problem summarizes: "An officer's overriding goal every day is to go home at the end of their shift."

Saw Something, Said Something

And that's only the beginning of the problems. Local and federal authorities had been contacted many times about the shooter. He was a known problem. He had been threatening others, accumulated weapons that he posted on his own Instagram account, behaving in scary ways. Citizens saw something and said something, as the airport posters tell us to do. "I know he's going to explode," a woman told the FBI tip line. He might resort to slipping "into a school and just shooting the place up." Another caller to 911 said, "He could be a school shooter in the making." Even the shooter called the authorities to give what amounted to a warning about himself.

You look through this sequence of events, and it seems impossible to imagine conditions that would have been more perfect to allow law enforcement to do a great job in protecting the students at the Marjory Stoneman Douglas High School. It was the perfect setup to illustrate why government should not be given monopoly control over weaponry and security services. The actual result is an astonishing failure at every level. This goes far beyond incompetence. It reveals pervasive and systematic loss of even basic functioning of the core functions of government.

And yet, even after all this news has poured in, what do we hear hour by hour on the mainstream news? We hear that the NRA — the main job of which is precisely to train people in gun use and safety so that we can live in a less violent society in which people like this school shooter cannot destroy lives — is the real problem. This messaging suggests a crazy mixed-up worldview that denies the incredibly obvious and puts blame for the problem on the actual solution.

Forced to Be There

As we listen to the student survivors from that bloody day, we hear expressions of this mixed-up worldview, which is entirely understandable. Recall two things about their lives as you hear them speak.

First, they are forced to be in school, thanks to compulsory schooling laws that consider a kid to be criminally truant for failing to show up. This compulsory approach has been around for more than a century and is so unquestioned that there isn't so much as the smallest effort to repeal these laws. Last year, an Arizona lawmaker made the case for repeal and was immediately subjected to a national grilling by the media for daring to question a central tenet of the American civic religion.

Second, the status of gun-free zones, a part of federal law since 1990, works like an advertisement to any violent criminal: no one in this place will challenge you. Just imagine if you had a law mandating gun-free banks or gun-free jewelry stores or gun-free convenience stores. Do you think that you would see an increase or decrease in robberies in these institutions? This should not be so difficult to understand and yet lawmakers seem often incapable of thinking through any second-level effects of their well-intentioned plans.

Now we come to the issue of arming teachers. Is this the right way to secure schools? Many teachers are alarmed at the prospect. Some might want to be armed but this is not their vocation. Why should teachers and students be in settings where the threat of violence is so intense that one must always walk around with a weapon? I wouldn't want to live in an apartment complex like that; surely we don't want our kids to be forced to attend schools where the threat of violent death is so pervasive. The pushback from students and teachers is completely understandable.

Private Governance

If not armed teachers, if not gun-free zones, if not gun bans, if not granting to the government an exclusive domain for security and the threat of violence, what is the answer? The least satisfying answer is actually the right one: we do not know precisely how to secure schools. We — "we" as in intellectuals, pundits, or society in general — do not know how to secure banks, jewelry stores, shopping malls, or casinos. How can we find out? By devolving that responsibility to institutions themselves, you allow the emergence of security solutions that are adaptive to the particular conditions of time and place.

In Vegas casinos, for example, there is no one-size-fits-all solution for every institution. There are cameras, private police, monitoring stations, careful vetting of patrons, undercover cops, and so on. The remarkable aspect of this is that all of this is present even as the casino tries to maintain an atmosphere of fun, decadence, and carefree abandon. As anyone who has been there can tell you, the whole thing works. It doesn't feel like a police state. It feels like a party. In this case, the market for security truly works.

The key here is to reject the central-planning model for security provision. We need what Edward Stringham calls "private governance," which is to say to allow market signaling and individual decision-making to reveal the best model to us, and also allow that market to be constantly adaptable to new conditions, threats, risks, and scenarios. Centrally planned security doesn't work any better than centrally planned housing, groceries, healthcare, or technology. The rule here is freedom. It is always a better solution than top-down rule.

37

Earthquake Economics

My experience with an earthquake deeply affected me in ways I could not have anticipated. Life was going along normally in a 16-story hotel in Acapulco. Then the room began to move. I thought I was imagining things. Then the windows began to shake and make noise, which was proof to me that something was happening. The rumbling and shaking got worse, and then it was clear: I'm experiencing an earthquake.

My first impression can be summed up as a profound sense of the loss of control. There was nothing I could do either way. I could put on my shoes and run out of the building, but everything was happening so fast. There was no chance of making it to the stairs and out of the building in time. I could only stand there waiting to see how bad it would get. It turned out only to last about 10 seconds, and absolutely nothing and no one was harmed, but at any point in the middle of it, I had no way of knowing.

I imagined the entire building collapsing into rubble. I would be crushed by crashing concrete, glass, and steel. I would end up as refuse along with everything else in the building, a mass of rubble on the ground as dust filled the air. I could do nothing to change it. No choices I made in that instant could protect me. I could duck and cover but my demise would nonetheless be guaranteed.

A few minutes later, Google had all the information I needed about what just happened. "The February 16, 2018, M 7.2 earthquake in Oaxaca, Mexico, occurred as a result of shallow thrust faulting on or near the plate boundary between the Cocos and North America plates. In the region of this earthquake, the Cocos plate moves approximately northeastward at a rate of 60 mm/yr."

It might have been vastly worse. The same entry reports that a magnitude 8.2 earthquake hit last September 8, and "caused at least 78 fatalities and 250 injuries in Oaxaca, and a further 16 deaths in Chiapas."

So it is all about the magnitude that determines damage and death? Not so much. "Eleven days later [last year], a M 7.1 earthquake struck closer to Mexico City, 230 km northeast of today's earthquake, resulting in over 300 fatalities and significant damage in Mexico City and the surrounding region."

What this means is that the earthquake I experienced might have been vastly worse and more deadly but for the crucial factor: the building I was in — and all the others in the area — have been made to withstand earthquakes. It's all about physics. These buildings bend and adapt to dramatic shifts under the earth. It's not always the case. If the construction is not earthquake resistant, the building comes down hard.

We too often take this for granted. It was for the justified fear of natural disasters that buildings in cities did not become skyscrapers until the late 19th century. The crucial invention here was the commercial viability of steel.

The Council on Tall Buildings and Urban Habitat explains that the first all-steel building was the Rand McNally building in Chicago, built in 1889 and taken down in 1911. The success of this building inspired many more. Steel is ideal because it is lighter weight and more adaptable than iron or concrete. It changed the way we live, the shape of cities, and the look of civilization itself. The iron age became the steel age, and then the physicists and seismologists got into the action and created glorious structures that molded themselves.

A few weeks ago I was in New York and looking across the skyline from a very tall building. I was looking down on what was once the tallest building in New York: St. Paul's Chapel of Trinity Wall Street. Churches throughout Europe similarly strived to be the tallest as a way of showing the centrality of faith in the building of civilization. That symbolism came to an end during the Gilded Age in the US, and it spread throughout the world, with the skyscraper standing as a marvelous tribute to human achievement.

The history of the earliest skyscrapers is marvelous to contemplate. Many technologies besides steel had to come online. We needed indoor plumbing. We needed electricity as the source of lighting (there was no way the new buildings could function with gas lighting). We needed a new modern sophistication over physics. And we need seismology to protect against the earth shifting beneath our feet. All these came together at that crucial moment in history to change the way we live and work. Today we think nothing of them.

But how is it that they all came together and why did it all happen in the 1880s? Here we need to reflect on economic institutions. It came at the end of what has been called the age of laissez-faire, a period that extended from the end of the Napoleonic Wars through World War I. There was no income tax. There were no passports. Property was protected against invasion by the state. Capital accumulation led to the complexification of the division of labor and structure of production. Money was sound and stable, rooted and conventional in gold. This inspired entrepreneurial risk taking to serve a hungry consuming public. Progress was the rage.

With all of this, humankind took major steps toward overcoming the exigencies of life itself. Crucially, all of this happened before the state grew to anything like its current level of intervention in the economic life of the citizenry. This was before income taxes, interventions in labor, zoning regulations, the draft, inflation, and all the rest of the problems that came later, introducing what we might call artificial uncertainty. The state had begun the great experiment in power, presuming to have more intelligence and wherewithal than entrepreneurs and society.

Let us not forget the contribution of free economies to making life safer. It wasn't the regulations that made the difference. It was the innovations in the context of free enterprise.

I never stop thinking about this reality, and as the 10-second earthquake hit, I found myself immediately reflecting on the relationship between economics, freedom, modernity, and the history of the great discovery of liberalism. My mind raced back to a time at the earliest years of the birth of modernity and the very notion of progress itself. The last black death in Europe was over. The Medicis were banking. Prosperity was growing.

The only piece of music I know from the period that relates to natural disasters is the "Missa Et ecce terrae motus" (Earthquake Mass for 12 voices) by Antoine Brumel (1460-1512). I recalled that it was remarkable. I always imagined that the composer had three tasks: characterize the terror of the moving earth, mourn the dead, and celebrate the living. As soon as the earth stopped moving, I jumped to my computer and played the entire piece from beginning to end.

38

The Long Life of the Mercantile State

I was digging through the archives of the American Institute for Economic Research and ran across a speech by founder EC Harwood from the early 1940s. He opened by recalling the circumstances surrounding the passage of the disastrous Smoot-Hawley tariff of 1930, an act that turned a predicted (and predictable) stock market correction into a macroeconomic depression. (AIER was founded in 1933 to oppose government intervention.)

Harwood pointed out that more than one thousand economists signed a letter denouncing the tariffs and calling for free trade. It might have been the largest and most organized effort by economists to weigh in on a government policy until that point in history. Looking more deeply, there is a substantial body of research recalling the circumstances behind this tariff and celebrating the opposing forces. It is a case study of how expediency triumphs over rationality and thereby produces social and economic ruin.

Principled Economists

The letter that came from the economists was very inspiring:

> "We are convinced that increased protective duties would be a mistake. They would operate, in general, to increase the prices which domestic consumers would have to pay. By raising prices they would encourage concerns with higher costs to undertake production, thus compelling the consumer to subsidize waste and inefficiency in industry. At the same time, they would force him to pay higher rates of profit to established firms which enjoyed lower production costs. A higher level of protection, such as is contemplated by both the House and

Senate bills, would therefore raise the cost of living and injure the great majority of our citizens.. We would urge our Government to consider the bitterness which a policy of higher tariffs would inevitably inject into our international relations.... A tariff war does not furnish good soil for the growth of world peace."

Economist Frank Fetter recalled what a striking moment it was. "Economic faculties that within a few years were to be split wide open on monetary policy, deficit finance, and the problem of big business," he said, "were practically at one in their belief that the Hawley-Smoot bill was an iniquitous piece of legislation."

President Hoover ignored the letter, as well as the pleas of top bankers and corporate executives. He signed the law that made a bad situation worse and kicked off a global trade war that no one won. Paul H. Douglas, the primary author of the letter, later recalled, "I think poor Hoover wanted to take our advice. His party was so strongly committed to protection, however, that he felt compelled to sign the bill, with the result that all our predictions came true."

To be sure, Hoover was under the sway of some small sectors of industry that benefited from trade. More pressingly, he was just trying to do something to patch things up and there is something about the idea of protectionism that appeals to a person assigned to be in charge of the nation state. It's a strange intuition that emanates from people in charge: keep the foreign products out and let's make everything here at home. No matter how often the plan fails, it keeps coming back again. The economists still object but somehow the chief executive hunts down the one economist who is willing to say what the executive wants him to say.

Unprincipled Economists

In this case of Donald Trump's tariffs, he found Peter Navarro as the economist who was willing to consecrate bad policy as holy and good. We know from testimony from people there at the time that Navarro became the man because someone on the staff searched Amazon books for some economist who was worried about China. The book "Death by China" caught the president's eye, and the rest is history.

For his own part, Navarro shares none of the president's interests in tax cuts and deregulation. He is a registered Democrat who opposes fossil fuels and favors product bans in the name of environmentalism. He is also an isolationist and protectionist (not unlike Bernie Sanders). None of which is surprising. Trump cannot claim to "drain the swamp" while filling the swamp back up with the torrent of trade lobbyists who are now begging the powers that be for some form of exemption.

The general goal of free trade as a guarantor of peace and prosperity has been one of the few consensus points of politics that has been consistent since the end of World War Two. Now, we suddenly find that we can no longer take this for granted, not when the President of the US is tweeting that he would love to start a trade war.

And thus does the world now find itself embroiled in the chaotic politics of protectionism, complete with panicked lobbying, retaliation threats, and shock and awe from anyone who possesses even the slightest knowledge of the history of mercantilism.

The rumblings are all around us. A new kind of uncertainty has come to the world: discretion is displacing the rule of law in international trade. Europe has produced a full list of American products it plans to target for retaliation. Basically, it is all the stuff that Americans are known for: trucks, blue jeans, corn, makeup, tobacco, and bourbon. You can browse the entire list of products that could soon find themselves unwelcome in the Old World, at least not at market prices.

Think about the implications of this trade war: American consumers and producers pay higher prices for millions of products and then American producers are blocked from access to markets abroad, and the retaliation starts again. Oh, what a beautiful war. What does it achieve? Nothing desirable from the point of view of the common person on either side of the border.

All mercantilism relies on a fundamental fallacy that confuses wealth with money and thus attempts to keep as much paper (or gold or whatever) as possible in the country. The mistake is the failure to realize that wealth takes many forms, including goods and services; money is only there to facilitate trade, which is the real source of rising prosperity. The particulars of the political geography of that trade matters not at all from an economic perspective.

State Building

By coincidence, I'm watching the second season of a wonderful show on Netflix called Versailles. It tells the story of the reign of Louis XIV in France, the Sun King, and his incredible imperial ambitions. The show revolves around life at the palace, which the King (who believed that he ruled by Divine Right) constructed to ingather nobles from all over France so that he could watch and pacify them, disarming them as potential threats to state power.

The show was conceived before President Trump was a reality but somehow it all rings familiar in our time, down to the Sun King's treatment of subordinates, his incurable paranoia, his insatiable desire for more power, and even his war on drugs and leakers in the palace. Staffing changes at the palace are driven by one consideration: loyalty to the King.

The show doesn't focus on Louis's mercantilism but you can pick up hints of it. The real history has Louis finding at least one economist in France he could rely on to feed his fear of imports, which he dreaded because he believed imports meant gold outflows and thus impoverishment. His name was Jean-Baptiste Colbert (1619-1683) who served as the French minister of finance. His litany of preferred policies sounds like it comes from today's White House: high spending on infrastructure, high tariff walls, an imperialist push for exports, and the creation of industrial guilds.

Colbert ended up presiding over economic stagnation of the country even as the palace and the royals lived ever more opulently. Colbert was no socialist. He is more properly considered to be a proto-fascist because his views on economics were exactly what we came to expect from mid 19th-century advocates of protectionism, industrial control, and centralized statism — an ideology that grew like cancer for a century until culminating in the interwar period in Europe. The goal of such an outlook on political economy is not prosperity as such much less freedom for all. The goal of the mercantilist state is the celebration, enrichment, wealth, and glory of the head of state.

The object of Colbert's service was the Sun King but the experience proves the rule that there is nothing new under the sun. Every departure from liberalism is a push for one or another form of centralized statism. The goal of feeding the power of the chief executive is always the core motivation of all forms of mercantilism, whether in the 17th century, the interwar years, or our own times.

39

No One Wins a Trade War

The politics of international trade rarely follows typical partisan lines. For centuries, free trade has been a cause for new businesses, transport companies, bankers, retailers, consumers, and wholesale manufacturers. Protectionism — which is a throwback to mercantilism of the Middle Ages — appeals to legacy big businesses threatened by competition, labor unions that want to preserve inflated wages, cultural groups that thrive on nostalgia, and ambitious politicians who build careers on the fear of foreigners.

If you understand that, perhaps it won't surprise you to know that Elizabeth Warren and Donald Trump — despite gigantic political differences on so much else — agree on the need for tariffs. She has been visiting China, and reports back, with support for the escalating war: "U.S. policymakers are starting to look more aggressively at pushing China to open up the markets without demanding a hostage price of access to US technology."

She is a voice for organized labor, which enjoys something of a monopoly privilege in the labor markets. She has also fashioned herself as an opponent of anything that looks like free enterprise. He is an investor in legacy brick and mortar that is being threatened by new forms of production and distribution. Both believe that a vibrant market for international trade, with products distributed by online platforms, could potentially kill their preferred models for professional success.

Brick and Mortar

In the case of Trump in particular, his real estate holdings are bound up with the old model of retail. "Trump's real estate holdings, specifically those in New York City, have taken a big hit in the past year, as retail values are struggling in response to Amazon's e-commerce gains," reports Fortune. "The loss has him moving from 156th on the [richest people] list down to 248th." It is for this reason that he is trying to turn back the clock.

Why not use the power of the presidency to do something about it? The best reason to eschew that path is that such efforts are futile in the long run. Technologies move forward. Financial losses cannot be covered using artificial methods. Markets eventually clear. Attempts to forestall that are extremely costly for consumers, and it drives down productivity over time. The special interests benefit temporarily but the price is huge for everyone else.

The language of national interest resonates because the US has indeed lost the title of the world's largest economy. To be sure, you can't really trust the Gross Domestic Product numbers of either country. By some measures, and adjusting for purchasing power parity (PPP), the Chinese economy is already bigger. In this case, we might be looking at the typical behavior of an empire in decline: lash out at foreign countries and demonize their tactics and methods as a way of distracting from domestic economic concerns.

Observe how the language has already devolved. Now every patent owned by an American company is "US technology," as if companies themselves are incapable of negotiating their own deals so the US government has to do it for them. This part of the discussion is all about the claim that China is stealing "our" technology.

But concerns over IP are not the dominant excuse to tax imports from China and thereby prompting China to tax imports from the US. The reasons have been the usual list from the trade-war playbook. China pays workers too little. They are rigging the game. They threaten our national security. They are manipulating the currency. The trade deficit is too high. Sometimes it is easy to spot a deception: there are just too many excuses for this policy and not one solid one.

That Deficit

Consider the trade deficit, which Trump talks about incessantly. He cites the incorrect $800 billion figure and says that it proves that China owes us something. But all it really means is that in dollar terms, the US buys more from China than the reverse, which tells us about as much as the fact that you buy more from WalMart than WalMart buys from you. It is a piece of data without any substantive economic significance.

But as with GDP, you can't really trust these numbers either. They are calculated based on declaring a country of origin for every good, and this, in turn, depends on discerning something the trade bureaucracies call "substantial transformation." Most things today are produced with the cooperation of people from many lands, while trade numbers depend on isolating a single country as the responsible entity by virtue of the locale in which the product was substantially transformed.

Let's consider just the coffee cup on my desk. It is branded with the logo of a local brewery, which conceived of the cup, designed the cup, and sells the cup to people who visit for tours, right here in the USA. To actually make the cup and sell it at an affordable price, the brewery outsourced production to China, where workers made it happen and sent it back. But the cup wouldn't exist much less be sold at all were it not for the local brewery with the idea and the marketing prowess.

Still, trade numbers count this cup as an import for purposes of the trade deficit. Because China put it together and sold it back to the US, does China thereby somehow owe someone something? This makes no sense. It's just an exchange like any other: all parties benefit.

For this reason, Zachary Karabell writes in Foreign Affairs: "If trade numbers more accurately accounted for how products are made, it is possible that the United States would not have any trade deficit at all with China. The problem, in short, is that trade figures are currently calculated based on the assumption that each product has a single country of origin and that the declared value of that product goes to that country."

How to fix the numbers? Economists have been working on that problem for many years, and the answer has to do with the calculation of the value added at each production stage in every country for every good and service on the planet earth. That works in theory. In practice, this would be impossible, unless half the world's population became economists and dedicated themselves to counting. As Karabell writes, "All indicators suffer from the same flaw: they try in vain to distill complicated, ever-changing economic systems into a single, simple figure."

No One Wins

Trade between nations dates back as far as we have historical records, whereas trade deficit figures are a mid-20th-century invention. Trade does not depend on having statisticians available to calculate the comings and goings of the products and services of whole nations. That this trade war is being conducted with the excuse of these statistics reveals just how pernicious they can be in practice.

The results of this war are as follows. US consumers get to pay more for imports from China. American companies lose markets as Chinese consumers and importers turn to other countries to provide wines, pork, and fruit. And this is only round one. The financial markets have suffered a terrible quarter one, just as all this interventionist rhetoric picked up steam. We are doing ourselves no favors here.

This is not how a nation becomes great again.

40

Two Trade Wars: 1807 and 2018

The legal uncertainties surrounding trade with China have sent people looking for historical precedent for this mess. One jumps out: the targeted trade embargo that the US imposed against Britain in 1807. Let's look at the parallels and lessons.

It's War

For months now, the Trump administration has been threatening every manner of taxes on imports from many countries but on China in particular. The policies would directly attack American consumers and producers of goods in which China has some role in the supply chain. China has responded with taxes on imports that would directly hit the economic prospects of Trump's political base.

Most recently, in order to escalate further, the president picked a big round number of $100 billion and sent aides out to round up enough products to meet that target. China, the spokesmen of which cannot say enough how much they would far prefer peace and economic cooperation, has retaliated with promises to close more markets to American producers.

Among the latest imported products from China affected are medical supplies and equipment, including pacemakers, artificial limbs, knee replacement parts, defibrillators, fillings for teeth, birth-control pills, vaccines, and that's just what is on the list. Many other secondary products and services will be affected. The supply of all of these will be restricted and hence the price will increase, provided you can get the products at all. At best it means raising health-care costs, which is pretty much the last thing Americans need.

To be sure, aides to the president, including his new adviser (however temporary; the last one resigned in protest against protectionism) Lawrence Kudlow, has taken it upon himself to tell everyone in public or private that this is not that serious really. The tariffs aren't yet implemented, though every American business that relies on imports and exports is working to retool for them to become real. The panic is unwarranted, says Kudlow, since this is all a negotiating tactic. Trump is just being a good businessman here, with his art of the deal and so on. The point is not to shut down trade but to extract concessions so that we can have even more. The end game, Kudlow implies, is freer and more open markets in all directions.

The problem with these assurances is the absence of evidence that there is truth to them. Consider the huge range of complaints about China that have been variously cited as a case for trade war: intellectual property violations, subsidies, currency manipulation, too-low wages, and the trade deficit itself, which Trump has erroneously claimed is a measure of how much China "owes" the US.

There is no possible agreement that could address all of these complaints. It seems like Trump is using all these conditions as excuses to roll back international commerce, essentially nationalizing economic production while letting the rest of the world go its own way.

Historical Precedent
One reason this feels so alarming is that there is almost no historical precedent for a US president using personal authority over trade and tariffs directly to target a single country to make its people (and our own) suffer as much as possible. "We haven't seen anything like this in centuries," confirms Douglas Irwin, the Dartmouth College professor and author of the most comprehensive history of American trade policy ever written.

Intrigued by this "centuries" remark? It turns out that American history does record an instance in which US ports were closed for both exports and imports, with the desire to harm Britain. The year was 1807 and the president was Thomas Jefferson, of all people.

The US was trying to stay neutral in a conflict between France and Britain (the latter days of the Napoleonic wars) but British ships started pilfering American goods and sailors for the war effort (still considering Americans to be subjects). Jefferson wanted to avoid a shooting war, but still wanted the US government involved to defend human rights against what seemed to many to be a form of terrorism. Jefferson was talked into using trade power (a supposedly more peaceful solution) in an effort to get Britain to stop.

The result was a near-total embargo, and probably the closest modern example we have of how national autarky would actually work in practice. Jefferson wrote in a letter that Congress has never been "more solidly united in what they believed to be the best for the public good." It's not possible to ramp up a trade war beyond a complete shutdown. In other words, this is a case wherein the president threatened trade intervention of a form far more extreme than has thus been proposed even by Trump.

The Results of 1807

The decision turned into the worst disaster of the Jefferson presidency. The trade war of 1807 led to the loss of lucrative trading routes, the breakdown of mutually beneficial trading relationships, a revolt among Jefferson's electoral base, a victory for the Federalist Party, the rise of black market trading activity, a huge rise in the price of imported goods and a fall in the price of exports, and huge popularity blow against the Jefferson presidency, which was supposed to be about reducing government's role, not cutting off business opportunities for the American people.

The entire trade-war effort failed and ended up undermining both American prosperity and the Jefferson presidency.

Irwin writes ("The Welfare Cost of Autarky: Evidence from the Jeffersonian Trade Embargo, 1807–09"):

> The highly controversial embargo was in effect for just 14 months. Growing domestic opposition to the trade restrictions, particularly in New England, forced Congress to repeal the measure in March 1809. The consensus among historians is that the embargo failed to achieve its objective because Britain and France refused to change their policies regarding American shipping. This was not due to the failure to eliminate trade, but the failure of the trade measures to weaken the political resolve in Britain to suppress neutral shipping in its effort to strangle the French economy.

So much for the politics of trade embargoes: it undid a presidency and bolstered the enemies of liberty. The tensions of this period continued into the next presidency and resulted in the War of 1812 in which the president had to flee the White House, which ended up being burned by British troops. The trade war became real war. The long-simmering dispute in American history between the nationalists and the decentralists ended up being lost by the good guys precisely because of a trade war.

The Economic Results

As for the economics, writes Irwin, "The embargo had a dramatic impact on prices in the United States, driving down the domestic prices of exported goods and driving up the domestic prices of imported goods." Further: "The best-guess calculation of the static welfare cost of the embargo is about 5 percent of GNP. The cost does not represent the total gains from trade, however, because the initial trading equilibrium was one of restricted trade. Still, the embargo inflicted substantial costs on the economy while it was in effect."

It's stunning to think of: fully 5% of national output. That's depression levels. These calculations are interesting but don't come near including the unseen costs of the embargo, the loss of trade routes, the ruined relationships, the diverted resources, the ruined businesses, and so on. All this wealth that was wrecked could have been invested or saved and formed new capital for business expansion during what was otherwise a time of great economic growth.

I personally adore Jefferson, the man of letters, the great champion of liberalism and human rights. But this was an egregious decision. Remember that he was the author of the protest letter called the Declaration of Independence. One of the indictments against the British king was "For cutting off our Trade with all parts of the world." Talk about hypocrisy! Jefferson's supporters made him and his party pay the price.

An Autarkist as President?

The great fear of financial markets today is that no one really knows what Trump is going to do next, much less why he is going to do it. My worry, which I expressed back in 2015, is that he is a convinced economic nationalist. He believes in national control of economic life. He is convinced that trade relations with foreign nations diminishes collective attachments to the nation and therefore to its leadership. This outlook is a rejection of everything we've learned about the economics of international trade since the 18th century. As with Jefferson, the people who will pay the price the heaviest price will be the president's main supporters.

Thomas Jefferson's motivation was not personal aggrandizement, nor was it the motivation behind the Smoot-Hawley tariff. But it hardly matters. International trade is a delicate business, with countless and unpredictable downstream effects. It can be upset profoundly with taxes and other impositions that disturb the commercial life of the nation. It can lead to depression and hot war. This is the history, and it doesn't bode well for our future.

41

Is Nationalism the Friend
or Foe of Liberty?

Israeli scholar Yoram Hazony is hitting the opinion pages (excerpts from his new book) with a provocative thesis: nationalism is not a threat to liberty but rather a guarantor of it. His argument is about stability under democracy. It requires mutual trust, fellow feeling, cultural cohesion, a sense that the other could be you because you share similar values, he argues. "Nationalism was the engine that established modern political liberty," he claims, and now we need nationalism to maintain the kind of political stability that undergirds freedom itself.

This is near impossible in what he calls "multinational states," by which he means a geographic territory too mixed up in terms of language, religious allegiance, and culture. He cites unsustainable states like Iraq, Syria, and Yugoslavia. Such mixing has worked, more or less, in the US because "the original American states shared the English language, Protestant religion and British legal traditions, and they had fought together in wartime." New additions to the mix (Catholics, Jews, and former slaves) were acculturated only due to preexisting cultural dominance.

He further argues that the national consensus in the US no longer exists, due to high rates of immigration. This has shattered mutual loyalty, so as regards America as an experiment in multinational diversity: "It's not clear that the U.S. is succeeding at this task."

Good and Bad Nationalism?
You might be thinking you have heard this line before. You have seen the memes from the far right, read the tweets, bumped into the fanatics at rallies. Such sentiments have been credited with getting the current president elected.

But Hazony is careful to distance himself from such movements.

Every nationalist movement contains haters and bigots (though not necessarily more of them than are found in universalist political and religious movements). But nationalism's vices are outweighed by its considerable virtues. A world in which independent nations are permitted to compete freely with one another is a world in which diverse ways of life can flourish, each an experiment in how human beings should live. We have good reason to believe that such a world holds out the best prospects for freedom, for innovation and advancement, and for tolerance.

If you had never read an argument for nationalism that is calm, reasoned, and rooted in history, you might find his point persuasive. Many liberals (and pre-libertarians) a century ago certainly did so.

Back then, the pressing issue, on which the fate of civilization rested, was the following: what should be the standard for the drawing of borders after the chaos of the Great War? It was a war for democracy, they said but it was the death knell for the old multinational monarchies of Europe.

Political loyalty in the Old World was based on dynasty, intermarriage of rulers, deal making, and religious control. In the New World, there is no question that democracy would be the watchword. The nobility would no longer rule; the people would be in charge. A unity global democracy is impossible. There must be states and there must be borders, so what constitutes the basis for nationhood?

Liberalism had a number of answers to the problem and most came down to precisely the terms that Hazony presents here. States should be organized along the lines of fellow feeling, mutual trust, and citizen identity in whatever form.

Liberal Nationalism

Ludwig von Mises, writing in 1919, was highly sympathetic to the nationalist project. What's a nation? Mises rejected the then-fashionable trope of carving up the human population by race on grounds that the supposed science of the project was "a thicket of error, fantasy, and mysticism." Instead, he wanted to define a nation specifically according to one overriding standard: language. Polyglot nations are unsustainable. Experience in educational institutions alone shows this. Attempting to fund and run schools with multiple language groups feeds resentment and hate. It's true for all public institutions. The only real answer is separation; that is, universal secession by smaller groups against larger groups. If national feeling feeds this, it is a friend of liberty.

What is the liberal attitude toward nationalism, in Mises's view? The true liberal rejects dynastic control of lands because it "rejects the princes' greed for lands and chaffering in lands." Further, it embraces the right of a people to determine their own fate: self-determination, in the phrase of the time. However, Mises clarified that there is nothing inconsistent between love of nation and love of universal well being. Liberal nationalism is always directed against the tyrant. It always seeks peace between peoples: "The desire for national unity, too, is above all thoroughly peaceful."

Now, keep in mind the year he was writing. It was 1919, before the rise of fascist ideology in Europe. The idea of forming states on the national principle alone was new, and Mises saw it as the only real path to preventing a new world war from being borne out of allied imperialism and postwar German resentment. His vision was to let bygones be bygones, leave people alone, permit any group or any part of a group to form its own nation (even down to the individual level, if that were possible), and move toward a world of free trade, free migration, and universal limits on power.

Mises's Mind Changed

The Misesian path was not the one followed, obviously. Mises's 1927 book on liberalism drops the endorsement of nationalism but retains the longing for self-determination. After the Second World War, following his migration to the US as a refugee, having spent six years being sheltered in Geneva, he was given the chance to revisit the question of nationalism. His new outlook appeared in 1944, in *Omnipotent Government*. Mises had completely changed his mind.

This book goes to great lengths to walk back his theory from 1919. In a world of statism, nationalism is a philosophy of aggression. Whether based in religion, racism, or territorial expansionism, nationalism is a threat to liberty itself and the project of human cooperation. It leads to migration barriers, trade protectionism, violence against non-nationals, and finally war. He no longer believed that nationalism could be a friend of liberty. The reverse is true: "nationalism within our world of international division of labor is the inevitable outcome of etatism."

What had made the difference? Life experience, for one. He watched his beloved Vienna be invaded by German armies. He saw the universities purged of intellectuals, particularly those deemed Jewish and liberal. He saw Europe enveloped in despotism, war, and mass death, in the name of territorial expansion and domination by the master race. He watched with horror as the nationalist principle, the one he imagined might be a source of peace, became the basis of the bloodiest nightmare.

What mistake had he made? As he put it, his nationalist idea was rooted in an underlying philosophical presumption of liberalism; that is, models of public administration that do not interfere in people's lives and property, do not seek war, do not restrict trade and migration, do not attempt to control racial and language demographics, and do not manipulate people's desire for belongingness to shore up the power and status of a "great" leader. In other words, the real answer is liberty; nationalism not only contributes nothing to the cause but is easily weaponized by any state that expands beyond its proper role.

Renan's Deconstruction

Mises, having witnessed the horrors of what nationalism wrought in his home and throughout Europe, sought out some theoretical basis for his new realization. He found it in a 1882 writing by the French historian Ernst Renan: What Is a Nation? Mises was right: if another essay has done as good a job in dealing with the issue, I'm unaware of it. Renan wrote it while the age of monarchy was coming to a close, as the rise of democracy was occurring everywhere, but still before the Great War unleashed such territorial confusion. Ideologies like socialism, imperialism, and "scientific" racism were vying to replace old-world understandings of political community.

Renan observes that people frequently throw around the word nationalism without unpacking what precisely it means. He delineates five conventional theories of nationhood from history and practice.

Dynasty. This view believes that ruling-class lineage forms the foundation of nationhood. It's about a history of initial conquest by one family or tribe over one people, its struggle to gain and maintain power and legitimacy, its marriages, wars, treaties, and alliances, along with a heroic legend. This is a solid description of European experience in feudal times, but it is not necessary for nationhood.

The dynastic sense of what nationhood is has largely evaporated in the 20th century, and yet nationhood is still with us. Renan saw that the dynastic view of the nation is not a permanent feature of the concept but only incidental to a time and place, and wholly replaceable. "A nation can exist without a dynastic principle," writes Renan, "and even those nations which have been formed by dynasties can be separated from them without therefore ceasing to exist."

Religion. The belief that a nation needs to practice a single faith has been the basis of wars and killings since the beginning of recorded history. It seemed like nationhood couldn't exist without it, which is why the Schism of the 11th century and the Reformation of the 16th century led to such conflict.

Then emerged a beautiful idea: let people believe what they want to believe, so long as they are not hurting anyone. The idea was tried and it worked, and thus was born the idea of religious liberty that finally severed the idea of national belongingness from religious identity. Even as late as the 19th century, American political interests claimed that the US could not be a nation while accepting Catholic, Jewish, and Buddhist immigration. Today we see these claims for what they are, politically illicit longings for conquest over the right of conscience.

In addition, what might appear at first to be a single religion actually has radically different expressions. Pennsylvania Amish and Texas Baptists share the same religious designation but have vastly different praxis, and the same is true of Irish vs. Vietnamese vs. Guatemalan versions of Catholicism. This is also true of every other religious faith, including Judaism, Islam, and Hinduism.

Race. In the second half of the 19th century, there arose the new science of race, which purported to explain the evolution of all human societies through a deterministic reduction to biological characteristics. It was concluded that only race is firm and fixed and the basis of belongingness. Renan grants that in the most primitive societies, race is a large factor. But then comes other more developed aspects of the human experience: language, religion, art, music, and commercial engagement that break down racial divisions and create a new basis for community. Focussing on race alone is a revanchist longing in any civilized society.

There is also a scientific problem too complex for simple resolution: no political community on earth can claim to be defined solely by racial identity because there is no pure race (Mises says exactly the same thing). This is why politics can never be reduced to ethnographic identity as a first principle. Racial ideology also trends toward the politics of violence: "No one has the right to go through the world fingering people's skulls, and taking them by the throat saying: 'You are of our blood; you belong to us!'"

Language. As with the other claims of what constitutes nationality, the claim of language unity has a superficial plausibility. Polyglot communities living under a unity state face constant struggles over schooling, official business, and other issues of speech. They have the feeling of being two or several nations, thus tempting people to believe that language itself is the basis of nationhood. But this actually makes little sense: the US, New Zealand, and the UK are not a single nation because they hold the same language in common. Latin America and Spain, Portugal and Brazil, share the same language but not the same nation.

There is also the issue that not even a single language is actually unified: infinite varieties of expression and dialect can cause ongoing confusion. How much, really, does the language of an urban native of New Jersey have to do with expressions used in rural Mississippi? "Language invites people to unite," writes Renan, "but it does not force them to do so." There is nothing mystically unifying about speaking the same language; language facilitates communication but does not forge a nation. Mises too embraces this view, thus reversing his position from 1919.

Geography. Natural boundaries are another case of nation-making in the past which, as with all these other principles, actually has little to do with permanent features of what really makes a nation. Rivers and mountains can be convenient ways to draw borders but they do not permanently shape political communities. Geography can be easily overcome. It is malleable, as American history shows. The existence of geographically non-contiguous nations further refutes the notion.

Americans speak of "sea to shining sea," but how does that make sense of Alaska and Hawaii? Also in the US, enclaves of past national loyalty are a feature of city life: little Brazil, Chinatown, little Havana, and so on. Even further, to try to force unity based on geography alone is very dangerous. "I know of no doctrine which is more arbitrary or more fatal," writes Renan, "for it allows one to justify any or every violence."

All the above have some plausible claim to explaining national attachment, but none hold up under close scrutiny. In Renan's view, nationhood is a spiritual principle, a reflection of the affections we feel toward some kind of political community — its ideals, its past, its achievements, and its future. Where your heart is, there is your nation, as Albert Jay Nock said. This is why so many of us can feel genuine feelings of joy and even belongingness during July 4th celebrations. We are celebrating something in common: a feeling we have that we share with others, regardless of religion, race, language, geography, and even ideology.

Renan: "Man is a slave neither of his race nor his language, nor of his religion, nor of the course of rivers nor of the direction taken by mountain chains. A large aggregate of men, healthy in mind and warm of heart, creates the kind of moral conscience which we call a nation."

Mises was clearly taken with this view, and hence his change of heart and mind.

Orwell on Nationalism

Around the same time, the always-remarkable George Orwell presented his own Notes on Nationalism in 1945. It's not as careful an essay as Renan's but consider the context: fury and disgust at the rise of Nazism, nationalist communism in Russia, and a ghastly war that wrecked so much of the world.

Orwell had it up to here with collectivism of all sorts.

His essay is in three parts. He first defines it: "the habit of assuming that human beings can be classified like insects and that whole blocks of millions or tens of millions of people can be confidently labeled 'good' or 'bad.'" Secondly, "the habit of identifying oneself with a single nation or other unit, placing it beyond good and evil and recognising no other duty than that of advancing its interests."

Notice that Orwell's definition is not rooted in the territorial issue. His nationalism is more ideological. It's the habitual and uncritical celebration of some group-based cause that one believes is specially blessed to solve all the world's problems. In this sense, the typical Communist is a nationalist, looking the world over for revolutionary movements to cheer on, such as the political pilgrims who look at a place like Cuba and Venezuela and find not tyranny but emancipation. He even finds nationalism in the works of G.K. Chesterton who celebrated a "little England" but found virtue in expanding imperialism so long as it took on the Catholic brand (Orwell was especially disgusted at Chesterton's defense of Mussolini).

Second, Orwell identified three nationalistic habits of mind.

First, **obsession**: "No nationalist ever thinks, talks, or writes about anything except the superiority of his own power unit. It is difficult if not impossible for any nationalist to conceal his allegiance. The smallest slur upon his own unit, or any implied praise of a rival organization, fills him with uneasiness which he can relieve only by making some sharp retort."

Second, **instability**. "The intensity with which they are held does not prevent nationalist loyalties from being transferable." It's a tribalist mindset and it can easily migrate. Thus were so many fascists recruited from the ranks of communists, and so many champions of the Pan-Germanism that bred Nazism came from the upper-class ranks of British society. In his view, nationalism is inherently unprincipled in this way.

Third, **indifference to reality**. "All nationalists have the power of not seeing resemblances between similar sets of facts…. Actions are held to be good or bad, not on their own merits, but according to who does them, and there is almost no kind of outrage — torture, the use of hostages, forced labour, mass deportations, imprisonment without trial, forgery, assassination, the bombing of civilians — which does not change its moral colour when it is committed by 'our' side."

He elaborates this prescient point that pervades the left and right today.

Although endlessly brooding on power, victory, defeat, revenge, the nationalist is often somewhat uninterested in what happens in the real world. What he wants is to feel that his own unit is getting the better of some other unit, and he can more easily do this by scoring off an adversary than by examining the facts to see whether they support him. All nationalist controversy is at the debating-society level. It is always entirely inconclusive, since each contestant invariably believes himself to have won the victory. Some nationalists are not far from schizophrenia, living quite happily amid dreams of power and conquest which have no connection with the physical world.

Orwell discusses other manifestations of this mentality, such as forms of identity politics. All salvation comes from the white race; all virtue is in the non-white races. All glory or evil resides in the Jewish people. Greatness/evil extends from one country. And we could go on with every list in the identitarianism of our time: misogyny/feminism, disabled/abled, Christian/Islam, rich/poor, and so on.

The nationalist is forever counterposing diverse societies with homogenous ones, as if the latter thing even exists. The word homogeneity should not even apply in any literal sense to any two members of the human family. No two people are the same; even twins have minds of their own. The chase for a homogenous population will always and everywhere result in forcing people into a group not of their choosing.

Orwell writes: "The abiding purpose of every nationalist is to secure more power and more prestige, not for himself but for the nation or other unit in which he has chosen to sink his own individuality."

What's most interesting about Orwell's essay is that he takes a broadened view of the nationality question, to the point that it is no longer about territorial politics alone and instead touches on the psychological impact of political rule itself. (Sigmund Freud has long ago identified this as a pathology in his overlooked Group Psychology book.) In this case, his analysis of nationalism applies not only to Nazism, not only to Communism, not only to Catholicism or any other religious or identitarian movement you can name. It could, conceivably apply, for example to libertarianism itself. No one, no movement, is immune from the virus. Reflect on that point to perhaps explain a lot that has happened to the "liberty movement" over the last ten years.

Back to Hazony

Our Israeli professor friend Yoram Hazony is not unaware of Orwell's writings, and addresses them directly. Still, he comes out on the other side, still arguing that nationalism is a friend of liberty. But what does he mean by liberty? He means democracy, stability, and high trust among society's members such that they have warm affections for the national state and see it as an essential source for social order.

"The national state leverages these bonds of mutual loyalty," he writes, "to get individuals to obey the laws, serve in the military and pay taxes, even when their own party or tribe is out of power and the government's policies are not to their liking."

This might be right — nationalism is certainly useful in manipulating people to intensify loyalties to the state — but is this necessarily the highest goal of society? Liberalism argued that the answer is no. The highest goal of society is realized through freedom that leaves people alone in their person and property to find their own path to happiness.

A century ago, Hazony's views might have been plausible. No more. Ludwig von Mises learned this lesson between his earliest and later writings. He lived through the experiment in controlled nationalism, and discovered the truth that it cannot be controlled. In fact, it can unleash literal hell as a propaganda device to disguise gross injustice and evil.

A nationalism that presents itself as a friend of liberty is one that must willfully ignore the most bitter lessons of the last century, while eschewing the greatest lesson of all: the only true guarantor of liberty is liberty itself.

42

A Second Passport, to an Island Paradise, Does Sound Pretty Sweet

W e tend to think of "industries" as steel, information delivery, and stuff like financials. What I had not realized is that citizenship itself, in particular, the acquisition of an additional passport, has become a real commodity and the basis of a $2 billion industry of its own.

And yet, when I was in the Caribbean recently, reporters kept asking about my opinion regarding the Citizenship by Investment Program. It has emerged as the top export of the gorgeous St. Kitts and Nevis islands.

Before attending this event, I didn't really have an opinion. Now I do. I absolutely love it. The market for second passports is one of the bright lights of freedom in the world today. It is legal. It is acceptable. And it is being used ever more. Rightly so.

The Escape

In a world of prison states and restricted mobility, a world in which nearly every human being is forced to beg and depend on the discretion of bureaucrats in order to exercise the basic human right to be mobile, the market for citizenship provides at least one safe haven against economic calamity, tyranny, and war. It's available only to the very rich today. It should be available to everyone.

"A lot has changed since 1984 when our Citizenship by Investment Programme (CIP) began as an ambitious start-up venture," St. Kitts Prime Minister Timothy Harris said at the Caribbean Investment Summit where I just spoke. He noted that there this is now a growing market in this product and industry.

"As to be expected, competition has surged along with interest in Citizenship by Investment Programmes — so much so that, within the past several years, Antigua and Barbuda (2013), Grenada (2013; re-launched in 2016) and St. Lucia (2015) entered the CIP market, and Dominica reshaped its CIP in 2014 after having launched it two decades earlier in 1993. Cyprus (2011; restructured in 2013) and Malta (2014) also introduced their own CIPs several years ago. As I speak, other countries are considering getting into the lucrative CIP market," Prime Minister Harris said.

I'm guessing that most readers when hearing about this are triggered to think of nefarious plots. Money laundering. Tax evasion. Protection programs. Secret plots. Actually, this is all nonsense. It's true that these places typically have no capital gains or income taxes (nor did anywhere have these before the 20th century). But both St. Kitts and Nevis have been removed from the grey list of list of tax havens by the EU.

The basis of the 2nd passport industry, especially the Citizenship by Investment Program, really comes down to the desire on the part of people to purchase an option to be left alone. It's really not any more complicated than that.

We think of the passport as normal because no one alive recalls a time when they didn't exist. Actually, the passport as a norm is a modern invention of World War I as a means of controlling people and their movements and binding people in a forced relationship to the state. They were unknown by most of the world — and would never have been tolerated — just one generation earlier. Such travel documents signifying the permission granted by the king had previously been associated with despots and caliphates.

The emergence of a universal passport was part of a complete suite of policies that emerged in those years, the purpose of which was to build a state-managed world. They fit alongside compulsory schooling, central banking, labor regulations, and income taxes as evidence that the noose was being tightened around the civilian population. The military model of wartime became the new normal for everyone.

Move Only with Permission

In recent years, the ability to travel and exit has become ever more difficult. The US is introducing exit scans when leaving the country, a program that is ready to go in every respect and is only missing universal application due to a shortage of machines and human resources. Getting a visa to visit the US or any foreign country is a more iffy proposition now than ever before. The US can deny any American travel rights for any reason.

It's not at all surprising that with the highly politicized environment of the US, with ever more controls, more people are looking for new ways to live a peaceful life. It only takes one visit to a paradise like St. Kitts to get the mind turning toward dreams of a new start, a life of peace and quiet. I completely get it. I was only in St. Kitts for three days and now I understand completely.

What does it take to gain a second passport to a place like this? A few years ago, the price was $200,000 plus all the fees associated with due diligence that is necessary to establish that you are not running from the law. Now the price is lower. You can buy in with a contribution of $150,000 or purchase a stake in real estate worth $200,000, in addition to other fees. There are people and companies all over the island who are ready to walk you through the process. Here is a brochure. And, no, you don't have actually to live on the island to enjoy citizenship.

Does this mean giving up US citizenship? You certainly don't have to. There are upsides and downsides to becoming an expatriate. The dream of not having to pay taxes sounds great, but there are large fees, huge compliance issues, and outright taxes associated with giving up US citizenship. Then you might have a problem getting a visa to get back in, even to visit extended family. Some 4,000-plus people do it in any case, partially because holding US citizenship is now a liability for many kinds of business relationships abroad. Many banks around the world shut the door on anyone with US citizenship.

But you don't have to be motivated by the ambition of renouncing your forced attachment to a particular nation. The Citizenship by Investment industry is booming because it serves as a hedge against unknowns in a world of state control, and provides a possible guarantee of safety, security, and a peaceful life. There is nothing particularly radical or strange about that. The only tragedy is that the privilege of enjoying that peace of mind is today available only to the well-to-do.

43

Economics Gave Unified Culture
a Mercy Killing

The broadcast of the Oscars this year had a record low viewership of 26.5 million viewers, which is down fully 19% from last year's previous record low. Donald Trump says it is because "we don't have Stars anymore." A more obvious explanation is the unbearable politicization of the presentations, with predictable and tiresome social-justice tropes flowing from the podium, alongside this year's misandric thematics. No one likes to be lectured on values and morality by this crew. I get it. There are better ways to pass the time.

That said, there is a deeper reason. The fall of the Oscars is only one sign of a larger trend. Technology fueled by economic considerations has given people more options than ever. We are curating culture according not to some mythical "national" sense of things but rather in accord with our individual preferences. This is happening now simply because we can. The economic trajectory of technology has made it possible. Any institution that strives to embody some mythical ideal of a unitary culture will fail.

Markets Speak Louder than Committees

The Motion Picture Academy is fighting the trend by choosing winners that are not market favorites. This is why so many of the winners of the fake competition this year were movies you have not seen. As the Wall Street Journal notes, "Between 1983 and 2005, every best picture winner was among the 25 highest-grossing releases during the year it opened." Today, it is different: "That string was broken in 2006 when "Crash" won best picture but came in No. 49 at the box office. That started a new streak in which just four of the last 12 best picture winners have been among their year's 25 highest-grossing releases, and none has ranked higher than No.15."

A gap has opened up between the way Hollywood wants to see itself and what consumers really want out of their cultural consumption habits. In the old days, we were stuck in the theaters and what films were released somehow thereby defined who we are as people. But as the volume has grown, the venues for watching have expanded and diversified, competition has driven producers to make movies that delight us in ways of which the elites do not necessarily approve. The decentralized model of cultural consumption is challenging the way we think about the concept of culture itself: it is no longer one thing but rather a deeply personal thing.

Episodic Shifts

The reason for the change traces to the way in which technology has collapsed time and space. Let's use music as an example, mainly because it is the field I know best. We think of music history as taking place in episodic swaths of time defined by a certain style. From the year 1 AD to 1200 AD, there was monophonic chanting based on a single narrative line of text. Thanks to the invention of the musical staff, that become polyphonic music with several parts, culminating in the early Renaissance of the 16th century, which eventually led to instrumental compositions, and the age of J.S. Bach and the Baroque. That led inexorably to the Classical period, the Romantic period, and finally the Modern period. Rightly or wrongly, but probably mostly rightly once you exclude folk traditions, this is the way we have thought about the history of music.

But notice what happens once you get recording technology, the rise of cities, population migrations made possible by technology, and radio and television. New forms of popular music entered the scene, especially after elite music culture became alienated from popular tastes (see atonalism, e.g.). Big band music took over the cities. Later came rock. Country obtained a mass following. Then the delightful chaos ensued. The genres split and split again, and again. When I was growing up, there was a tremendous and epic battle between disco, rock, and indie rock, everyone battling for the heart and soul of what would be the future of pop-rock. Little did we know that we were being buffeted about by a false sense that there has to be winner. There doesn't have to be.

The Collapse of Time

The idea that we had to rally around one style was heavily informed by scarcity. I could only buy so many albums. The space on my record shelf was limited so it became a big deal which artists, which symphonies, which pop stars I liked. Looking back, the intensity here was due to the limitations of the physical medium. We didn't know it but this was forcing on us all what would later turn out to be a false choice.

Today, I can ask my home assistant to play Lady Gaga, switch and ask for Palestrina, switch and ask for Tommy Dorsey, switch and ask for Schubert, and switch again and demand Metallica. I can do all of this in less than one minute. It has opened up an infinite range of possibilities for me to curate my own subjective culture. Democratize this tool and you enter into a new world, where all time happens in one instant. No more do we have to slog from one era to another as some kind of homogeneous blob. We can have it all, and no surprise: each of us does it differently.

So it is with news. In the 1930s, the information landscape was dominated by FDR giving his fireside chats. In World War II we watched propaganda films. In the 1960s and 70s, Walter Cronkite ruled the day and told us what is and isn't news. Today, information swirls around us like a sandstorm and it is up to us to decide what is and isn't fake news.

By analogy, we can see that the same thing has happened to motion pictures. The real best picture is the one that he or she likes the most. Period. Nor do we have to rely on the experts to tell us what we should like. On Rotten Tomatoes, there are two ratings: viewers and critics. In general, the people I know disregard the critics in favor of what the viewers say, same as we rally around Yelp for restaurants and Amazon reviews for product quality.

No More Experts

Technology has made possible the ultimate decentralization. The world of T.S. Eliot, who wrote about national culture having a top-down unity mass, trickling from the elites to the masses according to the designs of the clericy, has been completely smashed. It is the same with people today who complain about cultural collapse. They find things they don't like and characterize it as something everyone does. This claim is just wrong: in a market-driven, technologically advanced society like ours, you can choose your own culture.

While this is new in history, it is also the historical trajectory made possible by dramatic economic change. Nor is it anything to regret. The Academy and their award givers can preen, lecture, hector, and demand, but we no longer have to listen. It is the market that decides the winners, and that means you and I have just as much power and influence as the biggest of the big shots. The culture will no longer be unified, which means it will no longer be controlled.

44

What Our Frankensteins
Have Wrought

Mary Shelley's Frankenstein is all the rage, with the new book, the new movie about the author, an exhibit at the Morgan Library, and growing controversies about the personal and political ethos that a generation of radicals meant to their times and bequeathed to ours.

The occasion is the 200th anniversary of the publication of the book that never stops giving, but there is more going on. Shelley was a mighty intellectual force who foresaw the grave dangers of intellectual pretense (thus anticipating F.A. Hayek) and the unanticipated social consequences of what Thomas Sowell would later call the unconstrained vision.

The monster created in the fictional laboratory — readers are always surprised that he is a sympathetic character, only lacking in all moral sense — anticipates the unfolding of politico-technological history as it developed from the late 19th century through the 20th. Today we wonder whether innovations we rely on (social media, big data, personal tracking) will come back to destroy other features of life we value, like liberty and privacy.

The Person

This fascination with her work is also related to her intellectual pedigree. She was, after all, the daughter of one of two of the mightiest minds of the 19th century, William Godwin and Mary Wollstonecraft, thinkers who took the Enlightenment project into new frontiers of human liberation. Mary herself ran off with and eventually married the troubled but erudite Percy Shelley, found herself embroiled in an awkward relationship with Lord Byron, and experienced the terrible tragedy of losing three children while experiencing both cruel shunning and great acclaim.

Her thinking and her life were the product of late Enlightenment thought, infused by both its best (Humean) aspects and its worst (Rousseauian) excesses. Her lasting contribution was as a corrective, affirming the freedom to create as the driving force of progress, while warning against the wrong means and the wrong motivations that could turn that freedom to despotism. Indeed, some scholars observe that her politics late in life were more Burkean than Godwinian.

Her enduring contribution is her 1818 book, which created two enduring archetypes, the mad scientist and the monster he creates, and still taps into cultural anxiety concerning the intentions vs. the reality of scientific creation. There is a good reason for this anxiety, which we continue to experience.

She wrote during a period — it was a glorious one — when the intellectual class had a justified expectation that dramatic changes were coming to civilization. Medical science was improving. Disease would be controlled. Populations were on the move from the country to the city. The steamship was vastly increasing the pace of travel and making international trade more resource-efficient.

She was surrounded by the early evidence of invention. The beautiful movie about her life that just came out recreates the ethos, the confidence in the future of freedom, the sense that something marvelous was coming. She attends a kind of magic show with Percy at which a showman and scientist uses electricity to cause a dead frog to move its legs, which suggests to her the possibility of giving life to the dead. Thus did her first work explore the eternal human fascination with the possibility of immortality via science, controlling our world in ways that had never previously been possible.

The point here is not that science is bad or inherently dangerous but rather that it can result in unanticipated horrors when its deployment is tainted by the aspirations of power. As Paul Cantor puts it in his introduction to a new edition of Frankenstein:

> "Mary Shelley gives a gnostic twist to her creation myth: in her version the creation becomes identified with the fall. Frankenstein does God's work, creating a man, but he has the devil's motives: pride and the will to power. He is himself a rebel, rejecting divine prohibitions and, like Satan, aspiring to become a god himself. But Victor's act of rebellion is to create a man, and what he seeks out of creation is the glory of ruling over a new race of beings. Mary Shelley thus achieves a daring compression of Milton's story. Frankenstein retells Paradise Lost as if the being who fell from heaven and the being who created the world of man were one and the same."

What much of the modern scholarship about Mary Shelley is revealing concerns how much her work was informed by her own experiences. She married for love but found herself in a relationship defined by betrayal, neglect, anxiety, and instability. She bore children but was emotionally torn apart by their early deaths. The irrevocability of morality (dust to dust) consumed her thoughts. Her social circle was filled with people who loved humanity but couldn't manage even the modicum of decency with respect to their personal relationships.

All of these themes figure into the creation of her great work. It was as original as a horror novel can be, the story of a new human created in the laboratory barren of a moral sense who is nonetheless sympathetic even though he is responsible for ghastly death and destruction.

Modern Analogies

And so we look for later analogies to the monsters created by intellectuals later in history.

While consuming all this amazing content about her great work, I'm thinking this through. What were the monster's analogies that came later? My top candidates include terrible experiences that were hatched by academic elites who were sure they were doing the right thing. The Communist Manifesto appeared in print 30 years later — a blueprint for a new laboratory creation of a human being detached from any affection for property, family, or faith. Two decades later, eugenics became all the rage, and hatched decades of experimentation with sterilization, regulation, segregation, and state control. The ambition to bring democracy to the world by force resulted in this new thing called total war in which the civilian population was drafted to be killers and fodder to be killed. The interwar period launched nationalism and fascism as political experiments in making mad scientists into dictators who treated subject populations as lab rats, corralling, quarantining, and finally killing them.

Even following the Second World War, elite intellectuals were still busy concocting schemes for perfect social and economic functioning that produced results very different from what they imagined. Consider the Bretton Woods conference of 1944. The hope was for perfect mastery of the global monetary system, with a world bank, a new world currency, a clearing system managed by industrial and academic elites, and a lending facility that would enable the world to want for nothing. The actual results took decades to arrive but resulted in enormous bureaucracies that do nothing, vast expenses of resources that might have gone to building prosperity that instead tightened ruling class control, and hyperinflation that destabilized economic and political life. It couldn't last.

And even today, the headlines are filled with proposals for new creations that we know from experience will turn out very different from how they are envisioned. There is socialized medicine, the job guarantee, a universal income, a revival of mercantilism, the reemergence of nationalism and pretentious and coercive plans for controlling global climate through regulatory force. We keep doing this, gathering the raw material, going back to the lab, hooking up the idea to the power source, throwing the switch, and experiencing shock and regret at the results.

Two hundred years later, Mary Shelley's horrifying tale of the unconstrained vision continues to speak to us. It should also serve as a permanent warning.

45

A Hilarious Comedy
about Ghastly Evil

I share this with Joseph Stalin: a great appreciation for the musical genius of Maria Yudina. And I share this with Maria: a deep loathing of Stalin.

Maria never made a secret of her disgust and hatred of the Soviet regime. She let Stalin know, at great personal peril. He preserved her life and kept her safe because of her enormous talent (also she was never really a threat to his power).

Maria, who died in 1970, remains underappreciated to this day. No one has ever played Bach and Mozart the way she did, with all the enormous power, ferocity, and dramatic flair we associate with Russian arts culture. Her performances cared nothing for "originalism" or "authenticity"; she was interested in drawing out the drama in light of her understanding of the world.

The Death of Stalin

So I was absolutely delighted at the opening sequence of the strangely brilliant new film The Death of Stalin. Maria is playing a live radio broadcast of a Mozart piano concerto. Stalin hears it on the radio and orders that a recording of it be delivered to his apartment. There is no recording. Maria is told to play it again but she refuses pending a huge payment. She gets it. Once the record is made, she slips a truth-telling note in the sleeve of the record, accusing him of great crimes and the ruination of Russia. When the dictator reads it, he laughs uproariously but then has a brain hemorrhage.

The story might be apocryphal but it is true enough and the film captures her spirit well. It also brilliantly shows the wild jockeying for power that follows Stalin's death, with fantastic portrayals of all the important figures from this period: Nikita Khrushchev, Lavrently Beria, Vyacheslav Molotov,

Andrey Andreyev, Georgy Zhukov. It also serves as an excellent guide to what actually happened in those strange months that led to Beria's execution and the rise of Khrushchev to become General Secretary.

There is enough real history here to justly calling this film nonfiction. For example, it is rather obvious that Stalin's inner circle was thrilled to hear that the great man would soon kick the bucket. They waited a full day before calling a doctor because they had to meet in committee to make a decision. Plus there was another problem (again drawn from real life): Stalin had already ordered the death of nearly every competent doctor in Moscow so there wasn't anyone to treat him.

Another big event portrayed in the film was the funeral, which drew mourners from all over Russia, who were promptly shot as they left the trains and tried to make their way to the city center. It was this incident that prompted the gradual process of de-Stalinization that lasted many decades, culminating finally in the collapse of the Soviet regime itself and the loss of its vast empire of control.

Why Comedy?

But what's really remarkable is that the film is set as a dark comedy. How can one do that? Stalin's regime was guilty of mass murder of the worst sort, and not one person in his political orbit lacked dark blood stains on their hands. How can you make a comedy about this? You certainly have to obscure the horror going on and the film has been criticized for doing this. However, I will say this: a realistic presentation would be impossible to watch. Turning this to comedy actually makes it possible to discover this strange history in a way that doesn't completely repulse us.

For this reason, the film is hugely important if only to draw attention to this terrible history, and perhaps get a new generation interested in the truth about Soviet communism. It created a blood path, dictatorship, poverty, and fantastic amounts of human suffering. It's remarkable that anyone could, following this experience, proclaim an attachment to socialism given that this was the most spectacular experience in history that took place under the rubric of the ideas of Marxism.

The world is still in denial. Russia is too: this film was banned by Putin.

Ethics and Institutions

There is more here, however, than just a portrayal of the events. It's a portrayal of the darkest side of human nature. In the jockeying for power, acting on the ethics of right and wrong are out of the question. Everything is a lie. It is all about survival because it is pretty clear to all the players that they must either land on the winning side or be killed. Words mean nothing. Promises mean nothing. Right and wrong are slogans used to attack enemies. Malfeasance is a given. Words are propaganda and nothing more.

Now, you could watch all this come down and observe that these are all very bad people doing bad things. The question, however, might be turned around: what would you do under these conditions? Maybe you would be heroic and guarantee your martyrdom. Many people in history have taken this heroic route. But not even the most rigorous traditions of morality and spiritually have required heroism. Most stop short of mandating that in favor of merely not doing evil.

The story underscores a terrifying truth. Almost anyone is capable of ghastly evil under institutional conditions that forestall any good options. This truth is well illustrated in the case of a struggle for the control of government. There can only be one real winner and you have to figure out who it is in order to stay on the right side of the killing machine. Government is particularly adept at creating this win/lose scenario because government is not based on the idea of gains from trade or expanding wealth. It is a fixed pie and power is a zero-sum game.

The Dark Heart

Live long enough and you discover that this problem, and the ruthlessness it inspires in the human heart, is not limited to the Soviet government or other totalitarian systems. Power brings out the worst in everyone and drives normal human concern for right and wrong into the shadows. It can appear in any institutional setting in which winners take all.

If you see this around you enough — the way that envy puts a target on the forehead of the successful, the way friendship and loyalty evaporate in the face of palpable threats to position and power, the cravenness of the human personality when faced with the prospect of material deprivation, the shocking lack of concern that people can demonstrate for high ideals in practice, regardless of what they otherwise preach — you can develop a pretty dark outlook on life. Anyone can be a practitioner of betrayal and evil; anyone can be a victim.

At the same time, the preservation of civilization is bound up with a culture of respect for truth, human rights, the hope for justice, and the good of all. It's not just under Soviet communism where these ideals are invisicerated. They can disappear without notice even in seemingly civilized settings: church, business, family, and friendship networks.

It's an appalling realization to discover just how ephemeral the notion of morality truly is in practice. Your best friend could be secretly conspiring to destroy you; the recipients of your benefaction will knife you if conditions are right; your successes could be the very occasion of your undoing in the face of jealousy and envy; a person's ambition unchecked by principle can lead to grotesque injustice against you. You cannot really know the true character of anyone who has never been put to the test: what evil are you willing to practice in order to maintain your living standard or save your life?

Let's return to the brilliant Maria Yudina. She focussed on personal and artistic excellence. She never compromised. She fought Stalin at every step with profound courage and tenacity. She suffered enormously but kept her dignity. She left an amazing artistic legacy. Somehow she got through the worst of times, stayed alive, and thrived.

Maria's life shows us that not even the worst institutions can crush a soul that is indefatigably dedicated to truth and integrity as first principles.

46

Beware the Friend/Enemy Binary of Politics

Have you been part of a Twitter flame war over politics? A war to the knife on a Facebook group? Have a dinner party disrupted by some heated political argument? These painful struggles are mostly pointless, of course, but they reveal a deeper truth about politics in general. They set people against each other in a zero-sum game. That's mostly the whole point of contemporary politics, which is ever more defaulting to its most extreme forms.

In politics, winners take all. The losers lose all. They are supposed to be good sports about it, observing the beauty of democracy and acquiescing to the results. But something has changed since the election of Trump. The partisan wars are more intense and never seem to end. The divisions are growing deeper. Politics seems to divide the world between friends and enemies.

In markets, matters are different. We come together to trade. All parties benefit. Most of the material wealth around you comes from this win/win dynamic. Its discovery and development in the late Middle Ages would eventually restructure the experience of life itself. We take this all for granted today, with every trade ending in a mutual expression of thanks.

The Political Mind

We all know people whose whole lives are politicized. They seethe with loathing of their enemies. They come to the defense of their friends, defined by common enemies. You are trying to have a normal dinner with them and they keep lecturing people as if they are being filmed for a Sunday talk show. You just want to say, hey, can you please order a cocktail and chill for a bit?

What's puzzling about the contrast is how the same people behave differently in different contexts. Go to the mall, a local music festival, the club scene in the city, a farmer's market outside of town, or any chain restaurant. What you see for the most part is that people get along. The great political struggles of our time are nowhere evident.

Markets require that people play nice. Give these same people a forum in which to argue politics and they become barbaric.

Two Views

What we see here is a contrast in perspectives about how the world can and should work. Is it all about peace, trade, and progress for everyone? Or is it all about struggle, destruction, victory, and rule? Taking the pro-trade and pro-peace position are those once-called liberals, the conviction from Voltaire through Paine to your local merchant today that believes that commerce is the great palliative. Taking the pro-conflict perspective are many people who consider their personal identity and life mission bound up with left-wing or right-wing ideology (distinguishable by their cultural constituencies but not by their preference for statist means of social and economic organization).

The most famous theorist of conflict in the 19th century was Karl Marx, whose 200th birthday came and went on May 5 with floods of articles on his legacy. For a century and a half, Marxism has shaped what we call leftism. Less well known are his counterparties on the right, from Thomas Carlyle to Madison Grant to Carl Schmitt. Among this long lineage of pro-conflict right-wing thinkers, Schmitt is the most compelling, in my view, and the person to grapple with.

The Schmittian Way

If you believe in freedom and trade, it is worth your time to read the opposition. As it turns out, the theories of Carl Schmitt, whom Ludwig von Mises despised as that "Nazi jurist," was the leading opponent of freedom in Germany during the rise of the national socialists. He was their philosophical prophet. Even now, his is the voice behind the thinking of many political activists today. His own thought was influenced by Marxism of course, but the thinking of both traces to the Hegelian paradigm shift in German academia that took place in the early 19th century.

Marx emerged as the paragon of the left-Hegelians and Schmitt as the embodiment of the right-Hegelians. In a strange way, they agree on the essentials but end up applying it in different ways. At least Marx acknowledged the achievements of liberalism. Schmitt was not so gracious. His 1932 essay "The Concept of the Political" heaps disdain on the fathers of the liberal theory of life, precisely because they imagined a world of peace, prosperity, and progress.

Politics must demand "the sacrifice of life." But liberalism does not tolerate that. "Such a demand is in no way justifiable by the individualism of liberal thought," wrote Schmitt.

> "No consistent individualism can entrust someone other than to the individual himself the right to dispose of the physical life of the individual. An individualism in which anyone other than the free individual himself were to decide upon the substance and dimension of his freedom would be only an empty phrase. For the individual as such there is no enemy with whom he must enter into a life-and-death struggle if he personally does not want to do so. To compel him to fight against his will is, from the viewpoint of the private individual, lack of freedom and repression. All liberal pathos turns against repression and lack of freedom….what this liberalism still admits of state, government, and politics is confined to securing the conditions for liberty and eliminating infringements on freedom."

Keep in mind that this is what Schmitt opposes this view with every breath. True, it all begs the question: what's so awful about this? It's a no brainer to Schmitt. This would mean that life would consist entirely of trades and debates but no bloodshed. This would be "a world without the distinction of friend and enemy and hence a world without politics." He found such a world dreadfully boring, devoid of any philosophical meaning (in a Hegelian sense).

Such a world "might contain many very interesting…competitions," he observes, but "there would not be a meaningful antithesis whereby men could be required to sacrifice life, authorized to shed blood, and kill other human beings." His point is that the "friend-enemy grouping" is "ever present," "regardless of the aspects which this possibility implies for morality, aesthetics, and economics."

Now, you might observe that Schmitt is not only positioning himself against everything a civilized person regards as the good life; he further seems to be auditioning to be the high priest of a death cult. I don't think that observation is entirely inaccurate. His writings disparage liberty, cheer conflict, exalt dictatorship, and celebrate bloodshed. His fundamental desire is to turn back the clock on everything that makes life grand.

New-Found Appreciation

In our hyper-politicized times, when people are discovering new excuses to hate on others, when identity politics makes it possible merely to look at a person to discern him or her to be the enemy, and when the blood-sport of demonizing people based on competing ideological paradigms is on the rise, both Carl Schmitt and Karl Marx are enjoying something of a resurgence.

But by exalting these twin brothers of struggle, these champions of dehumanizing our neighbor based on political categories, let us be aware of what we are rejecting. We are tossing out the philosophical foundations of material progress, peaceful relationships, and the good life as liberalism has always understood it. We are throwing out the greatest innovation in ideas in history, the insight that human beings can cooperate to their mutual betterment without central management from the central state.

Read enough of these two, and you end up in a very dark place, only to be rescued by the delightful observation of Voltaire (a true voice of sanity) about the London stock market, a passage that would cause both Karl and Carl to scream in despair:

> "Go into the London Stock Exchange — a more respectable place than many a court — and you will see representatives from all nations gathered together for the utility of men. Here Jew, Mohammedan and Christian deal with each other as though they were all of the same faith, and only apply the word infidel to people who go bankrupt. Here the Presbyterian trusts the Anabaptist and the Anglican accepts a promise from the Quaker. On leaving these peaceful and free assemblies some go to the Synagogue and others for a drink, this one goes to be baptized in a great bath in the name of Father, Son and Holy Ghost, that one has his son's foreskin cut and has some Hebrew words he doesn't understand mumbled over the child, others go to their church and await the inspiration of God with their hats on, and everybody is happy."

Indeed, liberty does imagine and work toward a world of happiness. That strikes me as a much better model than Hegelians of the right and left ever offered, to say nothing of the social-media trolls who are trying to draw you into becoming a pawn in their illiberal ambition to make life ever more miserable.

Technology

47

In this Case, Nothing Beats Old Technology

I've lived through the age of non-stick pans, the new fashion for gleaming copper, the advent of every conceivable surface for skillets from glass to stone and a thousand synthetic concoctions, such that today you face a blithering array of choices at any cookware store.

Truly, despite it all, I've never found anything as wonderful as a cast-iron skillet. And not just for frying. It works for baking too. It's a case of how the oldest technology remains the best technology. I treasure my pan, which belonged to my mother's mother and perhaps hers before that. It is still in perfect condition, and will apparently remain that way forever.

I see now that there are many available on Amazon, most selling between $15 to $30, differing only by size and shape, because otherwise the quality is the same. It's just cast iron. Nothing more. And that is precisely what is so great about it. The wonders of the free market have put this beautiful item in the reach of everyone.

Your children will be fighting to inherit yours once you have left this earth.

In a time of improved everything, when I carry around technological wonders in my pocket, when I can access all existing music with a voice command and tell the same device to turn on the coffee pot, the cast-iron skillet stands out as a strange anomaly. So far as anyone knows, they were a thing in the ancient world. What we call the Iron Age lasted from 3000 BC to 1850 AD, finally ended only by the commercial availability of steel.

And yet here we are, needing to fry an egg or bacon, make cornbread, bake some fish, get a sweet finish on a steak, blanch some veggies, what do you reach for? The cast-iron skillet. People who know about cooking swear by it. I've personally never found anything better for all these tasks. So far as I'm concerned, when it comes to cooking, it is still the Iron Age.

What is the appeal beyond that it is a great cooking tool? Maybe it appeals to the primal in us. Maybe it makes us all feel like the frontiersmen were not. Maybe it represents a desire in all of us to touch what we imagine to be our roots, a getting back to what matters. Far better that we fulfill this desire through consumerism than politics. Cast iron offers us all a means of discovering who we are.

Proper Care and Feeding

Still, I've noticed friends of mine are slightly cautious about trying it out. There is a lot of mythology about it and people can be intimidated. For example, you hear that new pans don't work because it takes an arduous process to season them. This is completely untrue. Seasoning a new pan takes 30 minutes at most, in a hot oven, and continues with the use of the pan. The more you use it, the better it gets.

Another thing you hear is that using soap on the pan will ruin it. This is preposterous. Iron is nothing if not hearty, indeed indestructible. Too much can tear through the oils on the surface of the pan but it is easy enough to add them back in. And it's a beautiful thing, after so many years of fuss over what kind of spatula you can use on the delicate surface of your $300 pan, to dig into the iron hard with an old-fashioned steel utensil.

There is another secret to cleaning the iron skillet. Users know this. The point of the iron is that it breathes with the change in temperature. The heat opens it up. The cold closes it up. So when you are cooking with it and complete your tasks, you can unstick everything that is stuck simply by splashing some cold water in the pan. Another trick I use: grab an ice cube from the freezer and let it melt. The muck lifts off quickly and easily.

This breathing quality of the iron is ideal for deglazing. Let's say you have a steak cooking away and it is starting to stick. You put a few tablespoons of cold water on the surface and all the sugars are released and glaze the meat, giving it a sugary coating and a beautiful shiny finish. You can do this with pork, fish, or beef, or, really, anything you cook in the pan. This allows you to achieve gourmet status even as you have cleaned the pan.

Once the pan is clean, it needs to be dried before you put it away. Why? It's iron: it will rust. If that happens, it's not really a big deal. Clean off the rust and re-oil the pan. To prevent this, put the pan on the stove burner for a minute or so. This will take away the water. Then you have a surface for adding oil (I like to use olive oil but any cooking oil works). Once it cools off, you can put it away.

It's Back!

This might sound fussy but it is not. It becomes a beautiful ritual, one you are reenacting from antiquity. Nothing you do to the pan can hurt it.

It doesn't surprise me in the slightest that cast iron cookware is hugely fashionable again. The Lodge cast iron refinery is the last one in the US and it has been undergoing a huge expansion in recent years. The pans are cheap and the best investment you can make in cookware.

On the other hand, you can slip over to the local Goodwill and likely find a used one there. Some people are scared off by rust. But these can be restored very easily and quickly with some steel wool and some effort at re-seasoning it with oil. You can probably find one at any rummage sale too, for just a couple of bucks.

The continued popularity of the cast-iron skillet illustrates a point. The purpose of technology is not to be new. It is not to complicate your life. It is not to do something never done before. It is not to confound, confuse, or disorient. The purpose of technology is to make your life better than it is. In this case, technology can come from any age, even the ancient world. As the slogan of Lodge pan company says, iron is forever.

48

Why the Dramatic
Decline in Crime?

O ne of the biggest stories of the year was not only not reported. It was misreported. Following the headlines, you would get the impression of rising terrorism in the US, police brutality and shootings, hate crimes on the rise and so on. But the big-picture data do not show this. Just the reverse. Large cities in the US today are recording the lowest-crime rates on record.

New York City is paradigmatic. In a news item that received few shares, because no one apparently cares about good news, the Times reports on a remarkable plunge in crime in the city. Killings in the city this year have fallen 86% from the number of killings in the city 25 years ago. In 1990, 2,245 people were killed; this year, it's 286. Overall crimes in each felony category are at a historic low.

This is a serious and notable trend.

Crime has declined in the city steadily for 27 years and the trend is accelerating. The city as a whole is feeling safe, as safe as the 1950s. As someone who visits sporadically, I too sense this. I spent a week in the city last month and never once felt a sense of threat or fear. Nor did I observe a large police presence.

True, the traffic is unbearable, the streets are loud and confusing, prices for everything are too high, and I can never find my way around. But at least I never once worried about being assaulted, stolen from, harassed, or otherwise threatened. The city felt safe.

And it's not just New York. The Brennan Center of New York University reports that "The overall crime rate in the 30 largest cities in 2017 is estimated to decline slightly from the previous year, falling by 2.7 percent. If this trend holds, crime rates will remain near historic lows." And it's not just in the US either: in most developed countries, crime has fallen by half in the last 20 years. Car theft, in particular, will soon be a thing of the past.

Why the Decline

It's impossible to report on crime without asking the question why. And this invariably turns to questions of public policy and policing. It's the natural association. The job of the police is to control crime. If crime falls, it surely has something to do with policing. Perhaps the police are just more vigilant and this is deterring crime?

In the case of New York, it has nothing to do with some Trump-like crackdown on bad guys that he called for in the campaign, complete with stop-and-frisk policies. Mayor Bill de Blasio has imposed a policy of less deadly force by police, making fewer arrests, and ending stop and frisk. There is just no evidence that the falling crime rate has anything to do with intensified policing; indeed, because of the many scandals over police brutality in recent years, police departments are more cautious than before, knowing that everything an officer does can be caught on camera and reviewed by public opinion later.

In all the stories on this topic, I've yet to see anyone raise what strikes me as the most obvious answer here. Technology has made us safer in every aspect of our lives. It's made our homes safer, our property more secure, and has made it much more difficult for bad guys to go about their business and sneak away.

In New York, for example, nearly every resident carries a walking movie camera in his or her pocket that can instantly reach the world with a video of what is going on in the immediate vicinity. This not only protects the individual. It means that everyone else has the incentive to keep a watch on events around us (who doesn't want a viral video?). It takes only one second to turn on a video to record anything that happens, massively increasing the chance of discovery.

This, more than the penal system and aggressive policing, has surely made a gigantic difference.

And think of our homes today. We've never been safer indoors. Every apartment unit has highly controlled access with keypads, fobs, gates, and several layers of locked access. It's true for businesses in large cities too. You are watched and access is permission only. Sneaking around with anonymity is ever harder. This can be inconvenient for people but the payoff for safety and security is high.

You Will Be Caught

So much technological development these days is about increasing security. You can cheaply get a seeing-eye speaker for the front door of your home that allows you to talk to anyone on the front porch, even if you happen to be away on vacation in some far-flung area. You can later watch a video of the Amazon delivery person or the UPS truck dropping off something. Our property too is protected with small tracers that make theft increasingly difficult.

I think, for example, of my new iPhone X with its facial recognition software. Maybe there is some high-level way around it, but I don't see how. Only my face can unlock the phone, and, barring some Mission-Impossible-style rubber mask, I don't see how it could be hacked. If I leave my phone somewhere, I can rest securely in the knowledge that my data can't be accessed. I can even remotely delete the entire contents of the phone with a click or two.

A few weeks ago, I boarded a plane without my laptop. I had left it sitting at the gate. In the middle of the air on the flight, I had the sudden realization. When I landed, I immediately instructed the entire machine to self destruct as soon as it got online, thereby protecting everything. As it turns out, the laptop was picked up by a nice man from Iowa, who sent it back to me. I decided to try the technology. As soon as I opened the lid, the entire contents of the machine were deleted.

With Electronic Tracking Devices, highly affordable, you can secure all your property. They can go on laptops, passports, wallets, and purses, and constantly broadcast whereabouts. Nothing is perfect but these devices go a very long way to confounding criminal elements. As for cars, any model made in the last few years has become basically impossible to steal. Gone are the days of hard-wiring cars and taking off into the night.

As for personal protection, mace and tasers are widely carried and available everywhere, for the price of a fast-food meal. What matters is not that everyone carries one but rather the uncertainty that anyone might be carrying one. Despite all the attempts to control gun access, technology has made it possible for everyone to carry devices to subvert robberies. This is a gigantic change. And once perpetrators are caught — which is far easier today with communication technology — they face massive public exposure and pay a heavy price even without the justice system being involved.

Free Enterprise to the Rescue

Put it all together and these technologies have done more to deter and thereby reduce crime than all the police crackdowns you can imagine. They have made the world more peaceful and life more secure.

It's true that people don't often even consider the role of technology in crime reduction. One of the few criminologists who see this is Tom Gash, who writes at Wired:

"For decades, politicians have been perpetuating two big myths about crime. Those on the right have argued that only ever-tougher prison terms will deter would-be wrong-doers. Those on the left have argued that crime will only fall when we reform society and reduce poverty and inequality. In fact, crime has fallen dramatically over the past 20 years, not due to reforms traditionally advocated by politicians, but due to the technological change which has made it harder to commit crime."

Contemplate the implications. For centuries, for millennia, we've relied on government to stop invasions of person and property. We live more safely than ever before, thanks to market-based technological improvements, not reliance on government. It was once believed that only government could provide security; this debate dates back centuries. Now we learn otherwise. We get security from the same source that provides us food, clothing, and shelter: the matrix of voluntary exchange and free exercise of human creativity.

49

Don't Blame Technology, Blame Yourself

An older woman and her middle-aged son were at a public restaurant for Thanksgiving. He spent the whole of the dinner flipping through his phone, without uttering a word. She did her best to maintain her dignity while looking past him and trying to pretend that this is what life is like. This tragic scene lasted until they paid the bill and left.

The scene was relayed to me by a senior in college who explains how her generation is figuring out the right and wrong ways to use new technology, correcting for the errors of their parents, who somehow allowed their lives to be drained by the newness of it all.

Zak Tebbal drew the perfect cartoon for how our relationship to our smartphones has changed over the last 10 years.

No one planned it. It just seemed to happen. The gadget scratched an itch. We have to know everything, to be in touch with everyone, to be everywhere at once. It's an everything box, miraculous in its own way. Why are so many people creeped out these days that we seem to have turned over the whole of our lives to our smartphones?

It began with Facebook's brilliant notification system. Your friends are contacting you, liking you, appreciating you, and surely you need to know that! Every application caught on. More buzzes, dings, alerts, reasons to stare and scroll. During this time, your device holds your primary attention, and interrupts anything else that is happening.

Hours and hours per day, adding up to a day or two in a week, a week in a month, and, ultimately, years and years of our lives, staring senselessly at things that matter maybe a little but not that much.

And at what cost? Disciplined reading, social engagement with those around us, our attention span, serious thought, and even our sleep. No one signed up for our lives to be put into total upheaval one step at a time, forsaking all human connection and conversation, and eschewing serious mental and emotional development, in favor of digital trivia 24/7. And yet, this is what it has come to.

And we are shocked to learn that all kinds of enterprises have an interest in what precisely we are doing. It's the greatest marketing opportunity ever conceived, and we've tacitly approved of it all every step of the way.

Some users are starting to catch on. Now we are reading guides all over the internet on how to detox from our addictions. Back in 2011, I wrote a book called Beautiful Anarchy that celebrates the merits of all the platforms that many people now find oppressive, myself included. As a result, I've felt the need to come to terms with the change. Did I make a mistake? Why did I fail to anticipate how much of a burden it would all become?

The thesis of my book was not that we should allow digital platforms to rule our lives; it was that digital platforms aid in helping us curate a civilization for ourselves. It's the curation part that has gone wrong. We just haven't been very good at it. I'm confident that we'll get there after fits and starts.

Is This Addiction?

I'm always suspicious of claims that we are addicted to this or that. Addiction sounds medical whereas what we are usually talking about comes down to bad habits. I had a bad habit of smoking. I did it for 30 years. Then one day something snapped. I didn't want to be a smoker anymore. That was it, not even one more cigarette since that day. The human mind can overcome even biochemical urges.

Surely we can deal with information addiction so that we can regain control of our lives.

We are too quick to blame technology rather than ourselves. The apps we love specialize in getting our attention and drawing it away from other things. Good for them. This is their job, just as advertisers' main job is to persuade us to buy the product. We don't have to. If we are manipulated into feeding false wants, that's not the advertiser's fault; it is ours for going along as if we don't really feel we have volition.

I'm thinking back to my childhood when I first developed a desire to have more stuff. I watched the ads incessantly on Saturday morning. I wanted everything: the Big Wheel, the Moon Boots, the Sit and Spin, Tonka Trucks, Sugar Smacks, Honey Comb, Hot Wheel Tracks, you name it. Every new toy had to be mine. I wanted every fun cereal. My parents bought me my favorite cereals and indulged my desires during the holiday season.

Then I gradually learned that this stuff was not all it was cracked up to be, and I gained control of the materially acquisitive part of my brain.

Which is to say: I matured. So too must we all with our digital devices.

Recall when cell phones first came out. It was like a miracle. We had our own phones rather than having to share the same phone in a household. No wires. We could talk to anyone from anywhere. Restaurants had early adopters sitting at tables alone yammering on the phone in a way that disturbed everyone around them.

It's been years since I've seen such rude behavior. The court of taste and manners ruled against it. People have come to comply.

Now we have a different problem. We can't get through a dinner with friends without half the guests checking their phones every few minutes. We have truncated conversations, stopping and starting because people can't keep up with the line of thought. Tiny little buzzes are everywhere. You can see it in people's eyes that they aren't really there. They are thinking about their smartphones and applications.

This was happening to me, I admit. Then I entered into a social context in which constant smartphone checking was verboten. It took some discipline, but I eventually adapted, with happy results. If you absolutely must pull out the phone, it's a simple matter of excusing yourself from the public space and then returning once your curiosity is satisfied. After a while, you realize that nothing is important enough to interrupt conversation with friends.

There still remained the problem of too many notifications. The fix was simple (once you figure it out), but it took active measures. I shut down several Slack channels. I deleted applications. Buzzfeed has no claim on my time. Neither does Wired. There is nothing on Snapchat that merits my immediate attention. Emails too can wait until a time convenient for me. I accepted only the most urgent ones, realizing that it is actually not important to know how many people are liking an Insta image.

With a few changes, I deleted 90 percent of my notifications and the constant buzzing came to an end. I got my life back rather easily actually.

Another way to put it is that I trained my device to act in accordance with a matured way of understanding its role. The providers of information services are trying to elicit from within me my seven-year-old inner self. I don't fault them for that. It's up to us to push back and behave like adults.

Economists have been arguing for a while about whether individuals make rational decisions or need nudges to make them behave in a way that is best for them in the long run. But there is a third option: we learn from mistakes and adapt our behavior in light of the consequences. We improve over time. Experience creates new principles and rules that we voluntarily adopt in our own best interest.

Every new technology comes with an awkward stage of adoption, during which time people get manipulated and break every kind of rule of propriety until they figure out a better way. This is where we are today. It's not that the technology is failing us. It's that we need to figure out how to become its master rather than the reverse.

The market forces that have put the whole of human knowledge in our pocket work best when we stop blaming technology and start taking responsibility for our own lives.

50

Remember What the
Internet Is All About

S ome great minds are remembered mostly for one moment in time, a momentous action or revelatory piece of writing. Such is the case for John Perry Barlow, who died on February 7, 2018. Born in 1947, he was a remarkable visionary, a lyricist for the Grateful Dead who later became a founder of the Electronic Frontier Foundation, which defends your rights as a citizen of the digital age.

He is the author of the Declaration of Independence of Cyberspace. I've just re-read it. It's a wake up call to the true vision of what the Internet can make possible. In fact, it is a map for what is actually happening to the relationship between the individual and the state. Look past the daily headlines and you can see the larger trend: the state as it came to be in the 20th century is in the long process of collapsing. It has lost public support. Its ideas have been proven wrong. It is losing control by the day. We are living ever freer lives. This is what the Internet has made possible.

Barlow's declaration was written in 1996 — the perfect timing. The web browser had just gone mainstream. The Clinton administration privatized vast swaths of the Internet almost by accident. Few people fully understood where we were headed and how this would change everything. Here it is not even a quarter century later and we can see how this one tool has opened the world and laid waste to the schemes of central planners past.

It's an amazing statement that helps us understand the dreams of that generation and inspires all of us to work toward the ideals he presents here.

Here it is in full. It speaks for itself.

A Declaration of the Independence of Cyberspace

Governments of the Industrial World, you weary giants of flesh and steel, I come from Cyberspace, the new home of Mind. On behalf of the future, I ask you of the past to leave us alone. You are not welcome among us. You have no sovereignty where we gather.

We have no elected government, nor are we likely to have one, so I address you with no greater authority than that with which liberty itself always speaks. I declare the global social space we are building to be naturally independent of the tyrannies you seek to impose on us. You have no moral right to rule us nor do you possess any methods of enforcement we have true reason to fear.

Governments derive their just powers from the consent of the governed. You have neither solicited nor received ours. We did not invite you. You do not know us, nor do you know our world. Cyberspace does not lie within your borders. Do not think that you can build it, as though it were a public construction project. You cannot. It is an act of nature and it grows itself through our collective actions.

You have not engaged in our great and gathering conversation, nor did you create the wealth of our marketplaces. You do not know our culture, our ethics, or the unwritten codes that already provide our society more order than could be obtained by any of your impositions.

You claim there are problems among us that you need to solve. You use this claim as an excuse to invade our precincts. Many of these problems don't exist. Where there are real conflicts, where there are wrongs, we will identify them and address them by our means. We are forming our own Social Contract. This governance will arise according to the conditions of our world, not yours. Our world is different.

Cyberspace consists of transactions, relationships, and thought itself, arrayed like a standing wave in the web of our communications. Ours is a world that is both everywhere and nowhere, but it is not where bodies live.

We are creating a world that all may enter without privilege or prejudice accorded by race, economic power, military force, or station of birth.

We are creating a world where anyone, anywhere may express his or her beliefs, no matter how singular, without fear of being coerced into silence or conformity.

Your legal concepts of property, expression, identity, movement, and context do not apply to us. They are based on matter, There is no matter here.

Our identities have no bodies, so, unlike you, we cannot obtain order by physical coercion. We believe that from ethics, enlightened self-interest, and the commonweal, our governance will emerge. Our identities may be distributed across many of your jurisdictions. The only law that all our constituent cultures would generally recognize is the Golden Rule. We hope we will be able to build our particular solutions on that basis. But we cannot accept the solutions you are attempting to impose.

In the United States, you have today created a law, the Telecommunications Reform Act, which repudiates your own Constitution and insults the dreams of Jefferson, Washington, Mill, Madison, De Tocqueville, and Brandeis. These dreams must now be born anew in us.

You are terrified of your own children, since they are natives in a world where you will always be immigrants. Because you fear them, you entrust your bureaucracies with the parental responsibilities you are too cowardly to confront yourselves. In our world, all the sentiments and expressions of humanity, from the debasing to the angelic, are parts of a seamless whole, the global conversation of bits. We cannot separate the air that chokes from the air upon which wings beat.

In China, Germany, France, Russia, Singapore, Italy and the United States, you are trying to ward off the virus of liberty by erecting guard posts at the frontiers of Cyberspace. These may keep out the contagion for a small time, but they will not work in a world that will soon be blanketed in bit-bearing media.

Your increasingly obsolete information industries would perpetuate themselves by proposing laws, in America and elsewhere, that claim to own speech itself throughout the world. These laws would declare ideas to be another industrial product, no more noble than pig iron. In our world, whatever the human mind may create can be reproduced and distributed infinitely at no cost. The global conveyance of thought no longer requires your factories to accomplish.

These increasingly hostile and colonial measures place us in the same position as those previous lovers of freedom and self-determination who had to reject the authorities of distant, uninformed powers. We must declare our virtual selves immune to your sovereignty, even as we continue to consent to your rule over our bodies. We will spread ourselves across the Planet so that no one can arrest our thoughts.

We will create a civilization of the Mind in Cyberspace. May it be more humane and fair than the world your governments have made before.

John Perry Barlow
Davos, Switzerland
February 8, 1996

51

Your Signature No Longer Matters

Ⓐll the major credit card companies have announced that they will no longer be requiring signatures at the point of purchase. "Later this month, four of the largest networks — American Express, Discover, Mastercard and Visa — will stop requiring them to complete card transactions," reports the *New York Times*.

This is to confirm what you have probably already discerned: your signature is no longer a useful guarantor of your identity. What is? Well, the other day at the airport, I had the creepy experience of having my personal identity at the airport confirmed by Delta's Clear system via a retina scan. I stared into a small camera and my identity popped up on a screen. I didn't know whether to be impressed or alarmed, but it did happen.

In other cases, it is all about what we know: last four digits of the social security number, the zip code, a passphrase or PIN number, mother's maiden name, and so on. All of these represent iterations of the great problem of knowing how to establish trust. It's about preventing fraud and securing the system's confidence that you can and will pay.

The Origins of Trust

As a young man, one of my father's first jobs was working in the newly born credit-card industry. He told me the story of its origins decades earlier. It began in single stores with customers that were well known by the proprietor. Rather than pay purchase by purchase, the customer could come in anytime and walk out with merchandise. He or she would receive a single bill at the month. The store could benefit from the convenience that the customer experienced. Everyone won.

This was apparent in the early fifties. All records of credit-card owners were kept by the accounting office. Over time, companies saw advantages in institutionalizing this practice. American Express had begun as a shipping company in the 19th century, became a money-order company, and finally started issuing cards. Visa came along in 1956 and Mastercard in 1966. As sophisticated as these became over time, the model remained the same: if you can be proven to be good for the money, you get a card.

I can recall my first trip to the college bookstore came with piles of offers for credit cards, which were extremely easy to get in those days. I got one, filled it up to my limit in a month or so, and paid high interest paying it off for the next year. I realized my mistake. Many friends of mine did not, and instead began to play credit-card roulette, rolling balances between old and new cards, and eventually ending up with a drawer full of cards and six figures of debt.

Delinquency Rates on Credit Card Loans All Commercial Banks

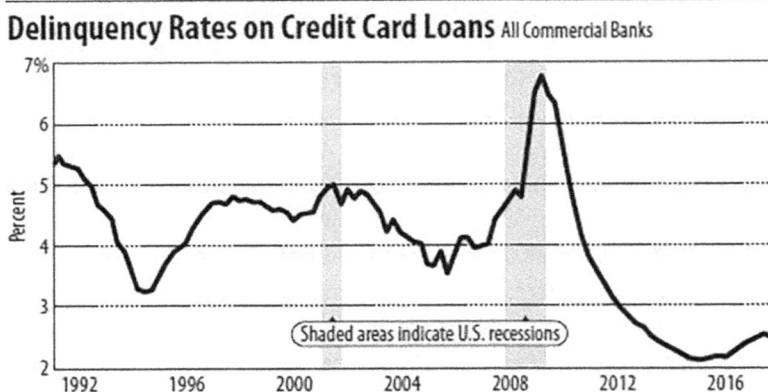

Source: Board of Governors of the Federal Reserve System (US); fred.stlouisfed.org

It's not so easy anymore. Banks clamped down after 2008 and, thanks to both risk aversion and new regulations, started getting fussy again, and for good reason. Now you can't get a new card without prepaying your credit line for a year, showing the bank that you can manage your money and pay your bills on time. The results are apparent. Delinquency rates are down dramatically since 2008.

The Signature Was Everything

In those days, the signature really did matter. Young people had to practice their unique signature, as if to define their personalities for life, except that it kept changing as the years went on. We must have admired the way our parents signed things with such elan, exactly the way the president signs executive orders today.

You can tell how much people invested in their signatures in the day. We sat in school and practiced them. We used them for papers, and, importantly, for yearbooks. Then the time came when we could sign for the credit-card receipts and its importance grew. Our signature was the way we ported our status as a human being from the heart and mind to the paper and thus toward the acquisition of goods and services.

It was our personality become art. We could reproduce it on demand as an extension of ourselves. Except that, over time, the status of signature started mattering less and less. I have a vague memory of realizing this at the grocery store when the electronic signature pad came along. It dawned on me — and probably millions of others at the same time — that it didn't matter what I scrawled in that box.

The advent of Internet commerce introduced a new challenge. Card companies had to deal with the problem of "card not present" transactions, further diminishing the status of signatures. It was controversial at first but progress demanded the change in policy. That unleashed an amazing amount of fraud but also the response in fraud-protection techniques. Rather than getting better, however, the problem is getting worse. Nearly half a million Americans report having their credit card numbers stolen every year, resulting in canceled cards and tremendous inconvenience, not to mention the constant threat of data breaches and billions spent to prevent them.

US Card – Present fraud losses
2011–2018

The expected reduction in CP fraud is due to the implementation of EMV in October 2015...

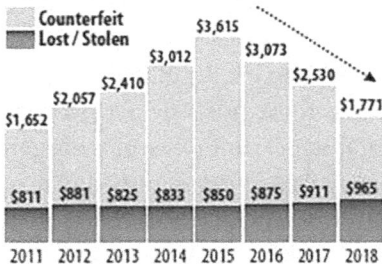

Counterfeit
Lost / Stolen

$1,652 $2,057 $2,410 $3,012 $3,615 $3,073 $2,530 $1,771

$811 $881 $825 $833 $850 $875 $911 $965

2011 2012 2013 2014 2015 2016 2017 2018

US CNP credit card fraud losses
2011–2018

...but the EMV implementation in the US is expected to lead to an increase in CNP fraud.

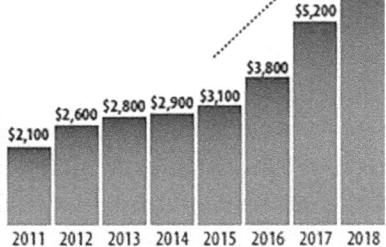

$2,100 $2,600 $2,800 $2,900 $3,100 $3,800 $5,200 $6,400

2011 2012 2013 2014 2015 2016 2017 2018

Source: FT Partners Research, quoting Aite Group interviews with payment networks and 18 large US Issuers, April to May 2014; creditcards.com

Trust or Verify?

Despite all the technological advances in the credit-card industry, including the newest recognition that a handwritten signature is completely worthless for verifying identity, the core model of credit hasn't changed since the industry began. Whether you can buy things online comes down to establishing an identity between the decision maker and the real person behind the identity.

This will remain true even if Amazon credit gradually comes to replace the function of banks, as Chloe Anagnos predicts. "Shopping with an Amazon checking or savings account would not only be convenient for customers," she writes, "it would cut out credit-card companies entirely—thus saving Amazon and consumers substantially on interchange fees."

Even so, it's all about who you are. Before blockchain technology came along, it wasn't obvious how this trust-based system could be replaced with anything. Then came the White Paper, which claimed to establish:

> A purely peer-to-peer version of electronic cash would allow online payments to be sent directly from one party to another without going through a financial institution. Digital signatures provide part of the solution, but the main benefits are lost if a trusted third party is still required to prevent double-spending. We propose a solution to the double-spending problem using a peer-to-peer network. The network timestamps transactions by hashing them into an ongoing chain of hash-based proof-of-work, forming a record that cannot be changed without redoing the proof-of-work.

As for signatures, yes, there would be those except digital using double-key cryptography. Fraud (pretending you are someone you are not), however, is prevented through a different technique: proof of both ownership and authority to access a distributed network is verified by evidence of your use of CPU power. In other words, with blockchain technology, it is not about who you are. It's about what you own and your authority to dispose of it. You don't have to rely on someone's truth or benevolence. In many ways, it is the largest leap in our commercial relationships in the postwar period.

The new system is still in its experimental stages, but we've already gained a glimmer of the possibilities, including money that operates outside the nation state or the necessity of third-party institutions, smart contracting, as well as the ability to raise capital for enterprises from the broadest swath of humanity.

The personal signature has a notorious history: J.S. Bach's on his compositions, the founding fathers on the Declaration of Independence, Picasso on his paintings, and the president's today on executive orders. Creating your own was a right of passage.

With credit card companies admitting the obvious that it does nothing to verify your identity, does it matter anymore? The signature isn't going away. It has just changed forms.

52

The Cash Register: In Memoriam

It still gives me chills when I'm in a small restaurant or coffee shop, and they ring up my tab on an iPad or iPhone, pushing my credit card across a small disk. No cash register. Maybe if I used cash, they would open the drawer for change but most customers do not. The whole experience still strikes me as futuristic, elegant, and generally beautiful.

I think the first time I saw a store without a cash register was at an Apple store. The employees walk around with iPhones. You pick out your product. Your card is charged while standing in the store. No lines. No big separators between the employees and the customers.

I know that technically this is no different from paying for gas at the pump with a card or swiping my card in a taxi. But somehow it feels different to do this at the restaurant or store. It's the same with the bars at airports that have the menu and "cash register" right at every single chair.

Even the self-checkout machines at the grocery store are a delight. No matter how you want to pay, there is functionality for that. As the machines have improved, ever less goes wrong, as scales, barcodes, and adaptable databases calculating discounts and member cards ring up the right totals and process payments.

That Ding

It's a new world. In my earliest jobs, a major task was learning to work the cash register. I remember the ding that would sound when the drawer came open. I learned to count change and give it to the customer in a way that he or she could count it too. This way everything stayed honest and open. The financial leakage was stopped. The books stayed balanced.

But that ding in the future may be no more. And that's fine. But it is worth exploring because that ding has been part of the retail experience for more than one hundred years. Thanks to Wikipedia, we can learn very quickly about the history of the ding.

The cash register was invented following the Civil War, as part of the huge wave of invention that characterized those years. They were amazing times. Between 1865 and 1910, we saw the commercialization of internal combustion, flight, domestic electricity, the availability of steel and the bridges and tall buildings that made possible the telephone, washing machines, book printing so that everyone could have a library, and so much more.

The cash register was part of that wave of innovation. It was designed for a particular purpose: to keep track of retail transactions to minimize theft and assist in balancing the books. The legend (which mostly comes from patent records) traces its invention to James Jacob Ritty, a saloon owner and shopkeeper from Dayton, Ohio. He had major problems with employees stealing money.

The Invention

Ritty is said to have taken an international trip on a boat. He saw that there was a machine that kept track of the turns of the boat propeller. This is where he gained the insight that the same kind of machine could be used to track inventory and prices in his retail shop. Four years later in 1883, he and his brother patented Ritty's Incorruptible Cashier. It did not have the ability to make receipts but it did allow employees to key in what was owed, what was given, and calculate the difference.

The drawer would open with a ding. Why? To alert the owner that money was coming and going. He could come over to monitor the transaction. There was also a psychological trigger here to the employee: be honest. Don't overcharge. Count out the change properly. Don't take any extra money out of the register because this will be balanced by day's end.

Also, the opening of the drawer is how this simple adding machine registered transactions, which is one reason that fractional pricing came along: $4.95, $2.99, and so on. The need to give change became a technological imperative.

Very soon, the patent was sold and then sold again, and landed in the company that became National Cash Register. This company exists today and is located less than a mile from where I'm writing now. But it has been a long slog from a century ago to today. In 1911, it had grown to have 6,000 employees. During the trust-busting craze of the Progressive Era, the company was found guilty of violating the Sherman Antitrust Act.

The Attack

The claim was that the company was battling back against the used cash register market by sending people into small towns to buy up the used models at inflated prices and thus taking them off the market. This allowed NCR to obtain a monopoly by selling new machines. It's a clever tactic that the market would have worked to subvert in time. But regulators weren't having it. The company heads and 25 employees were sentenced to one year in jail. The convictions were overturned in 1915.

It's a good history to recall if you think the attack on enterprise is only a modern problem. Here you have a case in which a company became big due to tremendous demand for its highly innovative product, one that was needed in every retail shop in the United States. It was rewarded for its public service with growth and profits. Then the government came in with criminal penalties and the public humiliation of jail sentences.

But that's hardly the end of the story. In 1981, NCR itself traded lawsuits with AT&T over patent claims. From the beginning, antitrust law has been a useful means by which companies attack each other over market share, with government regulation serving as the weapon of choice. In its absence, the forces of market competition would turn managerial attention toward the right approach to winning: serving others with better products at better prices.

Think about this when you see the attacks on Amazon today. It is a mighty company that grew from nothing through unrelenting service of the consumer. Now you have the president of the United States threatening every kind of legal action against the company, including, yes, antitrust investigations into its business practices.

A Seamless Garment

Some things never seem to change. Politics will be politics but innovation proceeds despite it all. The things we use in our daily lives come to us not descended from clouds, perfected and flawless, but through a trial-and-error process of learning, experimenting, and tweaking.

There is real inspiration to be had by looking at the iterative process of innovation, how that funny little machine from 1883 gradually evolved into the tiny payment processing units we use routinely today, an epic story of improvement in machinery in which the current stage is knitted to all previous stages through an invisible thread of passion for solving problems and serving others.

That iconic ding of the cash register can probably still be heard in country stores all over the country but there will come a time when it will finally fall silent, a stage of history ended and a new one begun. Indeed, you can visit the old spot of Ritty's first machine in Dayton, Ohio, today, and see all the new technology in operation.

What is the next stage? If you have ever processed a transaction using cryptocurrency — peer-to-peer, nearly instant settlement, no intermediaries — you already know the answer. We'll get there, without or without the approval of the regulations. They can slow down progress but cannot stop it. You can try it out right now with a contribution to AIER.

53

About this Proposal to End Air Travel

I'm driving down the road. I'm seeing all kinds of trucks. Many are driving food to grocery stores to put on shelves. That way, people can buy the food, take it home, and eat it as a part of living a happy life. The food was grown on land plowed by tractors that use internal combustion. Lots of it was flown in from abroad on planes that also use gasoline.

Thank goodness no crazy person is pushing for this to be abolished, by force of law.

Oh, wait a moment. Someone is. Many people are. I just read about it here.

In a couple of days, I'll board a plane that will take me in two hours to the completion of a trip that would have required months of travel 200 years ago — if I would have made it at all.

As I prepare my things, I'm struck by what I just read from a highly celebrated member of Congress, and endorsed by many of her colleagues. Using freshly printed and taxed money, she says the government should "build out highspeed rail at a scale where air travel stops becoming necessary."

So much for visiting Europe. Actually, so much for visiting anywhere outside your local community. So much for world trade. So much for eating food not grown in your backyard.

Actually, so much for life on earth as we know it.

The end of air travel and the end of industrial farming are just two pieces of "a massive transformation of our society" proposed in the Green New Deal, which is explained in a document which reads like a nightmare fantasy of the GOP.

Some of the strangest agenda points for government to do: "upgrade or replace every building in US"; "Provide job training and education to all"; stop "using fossil fuels for energy needs," which means ending 78% of current energy consumption; "reorient our entire economy to work off renewable energy," like sun, like wind, like the state of nature of starvation and early death; it won't happen because the tooth fairy will give us "economic security for all who are unable or unwilling to work," provided we "replace every combustion-engine vehicle" and pay for it with "a carbon tax" that would only cover "a tiny part" of the necessary mass confiscation.

What could go wrong?

It's almost hard to believe that an actual adult could produce this document without satirical intention, but there it is. What's more, the whole thing is too easily dismissed as a nutty childish fantasy. In a Democratic Party bereft of ideas, the gigantic socialist plan, which makes the Bolsheviks seem modest, could have a huge influence on the future. Once you come to believe that the state can best manage life on earth — provided the right experts are in charge and that all the necessary resources are unlimited — there is no turning back.

And yet I actually don't think this "plan" is that much of a danger to the modernity it proposes to abolish. Many people are critiquing the program on grounds that it is too expensive. It's true there is no magic money machine that can produce revenue without social cost. But even if such a thing existed, nothing in this delusional sheet should become operational. It would supplant market signaling and experimentation — and the consumer-driven process of discovering what should and should not be produced — with rule by an iron-fisted elite, ending anything resembling liberty.

And yet, it still raises questions, such as: why does this nonsense exist at all?

The Old New Deal

The last New Deal was much more modest. It sought to raise commodity prices, boost GDP, and reignite hiring. It didn't work; recall that the Great Depression didn't end until after the whole thing evaporated after World War Two.

Still, think about the state of the economy back then. From American Default: "Between 1929 and 1932, gross domestic product (GDP)…dropped almost 60 percent"; "production of durable goods, including automobiles, declined by 81 percent, and the value of agricultural production was down by 63 percent." During the same period, "employment declined by almost 50 percent — one out of every two people who in July 1929 had a job had lost it by March 1932." The number of unemployed: 15 million. Wages fell by 67 percent. Cash income in rural areas fell by 70 percent.

In other words, the collapse was inconceivable by today's standards. As bad as 2008 seemed, it was a blip by comparison. It is for reasons of this calamity, experienced in people's regular lives, that we can vaguely understand the lurch into the unknown, and the replacement of market signaling by government planning. It was a bad choice but emergencies are often the occasion for disastrous policy decisions.

Today, on the other hand, things are moving along swimmingly. The number of people employed has never been higher; the unemployment rate is rock bottom; financial markets have recovered from last year's panic over Trump's misbegotten trade war; new technologies are making life better; the environment is cleaner than ever.

Life is not perfect, and getting rid of the dead weight of the state would make for huge progress. But there is no sense in which a lurch into totalitarian insanity would seem justified in any respect. Not even the worst possible predictions of climate change would seem to provide an explanation or justification for utterly losing our minds.

Ideological Blindness

How to account for the existence of a document — widely trumpeted by the media — which proposes that we replace modern life for totalitarian government control? My only explanation is ideology. There is no idea so nutty that it can be ruled out by reason, provided we have the overlay of dogmatic ideology to blind people to obvious historical, empirical, and theoretical reality.

Ideology can be so corrosive and intellectually debilitating that it can convince even a person who has never personally achieved anything beyond obtaining a college degree that he can redesign the world economy. Amazing but true. And if there is no other vision to compete, even the most far-flung fantasy can prevail over time. This is how 20th-century totalitarianism came to be, and why it can never be ruled out completely.

I just typed that last sentence from an airplane, which is only in the air because people such as the authors of the Green New Deal have yet to get their way.

54

Your New Gas Can Still Doesn't Work

It's been a few years since I've looked at gas cans available for purchase. I'm looking now at WalMart. Nothing has changed. You still can't get one that works properly. Whatever you buy will not pour properly. It has no valve to release air so it blows up and shrinks depending on the weather. It is likely to spill when you have to use it.

Here's to hoping you saved your old cans before modern regulations ruined them. If you didn't, you are either going to end up with a non-functioning can or spend Saturday hacking your new can with one of these many kits you can buy online.

I love this reviewer's comment:

> I love using new gas cans with the safety, spill proof spouts as much as the next guy — I mean who doesn't love standing there with a full 5 gallon can inverted for 15 minutes while approximately one quart a minute flows out of the spout and no less than half of that quart escapes from every "sealed" seam, threaded fitting, and valve on the safety spout, spilling onto the top of your fuel tank, shoes, hands, and best of all, the still quite hot motor of whatever you're filling. But, that being said, I realized one day that I'm a grown man with better things to do, with children who need a father who isn't covered in third degree burn scars because some hippy in California is convinced leaking gas can vapors is what the real global warming problem is, and the industry is just as good at making leak-proof safety gas can valves as they are mousetraps, and generally speaking, dying in a burst of flames when a "safety" spout leaks fuel onto a hot exhaust seems like such an ironic and anti-climatic way to go.

That's some white-hot anger right there. Rightly so. The gas can is broken. The regulators broke it. Despite gazillion complaints on every conceivable forum, nothing is changing. The regulations sticks.

Regulations began in 2000, with the idea of preventing spillage. The notion began in California, spread, and was picked up by the EPA, which is always looking for new and innovative ways to mandate as much human misery as possible.

An ominous regulatory announcement from the EPA came in 2007: "Starting with containers manufactured in 2009... it is expected that the new cans will be built with a simple and inexpensive permeation barrier and new spouts that close automatically."

The government never said "no vents." It abolished them de facto with new standards that every state had to adopt by 2009. So for the last ten years, you have not been able to buy gas cans that work properly. They are not permitted to have a separate vent. The top has to close automatically. There are other silly things now, too, but the biggest problem is that they do not do well what cans are supposed to do.

And don't tell me about spillage. The reviewer above is correct. It is far more likely to spill when the gas is gurgling out in various uneven ways, when one spout has to both pour and suck in air. That's when the lawn mower tank becomes suddenly full without warning, when you are shifting the can this way and that just to get the stuff out.

There's also the problem of the exploding can. On hot days, the plastic models to which this regulation applies can blow up like balloons. When you release the top, gas flies everywhere, including possibly on a hot engine. Then the trouble really begins.

Never heard of this rule? You will know about it if you go to the local store. Most people buy one or two of these items in the course of a lifetime, so you might otherwise have not encountered this outrage.

Yet let enough time go by. A whole generation will come to expect these things to work badly. Then some wise young entrepreneur will have the bright idea, "Hey, let's put a hole on the other side so this can work properly." But he will never be able to bring it into production. The government won't allow it because it is protecting us!

Five years ago, hardly anyone even mentioned this problem. Now complaints are everywhere.

The main sites that seem to have discussed this are the boating forums and the lawn forums. These are the people who use these cans more than most. The level of anger and vitriol is amazing to read, and every bit of it is justified.

There is no possible rationale for these kinds of regulations. It can't be about emissions really, since the new cans are more likely to result in spills. It's as if some bureaucrat were sitting around thinking of ways to make life worse for everyone, and hit upon this new rule.

You are already thinking of hacks. Why not just stab the thing with a knife and be done with it? If you have to transport the can in the car, that's a problem. You need a way to plug the vent with something.

You can drill a hole and put a tire stem in there and use the screw top as the way to close the hole. Great idea. Just what I wanted to do with my Saturday afternoon. You can also buy an old-time metal can. It turns out that special regulations pertain here, too, and it's all about the spout, which is not easy to fill. They are also unusually expensive. I'm not sure that either of these options is ideal.

Ask yourself this: If they can wreck such a normal and traditional item like this, and do it largely under the radar screen, what else have they mandatorily malfunctioned? How many other things in our daily lives have been distorted, deformed and destroyed by government regulations?

If some product annoys you in surprising ways, there's a good chance that it is not the invisible hand at work, but rather the regulatory grip that is squeezing the life out of our normal consumer products.

55

The Solution to City
Transit Is Decentralized

Tell me if this has happened to you. You are in your car in a big city, moving at a snail's pace. You see someone walking and you think: would I be better off doing that? But traffic starts moving again. Fifteen minutes later you are stopped again and you see the same walker, now fully a block ahead of you. There must be a better way.

Uber has been a solid option to driving your own car. It has shattered the taxi monopoly and that's wonderful. It has been an exciting source of income for people who are between jobs or just discovering that gigging around is a better life than being chained to a desk. But New York City is now dealing with the reality that this solution is imperfect. Uber is still a car. It still needs the roads. Some people claim that ride sharing could make matters even worse.

Scooting Around

Here's what is amazing. Right now, on the street in midtown Atlanta, there are little electric scooters sitting around. I have a mobile app that tells me exactly where they are. I can walk outside the office and walk up to one. I scan the QR code on the machine. It unlocks. I step on it and push a lever, and zoom! I'm flying down the street, past traffic and toward where I'm going. I get to a restaurant or whatever and park it. Someone else comes along and snags it and does the same. So on it goes, all day, even all night, all over town.

These wonderful scooters cost $1 to ride and then 15 cents per mile. A single charge on a machine will go 15 miles at 15 miles per hour. You can sign up to become a charger and make between $5 and $20 hour just for plugging the thing in. How is it that they aren't stolen? If you try to move it without app authorization, the bike lights up and locks. These things go nowhere that the company cannot follow.

I personally find the whole thing amazing. Already, the company in question, Bird, has taken many cities by surprise by dropping hundreds all over town. There are two other companies doing the same (Spin and Lime). They are in San Francisco, Nashville, Austin, Atlanta, Santa Monica, Silver Spring, Washington, D.C., St. Louis, Charlotte, and so on. The companies are competing with each other for first-mover advantage. It makes sense for them to air drop the scooters before crawling to city officials to beg for permission.

And, yes, just as with Uber, there is already a pushback. People are upset that scooters are zooming all over sidewalks when they are supposed to be in bike lanes (if they exist). The sheer newness of the thing, as well as the thrilling fun of riding, is likely causing people to be rather ostentatious with their riding technique, thus annoying some people. Mostly some city governments are upset that no one came begging for the planners to plan before the business began operations.

Nashville, for example, put out a cease and desist order on a company. "Bird scooters have been observed by employees of the Metropolitan Government obstructing the public sidewalk," Metro attorney Theresa Costonis wrote in a letter to Bird's government relations director. How terrible! Plus some riders are leaving these things in strange places, mucking up pretty areas of town.

Just as with ride sharing in general, the ethos of "move fast and break things" doesn't sit well with everyone. But you have to admire the way the companies are proceeding here, perfectly aware that they have more to lose by failing to act than they do from getting in trouble with Councilman Joe and his bureaucratic cohort.

It was Uber who first rattled city administrations with the tactic of act now and deal with permissions later. Many other companies got the message. Despite all the PR and media frenzy, the tactic worked. Governments move much slower than markets. If you want to be a player, you have to act with courage and innovate with speed. Sometimes that means having to disrupt entrenched establishments.

This Is Part of the Solution

It is incredibly obvious once you try this out that this can be an amazing part of the solution to the problem of urban transit that has been part of city life for generations. What's fascinating here is the method by which the solution is being found. Countless attempts have been made in every city to plan from the top down with new rails, high-occupancy lanes, tolls, carpooling mandates, buses, and so on, but the problem has persisted.

Then came the Internet. Then the app economy. Then the possibility of using them to arrange transport via new companies with new solutions. Then ride sharing. Then micro-rentals. Crucially, we have international trade (China's Ninebot is a major supplier of the hardware). And now these dazzling little electric scooters popping up all over town. And as is typical in the private sector, the solutions are economically efficient, consumer friendly, effective, and fun too!

Actually, I didn't like typing the word "private sector" there. It makes no sense. This is a public solution, whereas the typical "public sector" solution feeds the selfish interests of politicians and bureaucrats. Really the words should be switched because the market benefits the public whereas government solutions so obviously benefit private parties. We use the terms as we do simply because market solutions are rooted in private property, but that property benefits everyone.

The rise of the city scooter as part of the app economy is a fantastic example of how markets generate solutions in the face of intractable problems. The more people tool around on these wonderful scooters, the lighter the traffic, the cleaner the city, and the happier people are. Note that no central planner came up with the idea. It has emerged out of discreet forms of market-based innovation using the best of modern technology combined with a perceived solution of a genuine use case.

Now on my scooter, I'm thrilled to buzz right past not only the guy walking but, incredibly, even the drivers on our crowded city streets. Be patient. The market will find a solution to our problems.

56

Scooter Nation

You have to travel around a bit to discover the astonishing way the dockless electric scooter has transformed urban life in America. Where I live in Atlanta, Georgia, their presence is growing by the day, so that they can actually be used as a reliable means of daily transport.

Right now, there are six outside my office waiting to be used. Another six are sitting within one block. In this area of town, there are literally hundreds. And that's just the ones available, while hundreds more are currently in use.

It's made a big difference in reducing traffic clogs in midtown Atlanta. You can actually be in a car now without being in stand-still traffic. For the users of scooters, it's a godsend. No waiting for buses. No hailing cabs. No having to wait for your Uber driver. Instead you just hop on and go.

And I just spent the weekend in Palo Alto, California. Scooters were everywhere, buzzing from place to place. I pointed this out on Twitter, and people started chiming in from all over the country. Scooters are transforming transport in America, in unexpected ways.

Think about this. There was no legislation that passed with great fanfare. There was no headline in the local paper about it. There were no enabling regulations that were debated by legislators and urban planners. One day they were not there and then, suddenly, they were there.

AIER has already run two articles on this topic from last spring. In the meantime, most markets have been penetrated by competitive companies. Bird and Lime are working in most cities. They are both profiting handsomely.

Market Signaling

What I admire most is how these companies are responding to market signaling. They know where their scooters are picked up and where they are dropped off. They know when there are too many at one location and not at another.

Their supply is responding to the demand, on a day-by-day basis, meeting the needs that consumers demonstrated on a daily and hourly basis.

And look how quickly all of this is taking place! A year ago, hardly anyone could have predicted that our cities would be flooded with electric scooters that work through mobile apps, are not docked in any particular place, and are available to anyone with a smartphone. Lots of things had to come together to make this possible but it is finally here.

I'm delighted by technological shifts that change our lives that are not anticipated by intellectuals or central planners. This is a good case in point. It's a paradigmatic case of permissionless innovation. It is especially delightful to consider that the science of urban planning, complete with central plans for how everyone should get around the city, has been a professionalized field of study and practice for the better part of a century.

In my lifetime, experts have busied themselves with all kinds of ideas for collective transport as a means of getting people out of their cars and behaving more like the hive. These have included mass transport schemes involving trains and buses, rules concerning vehicle occupancy, rewards for carpooling, and every conceivable scheme for discouraging individuals using their own cars to buzz around the city.

Billions in tax dollars have been spent to realize these plans. But they have all met with limited success at best. Americans love their cars, the claim has been, and nothing will ever change that.

Individual Choice

What scooter entrepreneurship realized is that it's not really about the car as such. It's about the control the individual has over his or her own transportation experience. It was Uber that provided the great breakthrough technology, enlisted average people to be drivers for other average people, with user and driving ratings as the governing source of order.

The scooter turns out to provide something similar, an individualized experience that takes care of most of what you need to do during the day in the city, whether it is getting lunch, going to the museum, swinging by the bank or Fedex office, or running various sundry errands. You are the master of the tool. You pick it up, you drop it off, and you control the payment system.

What's striking about the prevailing ethos is how much average people seem to be willing to inveigh against the whole phenomenon. People talk about how scooters are ruining the city, how dangerous they are for drivers, how annoying they are for pedestrians, and why we desperately need intense regulations on these things. Virtually anyone you talk to about these scooters will immediately tell you one of the above things.

Meanwhile, it's very clear that consumers themselves love these scooters. The whole thing is absolutely delightful. They are arriving in random cities in the middle of the night. You wake up in the morning and there are 500 of them strewn everywhere. People download the app. Within hours, people have found a new way to get around and have fun. It takes months for the legislators and regulators even to figure out what's going on.

Public officials are panicked. "They just appeared," Mohammed Nuru, director of the San Francisco Public Works, told the New York Times. "I don't know who comes up with these ideas or where these people come from." Spoken like a man who believes that nothing should go on in a city that doesn't have his direct permission.

We'll Learn

To be sure, scooters are not without problems. People can use them in a rude way, rushing pedestrians. They can buzz through intersections without considering the alarm they cause drivers. They can fly through driveways without taking precaution. That said, it is remarkable how few injuries and accidents they have caused given how new they are.

Every new technology arrives without settled norms governing its use. Remember when people used to answer phone calls in restaurants and speak loudly in a way that disrupted the dining room? That doesn't happen as much anymore because people learned how to use them properly. It will be the same with scooters.

And there is no question that this movement is going somewhere, even to the point that there will be more scooters on the road than cars. Who knows? The beauty of this revolution is that the market is driving it, which is to say that its future depends entirely on the wishes of the consumer rather than the plans of some powerful urban planner.

57

Thanks to Capitalism, You Can Now Sleep Sitting Up

O n an overnight flight from Los Angeles, I was looking around at passengers and their pathetic attempts to sleep. Mouths were hanging open. Heads were bobbing up and down, left and right. Snores were everywhere. No one was truly comfortable.

People would vaguely wake up from a thin sleep about every 15 minutes and try to get comfortable again. They would stuff clothes under their necks.

Many people had these U-shaped foam pillows designed for airplanes, but those don't really work. Kelly Conaboy, in a hilarious article for The Atlantic, nails it perfectly:

> Is there a pillow as useless as the U-shaped travel neck pillow? There is not. This half-ovate, toilet-seat cover-esque object reigns as King of Travel Accessories, while failing miserably at its intended sole use.

Rage against the U-shape all you want, but it seems like nothing else works either.

Ah, but on this flight, I, on the other hand, was as happy as I could be. I was using my new Trtl pillow that I snagged from Amazon for $30. This thing is amazing. It solves the problem. It is so compelling that if I could put it on you right now, wherever you are, you would immediately feel sleepy.

Maybe it is purely physical, or maybe it is psychological. Whatever the reason, this crazy gizmo has solved a problem everyone has had since the beginning of recorded history; namely, there doesn't seem to be a comfortable way to sleep while sitting up.

I'm trying to understand how this innovation came to be.

Not the Neck

Let me ask you: why is it that it is so difficult for you to sleep sitting up?

I looked up the question on Mental Floss, but the answer given here is pretty opaque:

> The partial paralysis and loss of muscle tone make holding the upright posture of a straight back and neck difficult. It may be why your seatmate tilts sleepily into your personal space, snoring on your shoulder, and why sleeping on a plane is just hard to do comfortably.

What answer would you give?

Until now, the usual focus has been on the neck. Surely we need a pillow to fill in that gap between the head and shoulders. Doing so would bring the most comfort. Right? It never really works. You put that U-shaped thing there and something is still not right. What is missing here?

10 Pounds

What is missing is that this doesn't actually deal with the root problem of trying to sleep while sitting up: namely, the head is really heavy. It keeps wanting to flop over. Stuffing a pillow against the neck keeps the head from falling entirely to the side, but it doesn't stop the need to lean over in an uncomfortable way and it doesn't stop the tendency of the head to flop forward.

Now, think of this. When you are lying down, the heavy head is not an issue. The flat surface takes the weight off the head, so all you need is a pillow to put your face on and perhaps fill the gap between the head and shoulders so you have a snuggly sense of comfort.

As soon as you sit up, you have a problem. The human head weighs about 10 pounds. To support that, you have to have engaged muscles. But as soon as you start sleeping, the muscles needed to support this heavy thing disengage, causing the head to flop around and thereby wake you up.

The Answer

The folks at Trtl began to think through this problem in 2010. What kind of device could take the weight off the head and support it while allowing the neck and back to relax? The answer seems perfectly obvious once you see it. We need something to support the whole head. What is that? A hard piece of plastic that flexes a bit in the middle. Wrap it in cloth and add a scarf to hold it in place.

Thus was born the Trtl pillow, the single greatest innovation in technology for sleeping while sitting upright. It's a complete game changer. You know it the instant you put it on. It's the most astonishing thing. Even while standing up, wearing it signals the brain to go to sleep.

There is the physical element here. Your head mostly stays upright with a slight tilt that recreates the feeling of lying down. And the cloth that wraps around your neck feels a bit like a blanket you pull up to yourself on a cold night. Thus it is part reality and part illusion, but the overall effect is the last thing you might expect. It really works.

I had to do a one-day round trip from East to West to East again, missing one and a half nights' sleep in my bed. With this pillow, my problem was solved. I actually slept, as in deep sleep, on the plane.

Entrepreneurship to the Rescue

If this solution is so fantastic, even obvious in retrospect, why hadn't anyone thought of it sooner and brought it to market? It's not as if this thing involves high-end technology as compared with a smartphone, for example. It is relatively simple, and the parts to make it have been available since the invention of plastics. Going back in time, a similar device might have been invented in the ancient world.

Why now? It's impossible to explain how it is that two students in Scotland finally hit upon an idea precisely at this time, and then acted on that idea (with great financial risk) to bring such a product to you and me. It has to do with the passion to invent, the drive to profit, the burning desire to improve the world that is unique to the human mind, and grants unto history its capacity to turn on a dime, disrupt the old, and usher in the new.

The unfolding process is called entrepreneurship, a term originally invoked by Richard Cantillon, pushed by John Stuart Mill, celebrated by Joseph Schumpeter, and refined into the purest theory in the works of Israel Kirzner. What it means is the capacity to imagine what does not yet exist and to bear the risk of making a judgment that the future can be improved with new ways of doing things. It is not subject to modeling. It is driven by intuition. It brings us goods and services we didn't even know we were without. Success is ratified by the market process.

The Brilliance of Simplicity

Some innovations are incomprehensibly complex. But what most presciently underscores the brilliance of entrepreneurship are those that are startlingly simple. The Trtl pillow is a case in point. At first it didn't exist, not even as an idea. It was an unmet need, one that a few determined to meet. Thanks to some serious thought and some willingness to take risk, it came to exist. It succeeded while making the innovators extremely rich, with profits serving as the sign and seal of a job well done.

Then we wonder why no one else came up with it.

The simplest solutions are the hardest ones to see. Once we do see them, we tend to dismiss the genius behind them. After all, it's just a silly pillow, right? No, it is the difference between a good life as a traveler and suffering with sleep deprivation when it is least welcome. This pillow is not only a tribute to good engineering and good sense; it is a credit to a commercial system that enables and rewards innovation in service of the better life.

58

Everyone Is Missing the Point of 3D-Printed Guns

The project of Cody Wilson's 3D-printed gun — the Liberator — has once again blasted into national attention. This is because Cody's company has (surprisingly) won a settlement with the State Department that had previously issued a restraining order against Defense Distributed, citing International Traffic in Arms Regulations.

There are echoes here with the long battle over PGP, which was ultimately won, to the great benefit of individual liberty and privacy. What saved the day was the cause of free speech. It might ultimately save the right to download and print a gun.

I recall the takedown order for the gun blueprint. Cody was now embroiled in a struggle at the highest levels. This was the battle he wanted. He got it. His life would never be the same.

That previous order against DD is now rescinded, thus permitting his company to release digital files that enable anyone with a 3D printer to produce a functioning handgun at home. This gun bypasses the usual regulations concerning serial numbers, registration, and regulation. That's way more than enough to cause a gun controller to panic.

The panic is not only about the mass distribution of unregulated guns; it's about the loss of control in general.

No More Control

This gun is a manifestation of the new digital reality: the physical world has become information-based. The only way to control it is to muzzle people, violate free speech rights, and fundamentally transform a principle we have come to believe about the relationship between the individual and state.

Keep in mind that Defense Distributed is neither producing nor distributing guns. It is only trafficking in information flows. It is a company and a website but maintains no proprietary relationship with the information it distributes. Every download can (and has been) duplicated and reproduced unto infinity using any digital platform: the mainstream web, the dark web, instant messaging, encrypted email communication, SMS, every manner of SMS-based application, or anything else.

You can try to control this distribution of information but not even today's most totalitarian regimes have succeeded. Information is a multi-headed hydra indeed, but not even that quite explains what we are talking about here. The only way fully to control information flows in a digital age is to take full control of thought itself, which is an ambition unrealizable in this world, even by the most complete and efficient system of thought control one can imagine.

Which is precisely the point that Cody was trying to make.

The Heady Days of 2013

Cody is part of a generation of intellectuals and activists that saw this world being born after 2008 and following. Many previously unimagined and unimaginable things began to happen in the digital world. File sharing on distributed networks released vast amounts of copyrighted material online. Government cracked down but to no effect: the system of distributed file sharing grew through the decades and continued long after the government's hammer fell.

Then in 2009, something incredible happened: money, the good and service that government had nationalized 100 years ago and largely dominated for thousands of years, entered into the realm of the information economy. This was the last piece of the puzzle, so to speak. We now had all the essential pillars of commercial and culture life ported over to the world of information, which is to say, migrated to the realm in which power was no longer effective.

The revolution, in those days, appeared to be unstoppable. In the first decade of the 21st century, these people were known as the cypherpunks, because they used code and cryptography to bypass and unsettle official channels of information production and distribution.

This later mutated and came to be crystallized in the movement known as cryptoanarchism. The point was not that we had to convince people of a philosophy. The point was to show how we had the tools today finally to make freedom a reality. We have learned how to bypass the two advantages of the state — its jurisdictional monopolies over force and its capacity to muscle and muzzle anything physical — and bypass it with tools of freedom that had no central point of failure.

There were 3D-printed guns before Cody Wilson. But his genius contribution was his willingness and desire to stand up and be the face of this paradigm shift. He knew that in order to press the point, the media needed someone to blame, someone to demonize, some one product (a gun!) to focus on, in order to write their stories and debate the implications. To inspire this debate was his whole pont.

Cody was and is not a gun nut; he was and is an information nut who saw what many of us saw. He chose to act on the new ideals. He was willing to be the poster child of a movement that, in fact, had no head whatsoever.

It's Not About Cody

The journalists who write about this subject have universally failed to understand the point. They are used to covering issues by focussing on people, institutions, and products, discerning and ferreting out the good guys and bad guys based on the doctrines of the civic religion. They are not disposed to cover large-scale paradigm shifts in the relationship between the individual and the state. They are uncomprehending of the implications of decentralization, the implications of the commoditization of information networks, and what this means for control of the world.

And this is precisely why the coverage of the first week of August 2018 has been so absurd. They want to focus on Cody and shine the light on this devil in our otherwise perfect garden of the neo-liberal, regulated, top-down social democratic welfare state. What they entirely missed was Cody's central point: the physical world that was once controlling is migrating to a different realm, the world of information that no one can control. The world of the future is uncontrolled and uncontrollable.

This was his core point. It was not about guns as such. It was not even about 3D printing as such. His core point concerned information flows and unviability of power in a digital world. Nothing will ever be the same. This is our current reality; it is not, however, our current politics or journalism.

To be sure, he and we underestimated the resilience of the reactionary forces in the world today. The paradigm is shifting but not without friction, not without victims, not without profound disturbance to the status quo, which would fight back with tools we know and some we do not yet understand.

We live day to day, experiencing only the passing scene we see on social media. But there are larger forces at work. There is no chance of finally censoring the future with any of the tools that molded the past. It's done, that great migration from a things-based economy regulated by the state to an idea-based economy regulated only by the choices of the individuals that make up society itself.

59

The Charming Luxury of Train Travel

The plane from Detroit to Las Vegas was taking longer than expected to take off. I happened to be sitting next to one of those people who is psychologically addicted to complaining. As we waited, every few minutes she would erupt into a variety of audible protests.

"Why is it taking so long? What's with these people? Come on! Let's go! I can't stand this wait anymore."

Amazing. And yet it is true that plane travel these days is enormously frustrating. Old timers will tell you that it is entirely ruined. The security searches, being treated like a criminal, the long lines, the crowds, the unreliable schedules, the cuts in amenities, the nonstop demands for proof of identity, the high cost of everything in the airport — it all adds up.

The time you spend in the apparatus of travel is two, three, or four times as long as the travel itself. That's crazy, if you think about it. Still, it's no excuse for bad behavior on the part of consumers.

Here's another case of postmodern impatience. I was turning into a grocery store in a town I didn't know that well. As I turned, the woman in the car behind me had her arms up in the air, screaming and yelling at me. As soon as possible, she floored it in order to make up for those possible four seconds of life that she could not otherwise get back.

What a world we live in. The impatience is justified if you think theoretically: we would all rather live in a zero-transactions-cost world. We would wish we were in Paris and, poof, we would be there. Want to go to the beach? Blink and the ocean would appear before you. Humanity won't rest until we get to that point.

Still, for now, travel takes time. There is a question of how you want to spend that time.

The Train!

I have my answer: the railroad. Because I've lived most of my life in Texas and the Deep South, trains are not too much on the radar. Automobiles are the way you travel. There is no particular reason to change.

But the Northeast, where I now spend swaths of time, is different. Train travel is normal, even essential, mainly because cars, while useful for local travel, are nearly impossible to drag into a place like New York.

In case you have never done this, let me describe to you how it goes. I arrive at Penn Station in New York City. I find the right place to grab the train to Hudson, New York, which was my destination. People are surprisingly helpful in the train station, by the way, even in this famously difficult city.

You don't have to arrive two hours ahead. You can get there exactly at boarding time. My train was boarded at 8:15 a.m. At this time, a line formed to go to the platform. You choose your car, choose your seat, put your stuff away (plenty of room!), and settle in.

Wait, you say. You might be wondering about security. It seems like an inconceivable luxury, but there is none at all. You just walk into the station and onto the train like a normal human being. You look around you and see other normal human beings. You show your ticket to the person who walks by after the train is already moving, and the person prints a ticket and sticks it above your seat. This really happens.

The whole thing is stunning and super relaxing.

Once the train begins to move — it all happens very quickly — you are not barked at with orders to sit this way or that or stuff your computer at your feet. Instead, you ... do whatever you want. The wireless internet connection is pretty good, and there are electric outlets for your computer, phone, or anything else.

You can get up and walk between railway cars — it makes me feel like I'm in a film noir scene from the 1940s! — and saunter up to the cafe. There you can order food or coffee, or indulge in a bit of morning drinking with a beer, wine, or cocktails. You walk back through the cars to find your seat again.

The trip from the city to Hudson is remarkably picturesque. You watch the Hudson River most of the way. The train moves at a steady pace that feels relaxing as compared with a car, and the experience is far less abstract than that in a plane because you actually observe the landscape. The scene in the foreground is fast: trees and pretty bushes and older homes on the river. In the background is a hill with a view of the sky. Between them is this river that has been so important for the commercial development of the United States since colonial times.

The train makes other stops along the way, so it's best to set your alarm so you know when you are arriving. You have to hop off pretty quickly, unlike when traveling by plane.

Imagine arriving at your destination more refreshed than when you embarked on your journey. This is truly what happens. Then you step off the train and feel like a character out of Anne of Green Gables. You smile and look at the beautiful sky. This is how travel could be — and it still is in the Northeast. (I can only imagine how much better it would be if Amtrak were truly privatized.)

The Hudson train station is especially charming. Indoors features lots of woodwork with a ticket window with iron bars and an old sign above it that says: TICKETS. There are benches around the periphery. You expect to meet an old guy there who is complaining about the policies of President Harding.

Time and Travel

The experience is a reminder of how dramatically train travel changed life for Americans. Here are some maps that one writer found in the 1932 Atlas of the Historical Geography of the United States. The lines on the maps signal not routes but geographic space with the starting point of New York.

He writes: "In 1800, it took a whole day to barely get outside of the city; two weeks to reach Georgia or Ohio; and in five weeks, you could just about get to Illinois and Louisiana."

Just imagine taking off a full month just to go from New York to New Orleans — and doing it without wireless internet.

By 1830, things had changed. "Train travel in the U.S. was almost twice as fast (a huge improvement!), but still quite slow by modern standards. Rather than taking two weeks, going to Georgia or Ohio from New York City took one week, and in two you could get to the state borders of Louisiana, Arkansas and Illinois. Getting to Minnesota would have taken about five weeks!"

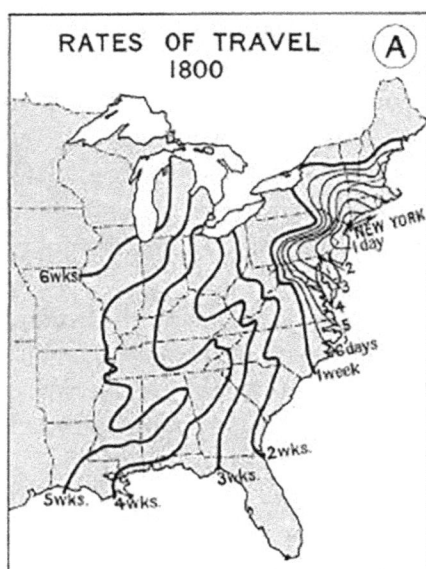

RATES OF TRAVEL
1800 (A)

NEW YORK
1 day

6 wks

5 wks. 4 wks. 3 wks. 2 wks.

By 1857, you could "do in a day or two what used to take a couple weeks. With a week's travel you could get to the eastern border of Texas, and in about four weeks you could get to California. Only the Northwest took longer than a month to reach from New York City."

RATES OF TRAVEL
1830

By 1930, you could go across the entire United States in two days! These days of course we would all find that intolerably slow.

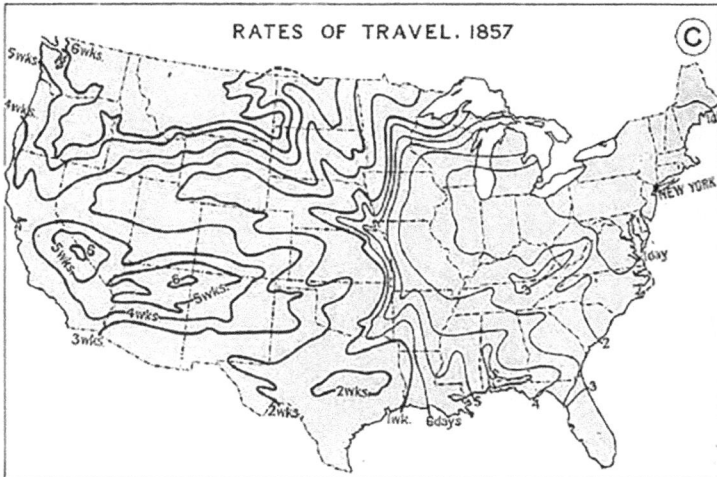

RATES OF TRAVEL. 1857

So let us remember just how dramatically trains improved our lives. They changed our conception of space and opened up new possibilities for progress. It is something striking that even now, they are the most luxurious travel I've experienced, and this will probably be true so long as there is no commercially viable market for flying cars.

Back to the pathological complainer on my flight to Vegas. It's very much possible that she would be less crabby had she been on a train with a nice view and a stiff cocktail. At least the rest of us wouldn't have had to listen to someone complaining about spending only a few hours on a trip that 150 years ago would have taken the better part of a month.

60

The Mystical Magic of the Mechanical Clock

There we sat, four of us in the ballroom, in silence, except that it wasn't silent. There was a quiet but penetrating voice in our midst, and it had something more compelling to say than any of us. We would not interrupt. So we were silent. And listened. The room was filled with a sound. It was a mechanical clock built in 1907 in Connecticut, the kind you have to wind with a key.

I found it in an antique mall in Hudson, New York, sitting tilted on a chair, neglected and dirty, its face yellowed with age and a thick patina of dust filling the crevices of the wood. I offered $75, and the merchant took it. It came with a key, which is rather unusual. I had no idea whether it actually worked.

We took it back to the Stone House at the American Institute for Economic Research, and put it on the mantle in the ballroom. There are two places in which to insert the key: the left hole, which turns right, and the right hole, which turns left. We had to stop speaking to hear it, and then the lovely sound began. It had come to life, speaking for the first time in perhaps decades.

There are plenty of electric clocks that affect a ticking sound. This is completely different. The sound is generated by a physical action inside, and the wooden box operates like an acoustic amplifier same as a violin or guitar. There are two sounds per second, one higher than the other. They seem almost like pitches, and my ear puts them about a third apart, though I'm not sure whether I'm imagining that or not.

All ticks sound the same, but they are not. Each sound is unique because it occurs in a different slice of time in the forward trajectory of history. But then the mystery strikes you. Is not the clock itself creating the very time linearity that causes each tick to become unique? How can this clock both create and inhabit the same perceived forward motion of history in what would otherwise remain an abstraction? It's unclear intellectually, but physically we experience it. We believe it is true because we hear it. The machine is providing evidence to our senses.

It's the sound of progress. Humankind only heard this sound in the late 13th century for the first time. It was a foreshadowing of the material progress that would sweep Europe a century later, but there was terrible darkness before the dawn. In 1350, perhaps half of Europe's population was wiped out by the black plague. It was the last horror of the Middle Ages. Then sanitation improved. Travel became safer. The skylines of the city came to be dotted by cathedrals. Painting became beautiful. Music improved. Mechanical inventions were spreading. And speaking. Singing.

The medieval clock, its chime once ringing over cities of danger and death, became the soundtrack to progress, chronicling the gradual end of feudalism and the advent of capitalism that would spread prosperity to the average person. So too did clock ownership increase. Every town needed one. Every large estate. It was a living symbol that humankind had improved its capacity to track the motion of time, for now history was in motion, creating events worth tracking.

By the 19th century, average people could gain access to material goods once reserved for the elites. Mirrors. Fancy clothing. Books. And clocks. In the United States, Connecticut became the center of production.

> In 1850 Connecticut clockmakers produced 511,000 clocks, with Bristol producing more than any other city in the state, making it the leading clock-producing center in the country. The increase in production spurred production of clock components including weights, bells, dials, painted tablets, and springs by small manufacturers. The presence of many small spring manufacturers in Central Connecticut today is an outgrowth of that phenomenon. Women often worked at home painting dials and tablets.

— www.ctexplored.org

Then came watches, as the inevitable stage in the inexorable trend toward the individuation of technology. First town, then community, then home, and then the wrist.

With electricity came increased accuracy and efficiency, but there was a cost: the absence of the mystical magic of that endlessly intriguing tick-tock sound that quietly reverberates through space and time.

I now recall it because my father's mother loved that sound. I now realize that this is why her home always felt to me as a child to be especially warm and comforting: she had a mechanical clock in every room. There was a mantle clock for the fireplace, a cuckoo clock for the dining room, a table clock for the living room, and a grandfather clock in the hallway that dominated them all.

I could barely sleep… or maybe I slept better than ever. I recall hearing a tremendous racket every hour, and waking to see my grandmother add another blanket to my bed. God how she loved me. How I loved her. The clocks gave me a sound to animate that love, an audible memory as powerful as perfume, so that when I just heard it again, I could recall her warm embrace, her smile, and those last days when she cried that her son, my father, had died before she had passed from this world to the next.

The forward motion of time, Kierkegaard called it, is something we intuit but don't fully understand. It is stable, or so we believe, no matter how often we hear Henri Bergson claim it is not. It roots us, gives us a sense of direction, allows us to track our progress, and draws attention to the thing we do not like to think about: the end of days. They will end. They did for my father, his mother, and they will for me.

And so what do we do with this thing we call time? We make the best of it. We make it matter. How much? As much as we can comprehend. The mechanical clock, by dividing the thing we call the second into two parts, tick and tock, allows us to discern that our life is limited, that we cannot waste it, that the clock will go on long after we too pass from this world.

All these truths are embedded in this wooden box that operates without our volition. And yet once per day we must stick that key in and turn it. Only then can we experience the magic. In the end, it happens only because we, with human hands, make it happen. So it is with the narrative of history itself, forever making itself available for us to control but never finally adapting to our liking.

This little box sat lonely on a chair, its face yellowed, its functionality neglected by every buyer, given life through the commercial exchange, and finally brought to our audible senses through a turn of the key. Both history and the future come to life.

61

Imagine a Clock that Doesn't Surveil You

Warning: this article continues with my clock obsession.

Our phones today are also clocks, plus dictionaries, health trackers, music devices, cameras, social tools, payment methods — and, apparently, the method by which we choose to be surveilled and politically manipulated. It's all rather remarkable, but hardly the first time in history when device mania swept the population. It's a luxury of being relatively rich, for every household or every person to acquire the things once limited to the elites.

In the eighteenth century, there were clocks in homes of the very rich, grandfather clocks that boomed the time all over the house to signal tea time and dinner and so on. Ah, to be a member of the leisure class! The clocks were extremely fancy. I was looking at originals just now at a high-end clock shop and they run about $17,000. It's hard to know where most people would even put them today.

What changed in the second half of the 19th century — when Karl Marx and the rest of the bitter crew was scribbling about how the masses were being oppressed by capitalism — is that clocks started getting smaller, cheaper, and more accurate. By the beginning of the 20th century, America distinguished itself for its industrial capacity to produce clocks that were within the budget of every person. At its height, the Connecticut clock industry alone employed 35,000 people.

The American clocks were gloriously practical, made of wood and springs, in contrast to the older European ones made of stone and operated with weights. It was classic American ingenuity at work, serving the common person.

One thing I was missing in this story of history was a practical reason for why every home had to have one. I get that gizmos are fun and telling time is awesome but why the urgency on the part of consumers to buy one to the point that a massive new industry sprung up in the course of a few decades?

I threw the question to the mighty owner of Classic Clocks of Atlanta. Bernie the owner has been in business for 40 years. His bookshelf is a comprehensive library on the history of clocks. He seems to know everything. He can tell the period, country, and year of any clock with a glance. He lives and breathes the history. He loves every tick, every chime. And he loves to talk about clocks — in other words, a classic merchant who made a viable business out of a personal obsession.

So I asked why so many people in the late 19th century felt the need for a clock. His answer came quickly and it is so obvious once you hear it. People left the farms where the rooster and moon told the time. The seasons were what you lived and breathed because it was your job. But now their children were moving to the city to work in factories. Factories had strict hours. You had to get up at strange times, and you had to go to bed at a particular time. Their lives were regulated with more precision, so they needed a precision instrument to tell them what to do when.

This is when the clock became indispensable.

This revelation blew my mind because it makes just so much sense. This was the period in which the majority of the population shifted from one form of production to a completely different one. Their lives changed. Their homes changed. The way they thought about time began to change.

In my previous essay, I spoke about the late Middle Ages and the birth of progress. This, I said, drove the demand for clocks. But we can see here that there is far more to the story. The appearance of the small mantle clock in the late 19th century signaled a dramatic change in people's aspirations. No more would the household clock be limited to the large form, resting in the large hallways in the entryways of the well-to-do leisure class. Now they belonged to everyone.

And sorry, Marx, but blessed capitalism is what made this possible. The story of our material progress is embedded in the tools that became available for the masses of people. The new system of prosperity spread wealth to everyone in ways that were inconceivable even a century ago. And that beautiful story today survives in these small shops in every city where you can see it all on display.

Yes, the workers could afford to purchase the products of their labors!

And listen to the stunning beauty of the tick tock and chime. It is like a living thing in your presence. It speaks with great profundity, the erudition achieved through wordless regularity. The new (but old) clocks now in the stone house at the American Institute for Economic Research have changed daily life there. Now many people can sit in the same room and not speak and still have a lovely voice filling up the room. It's brought a new calm and elegance to the conversation. Then at the top of the hour, the chime sounds and everyone stops to listen.

Why not just play music instead? There is a problem: no one agrees on music choices anymore. You can't play anything that is everyone's first choice. The conventional choice is silence. The best option is the sound of a mechanical clock, its clean beat with a melody that is left to your imagination. The sound also causes philosophical reflection on the nature of time and the meaning of its passage.

And you know the notifications that are blowing up on your phone every few minutes, tricking you into believing there is some fake news you have to know or that some stranger somewhere is texting you something important, so that you can never really engage in conversation with others around you? It's annoying beyond description, for everyone.

The notifications of these old clocks — the chime at the top and bottom of the house — mean something important but do not deceive or distract you. They are purely revelatory, not designed to manipulate you, sell you anything, to upset you.

I'm almost certain that our current notification obsessions with our smartphones are going to pass and we are going gradually to build up a certain etiquette surrounding them — same as people no longer talk loudly on their phones in public restaurants. But that will take some time. Meanwhile, the chime on these mechanical clocks is there to reveal to us the operation of a gentle, sonorous, and humane tracking of the passage of time.

You can shop for them locally or on eBay, and it's remarkable how well they still work. And think of it: none of them are in the personal surveillance business.

62

The Strange Economics of Mechanical-Clock Repair

You are strolling around a thrift store — op-shopping, as they call it in Australia — and happen upon a beautiful mechanical clock from the turn of the 20th century. So charming! Here it sits alone and unloved, begging to tick and chime again. It needs you so badly. (If you are confused why, read my past two tributes to mechanical clocks.)

The dealer is asking $40. It's a steal! You adopt it, get it home, and then discover a few problems. It ticks but not reliably. The chime is pretty, but the gears are noisy. It loses or gains 10 minutes per day.

No problem, right? There is a clock repair shop not far from here. They can probably fix this while I wait.

Time Preference

Here is where the confusion begins. You have entered into the strange world of clock repair, where you can wait up to two years before getting your clock back, and you have absolutely no assurance of how much you will pay. Could be $100. Could be $1,000. Somewhere in between those two numbers, you have the realization that you could have purchased a newly restored clock that is sitting right there at the repair shop for $350. And you could have taken it home that day.

The wait times are heartbreaking. It's not unusual. Based on conversations I've had with other clock repair places around the country, a wait time of eight months is considered short. Why do people go along, rather than buy a restored one off the shelf? I suspect it has to do with the sunk-cost fallacy: you are so proud that you paid so little for the used clock that you are irrationally willing to pay vast amounts to prove you got a good deal.

Regardless, time is money. Maybe you would rather pay double the amount to speed up delivery. We do this with shipping all the time. The laundry or tailor will get your clothes back to you in one day, but you are going to pay a premium. It's fine, so long as we know.

The price charged is a reflection of what economists call "time preference" — which in this context takes on all new meaning. Everyone prefers to realize his preferences sooner rather than later. The extent to which that is true for any particular individual can be rendered in terms that codify the cost you are willing to pay. This is the interest rate in financial markets.

In the market for repairing clocks, it could be reflected in the price: $5,000 for a one-day turnaround, but $500 for one year. So far as I can tell, this pricing model hasn't yet made it to this industry.

High Skills

To be sure, the consuming public is wildly confused about what the required skill level is for clock repair. There are whole schools devoted to this. The masters of the craft combine skills of the jeweler and the engineer in what is really an obsolete technology. So, yes, I can understand how one must be willing to pay to engage such skill.

I spoke with one such specialist at some length. He was positively maudlin about the disappearance of the craft. He said that the people who go to school to learn are typically retired. Once they learn, they sit at home and fix their own clocks but have no interest in the disciplined life of showing up to a repair shop daily. Why no apprentices? He says that he is too busy repairing clocks himself to spend time teaching someone else.

Still, he does worry that his is a dying art. What happens when he is gone?

Money and Motivation

He, like most people in this industry, assured me that he is not in it for the money. He is devoted to the skill as art and the preservation of these amazing innovations of the past.

That's a beautiful thought. Then again, that might be the very source of the problem. The skilled craftsmen are so focused on the realization of the dream that they haven't noticed the most obvious thing: these wait times are intolerable. They wouldn't be tolerated in any other industry: not cars, not sprinkler systems, not clothing, not medicine.

Somehow we have the equivalent of Soviet-style bread lines for clock repair, and no one seems particularly enthused about fixing it.

The economist in me believes the answer to the problem is simply to raise prices. This is how you ration a scarce good or service. This shifts the quantity demanded. Fewer people will get their clocks repaired, but that is precisely what is needed. Instead of paying for repairs, people will turn their attention to the refurbished models sold on the sales floor. Then at a higher level of profitability, more people will be incentivized to enter the industry and the market can eventually clear again so that clock repair becomes affordable again.

Now, obviously there is no legal restriction preventing this from happening. So why isn't it happening? It strikes me that we have an evolved skill set here in an industry with a single maladaptive but persistent trait. This trait amounts to what my colleague Max Gulker calls a "cultural price control." It is sustainable only because the industry is not competitive in the perfect sense you find in textbooks.

Then again, let's forget the textbook model and observe that markets are imperfect, especially highly specialized ones like this. They never work in real life the way they do on paper. This is especially true of an industry that is geographically diffuse, and will necessarily remain that way, simply because people will always choose the local clock mechanic over the distant one. And it does appear that most cities have one or two service providers at most.

In other words, we have a case of local monopoly here. What's surprising is that the monopoly power results not in high prices but rather in extremely long wait times. This is a choice that the providers make, in a manner consistent with their preferred trade-off of revenue vs. job stress. It's not up to the economists to wag a finger of disapproval here.

That said, my own sense is that the industry could use a bit of commercial derring-do. Chelsea Clock, Clockworks, and Master Clock Repair seem to be moving in this direction. The limitation of all these services is that they require something of the owner. You need to submit a detailed request for an estimate, be prepared to disassemble the clock yourself, ship it off to them, and so on. It goes without saying that there are no house calls!

There is a lesson here. Even the freest market — I can't think of any regulatory restriction on these institutions — will be academically imperfect simply because we live in a world of information asymmetries, high transaction costs, and geographical limitation.

The liberal order never promised a fully stress-free world that makes every dream come true instantly. What we have instead is the best-possible world of the moment that is always trending toward improvement, provided the consumer demand and capital and labor resources are there to make it happen.

The lesson is revealed in the audible tick of these remarkable little machines, each tick and each chime uniquely different from the previous one because it exists in a different moment in time that the machine itself is dedicated to chronicling in the service of human life itself.

Blessed are the makers of clocks and those who repair them.

63

Five Reasons the Future Isn't Here Yet

Every conference on tech these days features confident talk of the future. Everything is going to change and the results will be amazing! I've given a fair share of talks like this, mostly focussed on distributed ledgers and their potential to disrupt the status quo in money, contracts, and investment.

Today's fashion for futurism probably compares to the 1893 World's Fair that shaped popular culture. Then as now, the question is: why is the future not here yet? We have the technology. It is deployed in a limited way. It mostly seems to work. It seems intuitively obvious that it is better. Under these conditions, it seems like the future should be now.

The most obvious case in point is cryptocurrency. It works today. How long do we have to wait for it to be widely in use?

Horses and Tractors

Here is a fictional story from the past based on the real American farming experience. The year is 1910 and a family farm is in full operation. It's been in the family for three generations. The young son comes to his father and suggests that they upgrade from horses to a new gas-powered tractor, which was becoming commercially available in a way that was affordable.

The father finds the idea ridiculous. They have so much invested in horses. A tractor is too expensive. If it breaks, no one knows how to fix it. The job is getting done now. There is no compelling reason to change.

The father sends the son away with the wave of his hand. Was he foolish? My argument is no. He knew that the time had not yet arrived.

I've experienced something similar in my own lifetime. The first time I heard about email, it wasn't obvious to me that it would be better than a direct connection through the modem. How would the person know to login and get a message? There aren't many people who have accounts so what would be the point? It's expensive for this service whereas my phone and modem are already paid for.

Maybe someday I would find a use case but not yet. I sent away the promoter with a wave of my hand (and later learned to get humble about these things).

Which brings us to the five reasons why the future, even if it is known, is not yet now.

#1 Current technology works. Technology is not an end in itself and there is no good reason for anyone to use any of the practical arts unless there is a task to accomplish that cannot be realized through current tools. If the job is being done with some reasonable degree of efficiency, switching is more costly than continuing with the status quo. Think about this with regard to cryptocurrency. Credit cards and banks work just fine right now. Yes, the improved product offers advances (cheaper, faster, more secure) and though these are all good things, there are still plenty of problems that make existing solutions more economically rational for the vast majority of people. Of course that could change. A currency crisis, a bank holiday, or mass identity theft could shift the calculation dramatically. These could all make the future hurry up and get here sooner.

#2 Future technology is too buggy. Remember how the farmer said that there was no one to fix the technology if it should break? Exactly. Things break. Sometimes it makes sense to wait for the second, third, and fourth generation before you adopt because developers learn from mistakes. A technology recruits people unto its ranks to fix and repair. New companies come along that specialize in replacement parts (think about the screen protector on your smartphone). But all of this takes time.

When to adopt is a rational calculation and different people have different levels of hunger for new things. Installing electric indoor lighting in 1890 was possible and affordable for many but only a few were ready to pay and take the risk of seeing their house go up in flames. Oil lamps persisted for many decades. Similarly, some people bought the iPhone 1. Others waited until iPhone 4. This gradual adoption allows developers, producers, repair infrastructure, and replacement parts to come online.

#3 Talent pool for implementation too limited. I had a friend tell me last week that the perfect use case for blockchain technology is the electrical system in Puerto Rico. Maybe he is right. But I can also think of another one thousand similar use cases. There is titling, health care, food and restaurants, contracts, credit, transportation, auction houses, and more, not only in one country but in every country. It would not be economically efficient for 10% of the labor force to leave their current positions to become blockchain codeslingers. Right now, everyone I know who can code in this industry is extremely busy and very well paid. This will gradually attract more programmers into this industry. But every retooling of labor resources has an opportunity cost. It's not always worth it.

#4 New technology must build on old. Legacy technology is currently in use. Technology must be woven into the existing fabric. It is never adopted in whole. For example, anyone today can build a website from scratch but it is much harder to take an existing website and build within it and from it to refresh its functioning. Most new technologies are designed for the perfect use case. There is no such thing. This is why there are so many "concept cars" that you never see on the road. In real life, new technology comes about gradually, feature by feature, as small problems are solved, success is realized, and the benefits of more radical restructuring become more obvious.

#5 Economics takes time. It's not always about risk aversion, network effects, bugs, and the workability of legacy systems. There is the plain fact of economics that all resources — land, labor, and material — must be apportioned in a way that is rational and socially optimal. Only a central planner pretends to know how things should be allocated and he or she is always wrong. You need the gradual unfolding of the market process to test new ways through trial and error. How are these tests graded? Through the system of profit and loss. The best and coolest technology that produces nonstop losses is clearly not ready to be implemented. There is a time and place for all things. It's not always now.

The interactions and feedback loops between invention, implementation, and full-on adoption is a fascinating process to watch. It can't be gamed. It relies on something no one can control: the price system, human choice, resource tradeoffs, and case-by-case circumstances of time and place.

Thinking back on my initial doubts about email, it took nearly 20 years for email to become a universal part of life. To be sure, the digital age has speeded up the process but we all know people who continue to be seriously alarmed at the pace of digital life. They look at an app store and nearly have a meltdown.

Meanwhile, I'm meeting young people today who can't even imagine life before cryptocurrency was an investment tool. Thus goes the unfolding of history. If you feel rushed these days, don't be intimidated by it. Let the risk takers subsidize the risk averse. Eventually, if a technology is truly worth having around to replace the old, it will come to you, and you will love it.

Money

64

Government Cannot Be Trusted with Control of Money

Immediately following his inauguration in 1933, President Franklin D. Roosevelt focussed on what his advisers told him was the real problem: the fall in the prices of everything. The theory, which is completely wrong, is that falling prices were causing the fall in productivity. They believed that by boosting the prices of stocks and other financials, in addition to commodities, profits and wages would rise and recovery would dawn. They would achieve this by wrecking the dollar.

It's a classic case of what bad theory can do. It produces terrible policy that makes matters worse rather than better. Wages needed to fall. Markets needed to clear. Institutions holding bad assets needed to pay the price. The price system needed to speak the truth, not be manipulated into telling more lies. At that very time, all of Washington became dedicated to the opposite.

Three Blows

FDR undertook three dramatic monetary moves. First, he shut the banks. With this action, he told all customers that the money in those buildings belongs to government and not the people. He wanted to boost confidence but the result was the opposite: people would not trust the banks again for a generation.

The second action was executive order 6102. This did what would have been unthinkable a few years earlier. It forbade the private holding of gold money. It demanded that people who had gold turn it in and get "lawful money" in return. A banking act passed by Congress the previous month had done the same but with this order came the teeth: a fine of $10,000 ($200,000 in today's terms) or ten years in prison. It was enforced. There were dozens of prosecutions.

It seems amazing in retrospect that government (in the land of the free) would ever engage in such an outrageously tyrannical act of seizing the physical assets that served as the foundation of the money system. It would not be legal to own gold as money until 1975.

The third action in 1933 was the devaluation of the dollar itself, from 1/20 a gold ounce to 1/30. The redefinition amounted to an instant 41% tax on dollars. Thus did this administration seek to wreck the money at the very time when monetary soundness was essential to recovery. Behind it all, again, was bad theory, the belief that falling prices were causing the depression rather than the reverse.

The Resistance Born

It was at this moment that Col. E.C. Harwood, then teaching at MIT, decided that he must speak out and he must do so from an institution that would be independent of both government and academia. He founded the American Institute for Economic Research in 1933. Its very first publication (1934) was "What Will Devaluation Mean to You?"

"Devaluation, or clipping the coinage, as the process was called in the days of the Robber Kings, is a subtle form of taxation," he wrote. "Like most other taxes, those imposed by this insidious method will be borne by the Forgotten Man…. The effects of devaluation upon the Forgotten Man, who is the warp and woof of our civilization, are of vital significance. He has a right to know what these things mean."

The monograph went on to make an entirely reasonable prediction. He expected prices to rise and rise, thus making everyone even worse off. He urged all Americans to take every precaution against this through massive thrift and personal protection of property.

It's pretty awesome to think of the risks that AIER was taking at the time with such advice. Washington was basically waging war on the public (invoking even wartime statutes from 1917 to do so). AIER and Harwood did not sign up. In fact, they became the resistance.

Failed Inflation

When you read the original document, you might also be struck that the prediction of inflation turned out to be imprecise. Prices did stabilize but the much-feared inflation never actually happened. Why was this? Both banks and the public became hugely risk averse, and this caused a collapse in money velocity after 1930 and following. The process of inflation under a central bank requires the cooperation of the industry and depositors. So, yes, "all else equal," the inflation would have happened, but the crisis environment dramatically changed public and business psychology.

Instead of a puffed-up recovery, what actually happened was the creation of a lost decade of prosperity, ending in war and all-round wartime economic planning complete with production mandates, price controls, the draft, and wage controls. It turned out that the economy didn't really recover from the Great Depression until the end of World War Two.

Later in 1934, Harwood and his associates noted this behavior and predicted correctly that the new savings (hoarding) would form the basis of economic recovery as soon as Washington stopped its interventions in wages, prices, and production. He was exactly correct about this.

1930 and 2008

This all might sound familiar to you if you lived through the 2008 financial crisis. The Treasury, the Fed, and two presidential administrations set out to manufacture a big monetary inflation, based on the belief that rising real estate prices and financials would restore confidence and economic growth. It didn't happen. What we saw instead was a huge fall in money velocity, new caution in lending, and a rise in savings — all of which conspired to keep inflation at bay. But just as in the 1930s, the result was to prolong the downturn for a full decade.

(By the way, if you are curious about the relationship of prices and money velocity, you would enjoy this great paper: "Money and Velocity During Financial Crises: From the Great Depression to the Great Recession" by Richard G. Anderson, Michael Bordo, and John V. Duca. The parallels between the two periods are striking.)

In both cases, policy set out to manufacture a huge inflation as a way of fixing the problem. In neither case did the policy achieve its aims. The reason was the same in both: risk aversion led depositors to hoarding-style behavior and banks to pull back lending, thus changing the relationship of money supply and demand. The widespread predictions of hyperinflation (I made one myself in 2009) turned out to be wrong. It's a great lesson in humility here, both on the part of government and those who would presume perfectly to predict economic outcomes of government policy.

Wall Between Money and State

It's glorious to live in times when we are seeing the gradual emergence of a new and competitive money system, rooted in private provision and management, and trending toward disintermediation. Cryptocurrency is capable of smashing the traditional government monopoly over time, and providing the ultimate protection against confiscatory government policy. FDR was able to confiscate gold and devalue the dollar because he was the head of a money cartel. Break the money and banking cartel and you go a long way to ending the greatest threat to prosperity we face.

It is for this reason, and in light of this long and grim history, that every fan of technology, Bitcoin, blockchain, and cryptoassets generally should fight against every form of government regulation, management, or involvement in this sector, and favor a rollback of every intervention thus far. It is no different now from 1933. Government cannot be trusted with the slightest ownership stake in money. It never ends well.

65

Blockchain Works Like
Money in Yap

I've sensed for some time that people tend to exaggerate the newness of cryptocurrency, as if it were a technology never before imagined or experienced, meeting needs that were heretofore never felt.

This is not true.

For so long as humanity has existed, there has been a need to have some method of knowing of and/or documenting ownership claims. You can hold your property (that you claim is yours) and defend it against invaders. Or you can go one better and develop a social consensus technology to record who owns what. This improves life for you and everyone.

This documentation can take place on stones, clay, papyrus, parchment, vellum, or databases. The problem with all of these methods is the same: centralization. If there is only one record and one record keeper, there is always uncertainty over fraud, manipulation, or decay in the record itself.

This is where blockchain technology provides a remarkable innovation. Ownership claims live on a ledger in the cloud. Rights are moved by proof of work and proof of authority. When the ledger is changed, everyone can observe the results. Algorithms rather than human discretion drive the system, thus eliminating the possibility of ambiguity and fraud.

This is a technical innovation. But it is not an innovation in how we aspire to live. There is a big difference. The blockchain allows people to achieve something we have always wanted to do but haven't been able to do until now.

If that is true, can we find other historical examples of blockchain-like technology? A new paper published by the Federal Reserve claims to have found one. It comes from the island of Yap, a tiny place among the Caroline Islands of Micronesia.

As I was reading about this place and its people, I kept thinking (forgive me) of the movie Moana and the struggles of these island people. The Disney movie didn't feature any money in the community; for all we knew the people live in a happy communism of some sort. I knew there had to be something wrong. Everyone needs property rights. Everyone needs money. Everyone needs a way to keep track of who owns what.

It turns out that the island of Yap provides an amazing example of blockchain technology…of sorts. The authors of the Fed paper state that the monetary system of Yap relies on a form of this very thing. And this has been true for thousands of years, and remains true today. It is known the world over as the Island of Stone Money.

The great Milton Friedman took an intense interest in the monetary system of Yap and even wrote a full paper on the topic.

The monetary base is called the Rai. It is a huge rock made of limestone. These rocks come from 400 miles away and are extremely difficult to transport. Over the centuries the people of the island learned to make them in the shape of donuts to make them easier to move. If you want "proof of work," here it is!

But if these rare objects serve as money, how is trade conducted? This is where it gets extremely interesting. They do not move physical stones. All stones stay where they are. They are revered and protected. What changes hands is an understanding of who owns what. You bargain with others and communicate the results.

All reports say that there are about 5,000 people on the island with a stable population. The people involved in trading with money are a small minority. The key here is everyone with a stake in the system shares information about changes and truly remembers how rights in the stones are allocated. Apparently, at some point in history, marks were made on the stones but once the system grew to a certain level of sophistication, this was no longer necessary.

This knowledge persists and lives throughout the community. You can call it a blockchain of the mind. If all of this sounds crazy, remember that such "primitive" communities can exhibit a ridiculously high level of intelligence in ways that people of the "developed" world cannot even imagine. That everyone can share knowledge of ownership rights in a particular kind of money, with full clearing and no counterparty risk, requires a high level of trust. The people of this island evidently have exactly that.

I appreciate this example because it illustrates that while blockchain is new technology, it solves a universal human problem. In this sense, it is like every great innovation in history. We've always wanted to communicate, travel, light our rooms with a switch, fly through the air, stay warm in winter, and so on.

Railroads, electricity, flight, and indoor temperature control did not create new needs; they solved old ones.

It is the same with blockchain. That we have a glimpse of a more secure way of changing and tracking ownership rights, making deals possible, facilitating trade and other forms of human engagement, is mighty impressive. This technology exists. Nothing government can do to regulate it is going to cause it to un-exist. Our lives will be disintermediated and different. We will love the results.

Maybe someday we too can be as "primitive" as life on the island of Yap.

66

Why Do We Need So Many Monies?

S o many aspects of our newly competitive world of money defy prediction. For example, we wake this morning to observe that Bitcoin's market dominance of the cryptoasset sector has fallen to 37%, from 90% five years ago. The great monopoly breaker itself has become subjected to some serious competition from other assets that use the same technology but offer different features. (The data set I'm using is skewed by the inclusion of Ripple, which has more in common with traditional payment systems than cryptocurrencies.)

The sector is becoming more diversified and rivalrous. King Bitcoin is facing a challenge the same way it pioneered as a competitor to national monies.

As for the alternatives, it's been difficult to know ahead of time which of the tokens will take on a life of their own and which will fail. You might think that a community that has watched Bitcoin go from zero value to a high of $20,000 in nine years of existence would realize that no outside observer can know all, much less dictate outcomes.

Humility in this space comes at a premium. Still, when the August 2017 fork took place that created Bitcoin Cash (BCH) with a larger block size, the howling and screaming didn't stop for months.

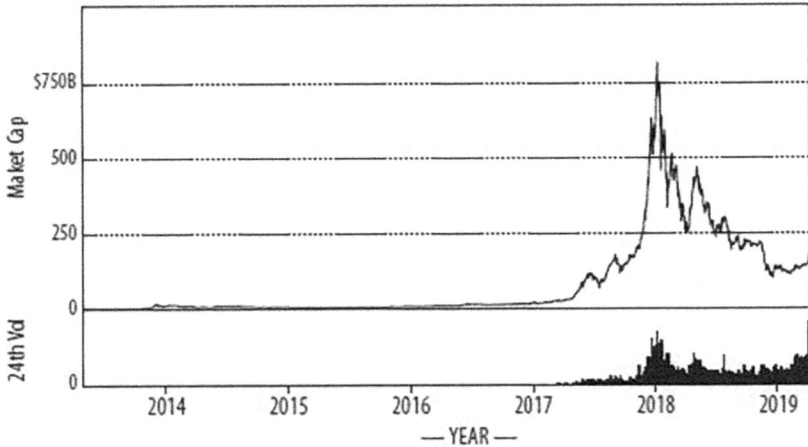

Total Market Capitalization Apr 28, 2013 to Apr 6, 2019

Source: CoinMarketCap.com

At some point, I sent a single tweeted suggestion that BCH might end up as a viable competitor to Bitcoin simply because Bitcoin had become so expensive to send and slow to transact. To me, this was no different from venturing a prediction about whether Coke or Pepsi would prevail in the market. Wrong. I can't recall ever having been hit by so much vitriol as this one tweet elicited. Not even at the height of the political campaign had I seen such mania. It was like stepping in the largest red-ant hill on the playground.

And yet look today: BCH has been adopted in the wallets within most major exchanges. It is a preferred sending and receiving method among many people because it recalls the old days of Bitcoin, when fast and cheap were supposed to be main selling points of cryptocurrency over national money. You can have all the technical discussions you want over block-size limits. You can decry user behavior. You can denounce the exchange ratio. You can call anything you loathe a pump and dump. But what you cannot do is dictate or determine market outcomes with your biases.

Why So Many Deodorants?

A few years ago, Bernie Sanders uttered a passing comment that elicited howls of laughter among believers in competitive markets. "You don't necessarily need a choice of 23 underarm spray deodorants or of 18 different pairs of sneakers when children are hungry in this country," he said.

Rather than merely laughing at the statement, however, let's consider the seriousness of what he was saying. It's not automatically crazy. We know what deodorant is supposed to do: stop sweat and stink in a particular area of the body. We know what sneakers are supposed to do: protect the foot from external stress. Why, precisely, are there so many brands? You could say because we all want different scents and styles, and that's true, but that doesn't cover all the options. Maybe these products are the same in all essentials.

The intuition, then, is not entirely crazy. Why don't consumers find the one brand that best fulfills the function at the best price and just make that the dominant one?

Why do we need this endless churning and upheaval and choice? Isn't this endless competition between similar products socially wasteful?

This has been the case against competition for centuries. The perception is that it is basically inefficient. If we could magically take all the resources that go into getting people to switch from one brand to another, we could produce more of the canonical brand and save consumers and producers money. That's not an intellectually preposterous idea.

For many decades, socialist central planners were persuaded by this kind of thinking. In a typical socialist grocery store in the old days, there was only one choice and they were named literally and without hype: beans, rice, coffee, sardines, bread, and so on. This was especially true with produce: tomatoes, bananas, and beets. Look at the efficiency! Look at the savings!

Why One Money?

You could say the same thing about money. We know what money is and does. Once we have it, we shouldn't change it. We only need the dollar. We only need the Euro. We only need one cryptocurrency. Or perhaps we need to centrally plan who needs to use what currency, discerning through the magic of econometrics what constitutes an optimal currency area.

It's true that we have now competition between existing national monies that operate within a defined government jurisdiction. What we do not have (for the most part) is competition between licit currencies within a country. Most Americans have never even considered money to be anything but the dollar. In other countries, the national money does compete with the dollar but mostly only in gray markets.

I can recall visiting Nicaragua at the height of socialist planning and encountering a huge black market for exchange rates between the national currency and the dollar. Kids as young as 12 were out on the streets making deals. They knew that tourists could get from them a better exchange rate than government exchanges. Tourists (even the socialist ones) love it. The math skills of these "child peasants" were better than most American college students.

But what about full-blown competition between currencies within countries? That is something that has been ruled out within all living memory. We've had socialism and monopoly provision for at least a century following the introduction of central banking.

Competition We Need

So let's just explore some benefits that come from real competition in monetary units and services. The case is the same as it is for competition in every other good or service.

To have no barriers to entry invites many producers to compete for consumers' affections. Rivals offer different features at different prices and invite the public to decide. This entails price reductions and quality improvements. This reduces producer profits over time but it also inspires innovation since any producer who can do better than the dominant player can win a higher rate of return and expand.

We can easily see this with, for example, pop stars. We need Taylor Swift, Mariah Carey, Justin Bieber, and Shawn Mendes, along with countless others, because each meets a different need, they learn from others, they get ever better through experimentation, and the process of competition here drives progress. There is also a healthy democratic element at work: which product, person, or service provider becomes dominant truly is the people's choice.

We do not know precisely what "pop music" is in its archetypal form, certainly not enough to codify it and legislate it. We understand that we need an unending process of discovery and creativity because it is music. But the same applies to every service or product. There is always a better way to mow your lawn, vacuum your carpet, or dry clean your clothes. There is always a better and cheaper coffee, mattress, or mouse trap.

A Better Money

And there's always a better way to do money. Realizing this is perhaps the greatest intellectual contribution that Bitcoin has made to the world. It has shown us new possibilities that most people — to say nothing of monetary economists — had not thought about. The usual historical trajectory of money starts with stones, shells, pelts. It moves to precious metals. Then it culminates in fiat paper managed by the central bank. Surely we have seen the best, the apotheosis of monetary perfection.

Bitcoin came along with some new propositions. How about a money and payment system in a single package? How about we get really strict about ownership claims and make these public, and enforce them not by trust but by proof? How about the system regulates the rate of creation of new units according to a public protocol rather than relying on the discretion of industry-connected insiders? How about a system of storage that is controlled by owners rather than third parties?

Ten years ago, most of this would have seemed impossible but now we know that it is not. We've come to realize that money as a technology should be listed among the practical arts, something to be improved and evolved through a market-based process of competition and entrepreneurship.

Among many huge problems with fiat-money central banking is that it stops the process of discovering new and better ways. It presumes that we know all we need to know. You could say the same about those who think there ought to be only one cryptocurrency and it should be Bitcoin. We can't actually say this. CoinMarketCap lists 1,372 cryptocurrencies. You can add a couple of zeros there and approximate how many exist today.

They offer different features, mining methods, and levels of privacy. Some are purely brands. There is nothing wrong with that. How many should there be? That is not for any intellectual much less central planner to decide. That is for the market to decide, same as with deodorant and shoes. At last we see that money is a product and a service that need never stop evolving to better serve human needs.

67

Crypto vs. Fiat: The Battle Is On

Y ou might be living in a time in which you will experience the end of central banking and perhaps even fiat currency, and their replacement by a completely new system.

Venezuela is a paradigmatic case. The official currency is the Bolivar, and it is in a permanent state of 4-digit hyperinflation. The government did this by printing endless money to try to make socialism work. The only result was to throw the entire country into poverty, chaos, and ruin. It is really difficult to create such a calamity in a once-prosperous and once-peaceful country but a regime that swears to implement socialism can actually achieve that. It's the only thing that socialism has ever achieved.

But my concern here is the destruction of the money. I'm thrilled to have received a first-hand report from my new friends at MonkeyCoin in Venezuela. They are on the leading edge of providing people in highly troubled economies a way to make, manage, and transport value, using cryptocurrency as the means. Without it, Venezuelans would have few hopes for surviving the incredible mess the government has made.

Two years ago, Bitcoin began really to catch on in the country but in 2017, Bitcoin's popularity bumped into a serious scaling problem that made it too expensive and too slow for hand-to-hand use. As a result, the country has become a major hub for alternatives. The most popular is Smartcoin but there are many competitors. The crypto community is thriving as never before.

All these currencies are actively acquired and traded as an alternative to government fiat, in exactly the way that Satoshi's White Paper originally envisioned it would happen. Crypto is money without counterparty risk because the payment system — final payment, not trust relationships — is embedded within the protocol of the money itself. Everyone can have access. Sending and receiving is cheap and fast. You don't need intermediation.

Keep in mind that addressing the problem of financial and banking crisis was a major reason for the invention of Bitcoin in the first place. While big bankers and ruling-class big shots in the United States called cryptos names like frauds and ponzis, regular people in Venezuela (and many other parts of the world) are using cryptocurrency as a way of protecting themselves from despotism and destitution.

What's fascinating is how the process has unfolded. Hard and soft forks aren't just for cryptos. There has been a hard fork in the way the government's fiat currency is traded. Digital versions of the Bolivar trade at a far lower rate than the hard version. If you have paper Bolivars, you can trade them at 3 to 1 for digital Bolivars, using the digital versions to pay bills, taxes, and so on. There is a thriving business involved in arbitraging between the two forks.

How is the government responding? It is pretty much bailing from the main currency and plotting to issue its own cryptocurrency called the Petro. It is structured as an authentic crypto, same as Bitcoin, but backed by oil, gas, gold, and diamond reserves. The presale of the token begins very soon, and it will trade on the usual crypto exchanges. The hope of the government is that this crypto will bypass the conventional banking channels and be censorship-resistant same as other tokens in this space.

There is some incredible irony here: a socialist government using a mega-capitalist, high-tech tool to save its economy from sanctions and its own bad economic policy. Will it work? My guess is that it will work for some people, namely the government and its connected interests. Everyone else in the country will continue to migrate savings and hand-to-hand trades away from fiat currency and toward this new form of hard money. But this won't be the Petro. It will be SmartCash, Bitcoin Cash, Dash, Monero, and so on. The Petro will be for official business.

This is the future of Venezuela but what about the other hundreds of currencies and central banks? They could go the same way but perhaps with less drama. This is nothing to regret.

F.A. Hayek spent a lifetime working for reform of the government's monetary system. At some point, he realized that reform needs to be more fundamental. In a 1984 interview, he presented the unvarnished truth. "I don't believe we shall ever have a good money again before we take the thing out of the hands of government," he said. Not reform, not a new system by and for government, but a completely market-based system.

These days, government seems to be doing its best to make this happen. This is because, at long last, at the same time central banking is failing as a model, we finally have a technology that can break up the government's monopoly on money. It takes many forms and it is still highly experimental but it is beating what government is providing. People now have options. Currency competition is actually working, and it is driving government provision of money into the ground.

The point of government monetary institutions is to exercise monopoly power. There is to be one national or regional currency, one legal tender. All money-based trades flow through the banking system, which provides final clearing for all transactions. The central bank is the regular and primary guarantor of the system. From there, experts conduct "monetary policy."

This system depends on being the sole provider of these services. Crypto and blockchain clearing do not need to actually displace the government's system. It only needs to become a viable competitor. Then the cartel is smashed and the monopoly is ended. This realization is precisely why so many voices associated with official institutions are warning about what's coming. They warn but they do not know what to do about it.

Here is why the Venezuela case is instructive. The end of the government money monopoly will result in some highly strange goings on: currency competition, forks in the fiat, a loss of the power over monetary policy, a possible abandonment of fiat in favor of a government-backed crypto, the end of monetary policy as a tool of politicians, a migration of many institutions from government money to private money, and the gradual depreciation and obsolescence of old-style monies to new forms.

The fiat money system has been fragile for a very long time. Indeed, it has been held together with tape and gum since its inception. The difference between our times and times past is that we now have an alternative, one uniquely suited to the digital age. We now have a way out, a path toward our eventual monetary emancipation.

68

How Cryptomining Could Change Internet Economics

There is no shortage of alarmism over the rising costs of mining cryptoassets, most famously Bitcoin but also thousands of others. But there is another way of looking at the problem: mining could provide the answer to rising problems in Internet economics, social media, and the commodification of information toward actual profitability. The height of ironies, one of the world's leading "progressive" (i.e. left-wing) websites is pioneering the new direction.

But let's begin at the problem that isn't. A typical case is a recent article in the New York Times: "Is Bitcoin A Waste of Electricity, or Something Worse?." That's a heck of a way to set up a news article! It's like "Is Bob torturing or actually killing his cat?" You are left with the distinct impression that, regardless, Bob is doing something very wrong. So it is the NYT's coverage of cryptomining. It would appear that there is absolutely no redeeming value to mining for cryptocurrency. It serves no positive purpose at all.

The article quotes the former head of research at the New York Fed. "It appears that much of our evolving digital infrastructure is devoted to activities, like the proliferation of cybercoins, that are worse than frivolous."

Why Mine?

The elevator response is as follows. Computers run the blockchain, the distributed ledger that is the real source of value. Mining is a metaphor. What this computer power is actually doing is confirming transactions. The CPU power used for this is effectively purchased by the protocol by granting ownership to new tokens. The creation of new tokens takes place on a strict schedule. The allocations need to adapt based on how many nodes are working the system.

The difficulty level of the mining algorithms has to increase to allocate new ownership rights. All of which is to say, the power used to mine — and the growing amounts of it — are absolutely essential to making the system work.

Our friend at the Fed seems oblivious to this. What I find interesting is how all this kvetching about the costs of mining is a blast from the past. The classic criticism against the gold standard is that it was too costly. Why are these guys wasting resources to suit up, dig into mountains, desperately seeking a finite resource, and slogging the results all the way to the Treasury Department?

This is all just silly, said the critics. We know how to make money: you print it. It's far cheaper to print than mine. A paper standard will save a tremendous amount of resources that can go to other purposes.

There is a plausibility to the claim. We do know how to make money substitutes that appear to work just as well as what we used to call money. The costs of mining operations are huge and discovering new deposits has to be funded. It involves speculation and drains financial and time resources, all to find the thing we already know how to make (more or less) with paper and ink.

Keynes Contra Gold

J.M. Keynes agreed with the critics of the gold standard. He wrote a monograph in 1923 ("A Tract on Monetary Reform") that condemned governments for depreciating currency, warned of monetary instability after the war, and then…dropped a bomb at the close of the book. He said that the gold standard is too inflexible for modern times. It has to go. Indeed it is a "barbarous relic" that should be replaced by a money wholly managed by the central bank.

Thousands of economists for decades followed Keynes's view, each of which imagines himself to be the central bank chief, ready to impose his own vision of what monetary power can accomplish.

Gold belongs to the past, not to an age of scientific central planning, or so went the refrain. The old-fashioned gold standard, with its limits and discipline and self-managing logic, just has to be destroyed. And so it was, for many decades, until 1971 when all that was left of it was demolished.

Digital Gold

There is a reason that Bitcoin is being called Digital Gold. It was structured to operate the same way as the classical gold standard minus the sponsorship of government. It requires no centralized management. You have to expend resources to become the first owner of the initial resource. There is a finite supply of the specie payment. Payments are finally settled when made. Bitcoin is the gold standard ported over to the digital age.

In gold mining, as the price of the metal rises, the inspiration for finding and mining more deposits rises, along with the profits of the mining industry itself. It is just the same in Bitcoin. During the mad runup in price of 2017, miner revenue went through the roof. It has settled back down again with the price drop from December 2017.

Now we are seeing the same argument against the gold Standard used against Bitcoin. It is said to be wasting massive energy. "The amount of energy used by computers 'mining' bitcoin so far this year is greater than the annual usage of almost 160 countries," says the Business Insider.

Salon rails against the trend:

> But what they might not have accounted for is how much of an energy suck the computer network behind bitcoin could one day become. Simply put, Bitcoin is slowing the effort to achieve a rapid transition away from fossil fuels. What's more, this is just the beginning. Given its rapidly growing climate footprint, bitcoin is a malignant development, and it's getting worse.

At current prices, mining is worth it, perhaps not for individuals but for whole mining pools. But what about the social and environmental costs? This is what concerns Salon.

Worth the Cost

To search for an answer, let's revisit the case of the costs of the gold standard. In 1983, Roger Garrison wrote an article on the topic. He points out that all costs are really opportunity costs: the thing you give up in order to get what you want. The gold standard is rightly contrasted with the paper standard that replaced it. What are the costs of the paper standard? This is a fair question if we are going to assess whether the gold standard is somehow worth it.

The alleged price-adjustment costs of a gold standard are identified by comparing the gold standard as it actually operates with a paper standard as it ideally operates. Such comparisons never provide a sound basis for choosing between alternative institutional arrangements. The comparison assumes away all the relevant costs of a paper standard. If paper standards were administered by angelic monetary authorities whose sole objective was to minimize money-induced disequilibrium, the choice between a gold standard and a paper standard would be much less consequential than it actually is. But actual paper standards have price-adjustment costs too. And as history teaches, the magnitude and costliness of upward price adjustments under a paper standard dwarf the magnitude and costliness of downward price adjustments under a gold standard.

Moreover:

> The true costs of the paper standard would have to take into account (1) the costs imposed on society by different political factions in their attempts to gain control of the printing press, (2) the costs imposed by special-interest groups in their attempts to persuade the controller of the printing press to misuse its authority (print more money) for the benefit of the special interests, (3) the costs in the form of inflation-induced mis-allocations of resources that occur throughout the economy as a result of the monetary authority succumbing to the political pressures of the special interests, and (4) the costs incurred by businessmen in their attempts to predict what the monetary authority will do in the future and to hedge against likely, but uncertain, consequences of monetary irresponsibility.

So the costs of the paper standard include the inflation risk, political opportunism, the explosion of government debt, the vast expansion of government power, the building of cartelized money and financial institutions, the politicization of money, the destruction of savings and investment (in light of zero-percent interest rates) and the rise of endless boom-bust cycles.

The experience with Bitcoin underscores other costs. Bitcoin works on a trustless basis that ideally requires no established credit or identity. That makes Bitcoin far more inclusive of unbanked populations. There is zero chance for identity fraud. There is no chance of someone acting like you to spend your money. To prevent this for national money and existing payment systems, the banking industry spends as much as $11 billion, which is five cents on every one hundred dollars spent.

Payment Systems

Even then, the fiat system is a disaster for your personal finances. You spend your money in an unusual way, you are nearly guaranteed to get a pushback from your credit card company. Even then, every few years, your cards are declared stolen and you have to get a new one and change the numbers on every online merchant website. If you have done this for 10 or 15 years, there is a huge paper trail of defunct credit cards on your websites.

In addition to payment-systems problems, there are the problems of the nationalized money system, which is so loose and confusing that no one knows for sure if we are in a boom or a bust or something in between or both.

The uncertainty of Fed policy has reached epic proportions, and makes the confidence expressed by Keynes seem laughable in retrospect.

Also, that mining Bitcoin is costly is not some arbitrary imposition. It's a fallacy to believe that the electrical costs are a waste. There is work to do to confirm transactions and operate the protocol. This will be true until someone can come up with some other system.

Put it all together, the gargantuan costs of the nationalized paper-money system, and compare it to the updated version of the gold standard, which is cryptocurrency, and the costs of mining Bitcoin don't seem so high after all. The acquisition of any resource worth having involves a cost. Paper money is nearly costless to produce, and destroyed so much for so many centuries. All the complaints about the costs of Bitcoin mining should be considered in that light.

Mining Is an Opportunity

How can mining be used as an opportunity for a website to earn money as a replacement for ad revenue? You might think it would be a free-market website that would first experiment with this. Incredibly, the pioneer here is…Salon, the very website quoted above. Rather than fighting mining, they have figured out how to use it to their advantage.

The trick goes like this. The site gains revenue from ads but ad blockers have hurt the stream. If the site detects that you are using ad blocker software, it prompts you to turn it off. But then it gives you another option. You can volunteer some of your CPU power to help them engage in crypto mining!

And what are they mining? A coin called Monero. It is doing very well actually. It has a $5.8 billion market cap. It was once associated with dark markets due to its anonymizing properties but it is going more mainstream now. It turns out to be very profitable to mine. Salon gets a portion of the revenue. I find myself in awe of the ingenuity here. Once you state the idea, it is obvious, like all brilliant ideas.

What if other sites did this? What if this strategy points the way toward flipping the economics of website use, from ad-driven to use-controlled? What if users become real partners with websites for content creation and consumption? Right now, news is getting ever harder to access, with more and more sites installing paywalls. It is starting to get frustrating. By having users volunteer the CPU power to mining, websites could find that they will earn more from mining than from subscriptions or ads. This could change everything.

Do you see what is happening here? Everyone says that crypto mining is a terrible waste. It might turn out to be the very thing to save the Internet. We just need the process of creativity to kick in to show us new ways that we aren't currently thinking about. The market needs to reveal to us new truths.

The criticism of the gold standard was entirely misguided. Abolishing it led to astonishing levels of debt, government growth, depression and recession, war, and loss of freedom. Let's please not go the same way with cryptocurrency. It is a beautiful innovation. Everything wonderful in life comes at a cost. The key is to turn the cost into opportunity.

I never thought I would say this but Salon is pointing the way.

69

Private Enterprise Can Manage Money Production

"The avarice and injustice of princes and sovereign states." This is Adam Smith's phrase. He said that this was what has been behind the destruction of money through the ages. Two-hundred years later, F.A. Hayek, after a career of pleading with governments to stop destroying the quality of money, said that the only way to protect money as a good from the avarice of governments was total separation. Money should be produced privately.

The debate is alive again today, with digital-age monetary inventions that are attempting to compete with government money. Debunkers are everywhere. Money can't be left to the market to produce and manage. It is a thing for the state to do. Governments have been in the money business for thousands of years. It must always be so. Georg Friedrich Knapp proved this more than one hundred years ago!

Let's consider.

Full Privatization

In 1963, Murray Rothbard wrote an anti-inflation tract called What Has Government Done to Our Money?. The effervescent prose and searing logic made it an instant classic, and a favorite of "gold bugs" for generations. If you had never thought about the nefarious effects of government control of money, this small monograph had an amazing clarifying effect.It certainly did for me.

But what's really interesting is that Rothbard wasn't really making a case for the 19th-century gold standard. What he was pushing was full privatization of money. He wanted it to be created and managed by the market. His push for gold was more predictive than normative: if government left the realm of money production forever, it is likely that the golden constant would be the victor, though other precious metals would likely circulate as well.

What truly blew my mind when I read it was his case for private coinage. Abolish the U.S. Mint, he says. Wow. He points out that the free market is perfectly capable of managing weights and measures. Markets were doing that long before governments got into the act. They can do it again. There are more than enough methods to tell real from fake.

As for banks, let them be regular businesses, competing with each other like any other business, he said. The issue of solvency will take care of itself. Banks that take too many risks or go too far out on a ledge, or just miss market trends, get punished. Those that are prudent and wise win out. They will be better calculators of their own economic interests without a government and central bank guaranteeing their survival and distorting the signaling systems of the market.

Private Coinage

It also sounds compelling. But what kept me puzzled was this claim that the private sector could be fully in charge. Who would get things going in the first place? As it turns out, the market is what creates money in the first instance, out of an existing good or service with a use value that people gradually come to acquire not to consume but to trade in another round. In this way, barter turns to indirect exchange.

We see this in prison environments all the time. Some valuable commodity serves as money, not because the wardens declare it to be so, but because informal markets in prisons cause something to emerge. It could be noodle packages, canned fish, or small soaps. It's hard to predict, but where there is a desire to trade, there will be money.

How can we know there would be enough available for everyone who needs it? Good money is divisible and its purchasing power adapts based on supply. The costs of producing money follow a profitability model. When it is worth it, we get more production. When it is not, money production falls. The price system of profit and loss — the entrepreneurial drive to get people what they need — works here just as with any industry.

What about a real use case? You can visit any high-end coin shop and see beautiful coins from ages past that were produced entirely privately. There is no lack of evidence that these existed.

The Button Makers

But has private production ever served an entire structure of production in any historical use case? A neglected book documenting exactly this comes from

George Selgin's Good Money, which tells the case of the factory system in the early years of the Industrial Revolution. Government minted high-value coins but there was a huge shortage of money to pay laborers in the factory system.

The Birmingham button industry saw an opportunity and started making money for factories to pay workers. The system worked beautifully — too much so. The tokens were much fancier and in demand than government currency. Government cracked down and re-monopolized the money.

The beauty of Selgin's book is that it provides the real history of Rothbard's robust theory. It could work. But there was one problem: it stopped working when government didn't like it anymore.

Here is the great issue in the history of money. How do you keep a perfectly good private system of money production from being trolled and finally destroyed by external entities? In the crypto world, this is the problem of the centralized point of failure. If there is a building to visit with auditors, a proprietary website to hack, a company to drag before Congress, a code that can be broken by darknet trolls, it is going to happen.

In the decade before Bitcoin, there were many attempts to create a digital unit or at least some private currency alternative: DigiCash, E-gold, the Liberty Dollar, and, even going back in time, the dream of the Gold Standard Corp to kick off a private money system (it didn't end well). Even PayPal began as an attempt to break free from government-produced and managed money.

Reasons for Failure

In the early days, I watched some of these companies come and go. There was always some issue, some problem that led to legal problems, lack of consumer interest, hackings and funny business, and so on. At some point, I had to conclude that the whole thing was hopeless.

What I saw as a long period of failure — proof that it could never happen — was actually something else. It was evidence of the indefatigable energy and creativity to figure out some solution to the problem of the government's money monopoly. In retrospect, I should have known that this is how market innovation works. Try, fail, improve, fail, adapt, fail. Then one day, it all comes together.

That eventual solution had many moving parts (internet dependency, a protocol governing money creation rates, a publically transparent ledger, double-key cryptography, hashing to provide proof-of-work access). This was all remarkable. But a feature that made Bitcoin different from everything that came before was its decentralization. Just as Bittorrent allowed peer-to-peer sharing of movies, with no central point of failure and therefore nothing to hack or take down, Bitcoin gave the world its first fully decentralized money.

Now there are thousands upon thousands.

What we've learned is that money can be privately produced. Hayek's dream of choice in currency can be reality. What form it will take in the future no one can know for sure. What's more, there is no end game here. The process of innovation will never stop. There might not be a final winner. But we've also learned that in order for money to be protected from the trolls both public and private — "The avarice and injustice of princes and sovereign states" — there also needs to be decentralization to make the enterprise durable in the face of attacks.

Napster was crushed, but Bittorrent lives. Uber will be regulated, but decentralized ride sharing is on the way. Many private and digital currencies — whether gold or crypto — fell before 2008. The new generation of decentralized monetary technologies have changed the game.

70

Green Stamps and the Long History of Other Money-Like Things

I needed a hotel overnight in a New Jersey town and had no time for shopping. I pulled up the travel app I use by habit. The first option was perfect. The price was even better: $0. Wait, zero? How can I stay in a nice hotel overnight and pay absolutely nothing for it? It turned out to be true. I stayed, paid nothing, and left.

You have already guessed the answer. My loyalty benefits were applied to his hotel that would have otherwise cost $127 plus tax. I had the option not to use my benefits (or "bucks," as they call them) but I couldn't pass up the chance for a free hotel. Now my bucks from this particular site are depleted a bit, of course, so there is a sense in which I did spend money.

Still, the fact for me is real: no dollars changed hands between me and the hotel. I "paid" my accumulated points to the travel app, and the travel app paid the hotel its set fee, with no dollar transaction that affected me at all.

Now, you can rightly observe that my loyalty points are not really money, and for two reasons: they belong only to me (to my knowledge, they are not transferable) and they are of limited liquidity. I can only use them on terms defined by the app. I can't take them to the store and buy a basket of groceries. That said, money is fungible. What I didn't spend that day became money I can use for other purposes.

The experience got me thinking about how many money-like things we use these days. They are all around us actually. Go to the drug store and you get a printout that entitles you to future discounts, and some even offer outright cash back on anything you buy. Some grocery stores offer much lower prices if you use a proprietary card. Some benefits accumulate. Then, perhaps most famously, there are miles you get from particular airline programs (you can transfer ownership but it is not easy and not cheap).

A question might be: are these money? Returning to the most reductionist possible definition offered by Ludwig von Mises — that money is that which makes possible indirect exchange — these do seem to behave a bit like money. They are marketed as money. We think of them as money and use them that way. As the consumer obtains and uses these loyalty points — things acquired not to consume but to trade for consumable items at a later times — they have the feel of money. However, the attribute of common acceptance is not generally present. Without getting overly theoretical or pedantic, let's just call them money-like things.

Green Stamps

This experience got me thinking about loyalty programs in general and the means of exchange that are created by them. When I was growing up, my maternal grandmother had a drawer full of green stamps. When I would visit the house, she would take out sticker books and a big pile of these green stamps and ask me to stick the stickers in the books. It was the kind of thing that was fun for kids but drudgery for adults.

My brother and I would work all day on the task. At the end, we would have a big pile of books filled with stamps. My grandmother would be full of glee, and then we would race to the green-stamp store to spend them. This was a rarified place with home products of various sorts, and all the prices were quoted not in dollars but in stamp books. We would get a toaster or a pillow or a figurine or two, turn in our books, and head home. It was for me an early experience in using money-like things to obtain goods.

Looking at the history of S&H green stamps, I should not be surprised that they got going at the height of the Gilded Age when mass commercial society as we know it was born into the world. The company Sperry & Hutchinson had the idea of selling its stamps to stores for them to give to customers. Why should a store buy these useless stamps? Because customers will come to value them because they can be traded for goods at S&H stores and using the mail-order catalog (which was as exciting as the Internet in the 21st century!).

In other words, S&H representatives had to persuade stores that by dealing in these stamps, customers would get hooked on them and choose their store over another. I can totally imagine that this was a tough sell. But eventually it came to work. It worked so well that the product became a wild craze and finally an American institution by the 1960s, dying out only in the 1980s. Amazing.

Box Tops

What's also striking is to realize that such loyalty programs date even much earlier, at the height of the Industrial Revolution, when some merchant stores began to offer little copper tokens that could be exchanged later at the store itself. (Wikipedia has a brief history of loyalty programs.)

As I think about it, when I was a kid, I would collect box tops from cereal to send it for special gifts. In fact, remembering now, my friends and I would trade these box tops.

Think about it. These box tops had no value as consumer goods. They were objectively trash. Subjectively, they were valuable. We valued them because we could trade them for something else. In other words, they functioned as money, at least for us, at least for the limited purpose of getting a disappointing plastic toy in the mail 6 to 8 week later.

Thus you can see that loyalty programs like we take for granted today, along with their money-like points, actually grew up with the rise of modern capitalism itself. Contrary to what you read in the Harvard Business Review, their market worth has been proven through a long history.

Repeat business is rewarded with a proprietary and money-like scoring system that can be spent later.

What this history should teach us is that what we call money, at least in an innovative and fast-changing commercial culture, is varied, changing, and adaptable, a non-stop stream of entrepreneurial innovation. It's easy to forget this now that nationalized monetary systems have defined the experience of so many generations. Now this is changing.

The invention and production of money is a universal product of human experience, and continues to be, produced not by the state or social contract but organically within markets themselves.

Every prison has a money. Many towns in the US have created local monies. In lucrative markets for illicit goods where dollars are difficult to obtain or launder, other options are sought after constantly. Our online shopping experience is replete with programs that reward us with points to be used as money.

Digital innovation, the globalization of commerce, and the new applications of creativity to the defining and redefining what it means to be a "means of exchange" will continue to reshape what we think of as a money-like thing.

Money is not just what the government says it is. The market has been struggling to create alternatives for a very long time.

71

It's a Snap to Abolish the Fed

arkets have been roiled of late by speculation over the Fed's monetary policy. Will the Fed raise interest rates too fast, choking the expansion, or too slow, thereby risking inflation? The president has repeatedly denounced the Fed for endangering prosperity. And it seems like the Fed's chairman has gotten cold feet too. Jerome Powell's passing hint that monetary policy won't be tightened that much has sent financials soaring.

The real question is how either the Fed or the president can know for sure what rates should be. It's not as if either politicians or monetary central planners have a stellar record in this respect. In any case, it's a myth that the Fed controls interest rates. It controls only the rate at which the Fed lends to banks, which influences only a tiny sliver of the yield curve. The market manages the rest.

The Fed never likes to admit it is not in control, however. Whatever the interest rate — credit cards, commercial loans, mortgages, Treasuries — the Fed winks and nods: "Yeah that's us." Sure, as if there is not a $30 trillion market for debt that might have some influence.

It's not even clear whether and to what extent the Fed really has a handle on the money supply. As George Selgin has shown, Fed policy often works at cross purposes. After 2008, the Fed ballooned the money base and then started paying interest on bank deposits at the Fed. The overall effect was nothing like the inflation expansion everyone was expecting. Was this the intention? Hard to say.

No Wizard

There is a disconnect between what the Fed says and what it does simply because the system is too complex to be run from the center. Money in circulation is determined by a combination of depositor/borrowing behavior and the risk tolerance of banks themselves. There is no money wizard in Washington who can operate the whole like some precision machine.

Which raises the topic: why do we need the Fed?

It manages a clearing system for banks but banks can do that themselves without help from Washington. It manages the federal funds rate because it holds overnight loans between banks. Here again, banks can perform those operations without help. It pursues a mandate to control inflation and unemployment — macroeconomic stabilization, as it is called — but the record shows that this has mostly been a failure.

What else does the Fed do? It backs the promise to make good on debt issued by the federal government, but municipal governments issue debt all the time without recourse to a central bank. Plus, Treasury debt should be subject to a default premium like all other debt. Without such market pressure, investors get poor signals about the real quality of the debt they are holding.

Anything else? The main Fed and all the regional Feds issue an amazing amount of research reports but surely the fine men and women who write them can find other outlets, such as the Social Science Research Network or maybe Medium. It's true that the St. Louis Fed has the best online tool for data reporting but how many people know that this is actually outsourced to a private sector firm? [Correction from the St. Louis Fed media relations: "FRED is a St. Louis Fed product, it is not outsourced."]

Money without Policy

There is plenty of downside to having a central bank. It tempts politicians to believe there is no cost to endless debt issuance. Without a default premium and rational investing decisions, there is no punishment for fiscal irresponsibility. Think of how state governments have to have balanced budgets. This is because they have no central bank to guarantee payment on the debt. Ending the Fed would do far more to restrain spending than pious speech or even a Constitutional amendment for a balanced budget at the federal level.

Imagine a world in which financial markets were not constantly buffeted between optimism and pessimism based on the words of the Fed chairman. The current system is not bringing stability but just the opposite.

I'm thinking too of the long history. The Fed was created more than a century ago. Its first great achievement was not ending "wildcat banking" but rather providing the funding for the first World War. Not a good beginning. That blew a bubble that popped in 1921. Then it blew another that popped in 1929. Then it botched an attempt to reflate from 1930 all the way to the second World War, which it also funded.

The postwar history was of endless screwups: inflation, recession, stagflation, and all-around mercy that culminated in the great pillaging of 1979. Then came the Savings and Loan Crisis, the dotcom bubble, the reflation after 9/11, the housing fiasco that blew up 7 years later, then the bailout of banks with balance-sheet manipulations, then the convoluted and contradictory regime that followed.

Finally, there is the grave political danger of the Fed. Every president wants lower rates. The only exception in my lifetime came in Reagan's first term when he demanded tight money to end inflation. I doubt we'll ever see those days again. Even the current president who denounced bubble blowing on the campaign trail is now pushing for the Fed to help his reelection prospects.

It's all too much. At some point, we should recognize that the idea of central banking is a relic from a technocratic/nationalist age that does have a role in an infinitely complex and global financial and monetary world. Unlike a century ago, forms of money, lending, and banking are hugely diverse. As a practical matter, the Fed and the banking system controls less and less of it. This undermines the whole premise of central banking. And yet this institution is still hanging around.

Here to There

How to get rid of it? I used to think this was a complex problem, that we needed some huge monetary reform to make it happen. A serious gold standard would be great. The trouble here is that sensible reform will require the cooperation of the people and interest groups that benefit most from the status quo. The best policy will be the one that has the least steps, remembering that the main point is to end the system of centralized, discretionary policy that is so subject to abuse.

The simplest solution would be to normalize the Fed's balance sheet (it's already happening) and then pull the plug by freezing the monetary base. No more printing via open-market operations. Let banks and other intermediaries take it from there, issuing their own branded and redeemable notes on a competitive basis in response to consumer demand. Competition, redemption requirements, transparency, and no more too-big-to-fail would prevent overissue and incentivize a system far more sound than the current one.

As part of this, we need liberalization of monetary alternatives, whether proprietary monies, precious metals like gold and silver, or permissionless use of cryptocurrency. We live in an age of innovation. The quality of money, banking, and payments systems should benefit from market forces rather than be monopolized by government.

Wouldn't the world fall apart? Not at all. I predict that the news would be front page for the usual 48-hour news cycle and then the world would move on. No big deal. There is no downside. And a huge upside. All it requires is some political courage.

Ideally, Congress, which created the creature in the first place, would step up and do the right thing. It's also intriguing to imagine what would happen if the president, famous for his edgy uses of the executive order, would shutter the place with the stroke of a pen.

Even if it doesn't happen, I am safe to predict the Fed's growing irrelevance in an age of innovation in cryptocurrency and ever more choice over depository institutions. Might as well call it now and end the Fed.

Stuff

72

What Has Government
Done to Our Bathrooms?

People who have traveled the world, or are of a certain age and have long memories, are conscious, however inchoately, that something has gone very wrong in our bathrooms. Maybe you are among those who have noticed.

You travel to Brazil or Spain or Israel, and you take a shower. The water pours down on your head. It feels like the first real shower you have had in years. You come back to the US. The water dribbles out. You stare up in disbelief. Is this all you got? Yep.

You wonder what has gone wrong. The shower barely gets the conditioner out of your hair. You buy a new shower head that promises much but delivers nothing at all. No matter how long you stay in, you don't feel like you are getting clean.

You long for Brazil. You wish for Mexico. Anywhere but the U.S. because none of these countries have gone what we've gone through since in 1992 George Bush signed new amendments to the Clean Water Act that mandated low-flow showerheads (2.5 gallons-per-minute max). No retailer can sell any showerhead that does not conform. You can buy them and hack them (I've become very good at this) but even then, there is a problem because the water pressure in our homes and commercial spaces is also restricted.

Hacking gets you improvements (the cheap showerheads are easiest to hack), but, even then, we are far from the ideal.

I'm staying for the week in a New England mansion — Edgewood, the historic mansion of the American Institute for Economic Research — built in the nineteen teens originally but with plumbing that dates from the 1930s, as installed by Crane Plumbing back in the day. The original fixtures are still here. Thank goodness no one had the idea of replacing them with "modern" and "efficient" fixtures.

You turn on the shower. It's Niagara Falls. Just imagine barrels of water being dumped on your head. When one runs out, another begins to pour. This keeps happening, the water all warmed to the most luxurious temperature. No matter how much I describe it, you have to experience it to believe it. If I could permit access to one person after another to such a shower as this, there would be some kind of revolution in this country.

And the toilet: the tank is gigantic, unbelievable. It would sell on the black market today for six figures. Why black market? Because it is illegal to sell such a thing on public markets today. Since 1994, all toilet tanks can only hold a maximum of 1.6 gallons. This explains why there must always be a plunger nearby. It's why you have to buy bleach capsules. It why one-ply toilet paper is so common. Anything else leads to embarrassing clogs.

With modern toilets, you are just glad when they accomplish the minimum most to achieve the task. Forget staying clean, however. There is not enough water running through them to achieve that. There's not enough water running through the system even to keep the buildup away from fixtures and pipes, so you are forever having to repair them.

No matter how much technology you deploy, there is no way to make a toilet work the way it once did by using only 1.6 gallons of water per flush.

But this toilet from the 1940s is a wonder. The initial blast takes care of the essential task. There is another round of water that cleans further. And yet a third comes along to wash yet again. The results are infallible, clean, and truly glorious. How many gallons is it? I'm estimating 8 but it could be 10 or more. It is huge and wonderful.

The only reason that this world went away is regulation. It has nothing to do with a water shortage. We've got the technology to consume all the water we need and are willing to pay for. Not only that: water is the ultimate renewable resource. It comes down from the sky, we use it for stuff, and it goes back up again. Round and round it goes.

The only restriction on water today is purely statutory. Even then, it is ridiculous.

On the campaign trail in December 2015, Donald Trump was challenged to mention a regulation he would repeal. It was this one that he named. "I'll give you one regulation," Trump said. "So I build, and I build a lot of stuff. And I go into areas where they have tremendous water. ... And you have sinks where the water doesn't come out. It's true. They have restrictors put in. The problem is you stay under the shower for five times as long."

He was exactly right.

What is the thinking here? It's always about conservation. The regulators see our use of shower water as amazing waste. Listen to this alarmism promoted by the EPA:

"Showering is one of the leading ways we use water in the home, accounting for nearly 17 percent of residential indoor water use—for the average family, that adds up to nearly 40 gallons per day. That's nearly 1.2 trillion gallons of water used in the United States annually just for showering, or enough to supply the water needs of New York and New Jersey for a year!"

My goodness, that sounds terrible. What decadent and wasteful people we are. No wonder there are flow stoppers in our showers.

But hold on a minute. A full page of seemingly scientific statistics at the EPA never actually raises the central question. What we really want to know is: what portion of overall water use do our showers actually drain? What difference are we making to the whole by degrading our shower experience in such an extreme way?

For this data, you have to head over to the Department of the Interior, and look at estimated water use in the US. It turns out that thermonuclear power and agriculture account for 78 percent of all water use. Public supply in general — meaning everything that could possibly be related to any domestic or commercial use where you live — is only 12 percent of the total.

We are being hectored daily about our water use, but it turns out that straight up domestic use of the public water supply accounts for a small fraction of total use. "During 2010, about 42,000 Mgal/d of freshwater was withdrawn for public supply, which accounted for almost 12 percent of the total water withdrawn." And how much of that is actual household use? "About 57 percent of public-supply withdrawals [which itself is 12 percent of total], or 23,800 Mgal/d, was delivered for domestic use, which includes indoor and outdoor residential uses, such as drinking water, sanitation, and landscape watering."

In other words, all the water use associated with every home in the US, including the washing machine, swimming pool, lawn watering, car washing, cooking and cleaning, plus flushing and showering, account for less than 7 percent, and probably close to 5 percent of the total. You can look through the report yourself and see but there is no estimate at all about flushing and showering because the usage is so small, even to the point of being negligible.

The amount of water you use for showering, flushing, washing dishes, and washing clothes is a tiny fraction of overall water use. Only by reporting raw numbers — and excluding the main uses of water for power generation and agriculture — can the public be convinced that submitting to a lower standard of living is achieving anything to save the planet.

Essentially, the public is being gaslighted here: "a form of manipulation that seeks to sow seeds of doubt in a targeted individual or in members of a targeted group, hoping to make them question their own memory, perception, and sanity." Water is scarce, true, but so is everything else. We have a system for dealing with scarcity: it is called prices. It applies to everything, water included. Water poses no special problems for economic allocation that do not apply to shoes, vegetables, or cars.

What, then, is the real point of all the scary data pushed by the EPA?

If you were into conspiracy theory, you might observe that the thermonuclear power industry plus big agriculture are pushing regulations on normal domestic water use as a way of reducing water consumption and lowering prices for their own use. Sounds like the plots of myriad movies like Rango and Mad Max.

The net effect of all of this has been to ruin our bathrooms. You might not realize it because the change has been slow, extending over 25 years. Only by encountering a bathroom with original fixtures from the 1940s can you perceive the full horror of what has happened. Our showers are lame, our toilets don't work, our pipes are dirty, and everything is less sanitary. Chalk it up as yet another thing that government has ruined.

73

Why Your White Clothing Is No Longer White

I'm sitting here today wearing the whitest shirt that's been on my back in years. My collar matches. It wasn't easy. It took a good part of the day. It's the culmination of years of trial and error to achieve what decades of government regulations have tried to prevent.

In a bit, I'll tell you how I achieved this, revealing every secret.

First some background.

Speaking at a Caribbean island this year, I was notified of a "white party" one night. I had never heard of this. Everyone must wear white, all the way to the shoes. I scrambled to buy some clothes, and I'm glad I did. The entire beach was filled with people wearing white, while the lights of the event were an ultraviolet hew. The effect was glorious.

But then again, this was an island that still knows how to get clothing white. In the United States, we seem to have nearly given up. This party would not have worked here for the reason that white clothing hardly exists — really white, bright white, blindingly white.

Back in my childhood, vast numbers of laundry commercials were about how this or that product would make your clothing white. These days, not so much. Look around at your friends and coworkers. Either they are not wearing white or the whites are vaguely dull and unimpressive.

What has changed? All the essential tools for making clothing super white have been deprecated, mostly by government regulations.

The water in our homes is no longer very hot because government regulations nudge us to use low-performing water heaters. It needs to be 140 degrees, whereas most "water heaters" come with 110 degrees as the default.

Our washing machines don't use much water at all, thanks to "high efficiency" standards that load from the front. You can't truly clean without lots of water.

Our laundry detergent no longer contains phosphates, which means that the soap stays in the clothing, making them ever duller with each wash. Bleach is an option, but it ruins clothing.

Finally, we no longer hang out clothing in the sun to dry. The sun is the most effective and natural bleaching agent. Now a clothesline is considered tacky, so we don't do that anymore. We stuff our clothes in a tumble dryer.

All of these changes have mounted gradually. The whites get ever duller. In a quarter century, we went from a country in which white cottons gleamed (and laundry doers beamed with pride) to one where most people are wearing dull shades of tan and gray. We think nothing of it. We don't even know what we are missing.

There Is Hope

And yet there is a path forward, through the thicket of government regulations.

The first element is hot water. To get whites truly white, you need very hot water. I've learned to boil water in the largest pot I have, and then add that directly to the washing machine. There should be steam coming out of that water before you add your clothes.

You need to treat your whites with Spray and Wash or Shout, on the collars and cuffs, before they go into the wash, letting them sit for five minutes and sometimes rubbing them to loosen up the stains.

There is no clean laundry — and this goes for colors too — without using trisodium phosphate. Everyone serious about laundry knows this now. The purpose of this is to break down the soap and whisk it away in the water. This was banned by government regulations some 20 years ago, to the detriment of all laundry. The ostensible reason was to save the fish from excess algae growth in ponds, punishing domestic laundries rather than the real culprit, which is big agriculture.

As for the problem with drying clothes, I've mostly given up and acquiesced to the machine dryer instead of the glorious sun. Sometimes when I know for sure that no one will see, I will string a clothesline and let my whites experience a glorious natural bleaching. But the occasion rarely presents itself.

There Is More

There is still one more step, and this one will probably be news to you. It was certainly news to me. There is a process of getting clothing extra super-duper white that is called Bluing. I'd never heard of it until two weeks ago.

Sure enough, looking through Amazon, I found the magic liquid: Mrs. Stewart's Bluing. This company, which is still family-owned, was established in 1883. It is a subtle blue dye. You mix a bit (just a few drops) in cold water and add it to your very hot water before adding your clothes. It adds just a hint of blue to your whites. You can't see it. It depends on a bit of optical illusion by playing with the color spectrum: our eyes look at a tiny bit of blue and instead see white.

The story behind this project is truly inspiring. It was discovered at the very height of the Gilded Age when people began really to care about getting clothing bright white. If you think about it, white clothing signifies the rise out of the state of nature. Everything in nature is dirty, grungy, dull. To wear white illustrates the advance of society, the achievement of cleanliness, the triumph over dirt and muck. It's a symbol because only in the late 19th century did this become possible for the masses of people.

The story of the bottle alone is fascinating. The old lady on the bottle was supposed to be the creator's wife, but this person refused to pose. So he grabbed a picture of his mother-in-law and gave it to the artists. She was then immortalized. The company tried to modernize the picture in the 1970s, but consumers raged in revolt and the image reverted. Now the company itself sells tee shirts (probably the lamest tee shirt in history, which makes it all the more awesome).

Bluing your whites is the final touch, and probably won't do the trick unless the other factors are in place.

Unlike in Bermuda, we don't have a lot of white parties to attend. But knowing how to make clothes white is a skill of its own, a way of demonstrating that despite all government depredations, and the conspiracy to make our clothing boring, you possess the wherewithal to nonetheless rise above the state of nature and achieve something truly extraordinary.

74

How IKEA Changed Our Values and Lives

Ingvar Kamprad, the founder of IKEA, has died at the age of 91. He is a remarkable example of how enterprise and visionary entrepreneurship can have such a profound effect on the world. Even now, walking into an IKEA store for the first time is a riveting experience. It invites you to reassess your life priorities, how you live, how you spend your money, what you seek to do in life. It certainly did that to me, and I've never let go of what I learned. In some way, as I think about it, Mr. Kamprad, though I never met him, has been my teacher for a large swath of my adult life. Millions of others can say the same.

In the houses of my growing up, furniture was always called an investment. There were pieces around my house inherited from previous generations, so my parents bought with the understanding that I would inherit what they had today. Every piece was huge. It was designed to broadcast a certain social status. It was to convey a certain permanence. The furniture was heavy and big enough to seem to be bolted to the ground, and the style was elaborate beyond anything necessary. The styles of the kings of old had been widely distributed among the bourgeoisie and we loved to flaunt it.

I can recall as a young boy shopping with my parents for what was called a bedroom suite. There was a gigantic headboard with big side railings, a chest of drawers, a big chest for the end of the bed, two nightstands, plus a big matching mirror. You bought it all as a single set, hugely expensive but mainly just big overall. The movers put it all in my room. It seemed inconceivable that it would ever be moved again, and this was part of the point. We were supposed to think of ourselves as rooted and secure. The furniture we chose underscored that.

Then the unthinkable happened. We moved because my father got a new job. Moving day was a nightmare. We tried to do some ourselves. Everyone was suffering just to pick the stuff up and get it to the new place. There was breakage of course and lots of the furniture didn't really look right in the new place. It seemed transplanted in some way. But we dealt with it because, in those days, your furniture was seen as the embodiment of the life of the family, physical symbols of who we are, almost like commoditized DNA.

Then we moved again. Then again. It was becoming absurd. At some point, my parents wised up and got a smaller home in a more urban environment. What used to be treasures started to feel like junk strewn about here and there, as if we had to find a place for this stuff because purchasing it in the first place seemed like such an epic event. You would never turn your back on this warehouse full of heavy wood else you might as well be invalidating your past.

At some point in this process, I began to despise furniture, though I didn't fully realize it. I was a teenager making my way in the world of sales, and I was very good in the clothing industry. I tried to port my skills over to the furniture industry because the money was better. There I encountered a serious problem. I couldn't sell it. Customers found me unpersuasive. And for an obvious reason: in my heart, I didn't really want people to find themselves in the position of my own family. I knew that they didn't really need all this junk. I also came to discover that the ticket price on the items reflected mostly illusion. I loved selling clothing but I despised selling furniture, and my numbers reflected this reality. I was the worst salesperson on the floor. I bailed before I was hurled out.

Years later, I found myself in an ideal position. I had mostly junked all my old furniture because I was tired of lugging it from place to place. I had a new space in Northern Virginia and it was mostly empty. Someone told me to go to IKEA for things like bookshelves and a sofa and so on.

Browsing that store challenged everything I thought I knew about furniture. It was not expensive. It was not heavy. It was not ornate. It made beauty out of the love of function. It does what it is supposed to do. There is an elegance in that. Even the showroom seemed to convey a completely different ethos than I had ever encountered. Today we call it minimalism. It is free of clutter, free of stuff and junk. Being in the presence of this settled my mind. It did more: it helped me rethink my life.

I snagged a few pieces made of simple pine wood, the smallest table, a bare-bones sofa, a stand for various odds and ends. I could put it all together myself. I could port it around in my car. I could move it around my house with no issues. And I became aware that if, when, I moved again, maybe to a new city, I could just leave all this furniture behind. No guilt. I could buy more at the new place for less than it would cost me to move. I fell in love with my new IKEA life.

Maybe you know this feeling after going to IKEA the first time. You sense that you have been doing it wrong. What these people are doing is doing it right. You buy a few items and take them home and look around. The place is stuffed with junk. You immediately feel the urge to declutter. You want to throw things out. You wonder why you have this huge sofa, this massive coffee table, this big chest of drawers, this ornate dining room table designed to expand to accommodate 12 people at the big dinner party you have never held.

Here's the problem with buying things for your home. At the store, it is an isolated thing and it seems attractive. You want that thing. But you get it home and it's not an isolated thing. It becomes just another addition to an accumulation of things that seem fine in isolation but terrible as a group of things. The whole room starts to feel like a pile of endless stuff. Then the whole apartment or house feels that way. It is disorienting, confusing, even mentally and emotionally rattling. You can't find a single thing to throw away but all of it together is diminishing your life quality.

What the IKEA showroom does is a reveal a different philosophy of life. Now just consider how remarkable and implausible this is: a huge store that makes you want to get rid of all your stuff and buy their stuff instead. That's a feat of marketing — or psychological magic. They made a business out of showing you how to live more simply. But the irony is penetrating: in order to live without, you have to buy their things! That's a brilliant business.

It's all not just a strategy. It is a real philosophy, which is why it feels so authentic. The New York Times reports

> All his life, Mr. Kamprad practiced thrift and diligence, and he portrayed those traits as the basis for Ikea's success. He lived in Switzerland to avoid Sweden's high taxes, drove an old Volvo, flew only economy class, stayed in budget hotels, ate cheap meals, shopped for bargains and insisted that his home was modest, that he had no real fortune and that Ikea was held by a charitable trust….
>
> Ikea had been achieved, he said, by frugality: building stores on less costly land outside cities; buying materials at a discount; minimizing sales staff to let customers shop without pressure; putting no finishes on unseen furniture surfaces, and packaging items in flat boxes to be carried away by customers for home assembly (instructions provided).

For millions of people, this whole approach changed everything. Getting rid of the clutter permits clarity of thought. Spending less saves money. Enjoying a clean and lightweight domestic environment focuses the mind on what really matters. And it helps wipe away this strange myth that accumulation and mass in material objects somehow reveals that quality of your life. It turns out that generations have made a basic error.

The less you spend on junk the more you can save to really boost the quality of your life in food and travel, getting out of debt, saving for the future, even developing a financial legacy that matters, one about liquid funds, not about huge amounts of stuff.

The wisdom of this whole approach to life has grown on me over time. I recall when my father died, I was tasked with finding something to do with the amazing amount of stuff (tools, books, knives, papers, and just…stuff) he had accumulated in the course of his life. The truth is that I didn't want it. It broke my heart but I held a yard sale. I saw strangers cart away my Dad's things for absurdly low prices. He thought of all of this stuff as treasure. The market saw it differently. I saw it differently.

I returned from that experience to rethink my own attitude toward material goods, much more in line with what Mr. Kamprad believed. He made a huge impact on the way we think, not just about our domestic furnishings, not just about the mobility of the things we own, but more fundamentally. He helped us to discover what really matters, and to dispense with the illusion that bigger, more expensive, and heavier equates to life quality. It doesn't.

There is delightful irony in knowing that he died as one of the world's richest men. For clarifying our values, the market rewarded him handsomely. As it should be.

75

The Glory and Majesty
of the Dreamliner

The downside of the jetway is that it denies you the chance to appreciate the sheer awesomeness of the passenger jet. You walk from one room with chairs, shops, and restaurants, through an enclosed hallway, and enter into another room and sit down. So mundane. You can't back away from the scene to appreciate the whole of what is happening. The experience of flying is reduced to looking out a small window.

That's why I'm always thrilled when instead I can walk downstairs from the airport lobby and enter onto the tarmac. Then you climb the stairs to the plane, just like in the old movies. Every time, it lifts my heart. You can stand close to and finally board a thing of beauty. In my experience, this happens most often in airports in foreign countries.

It happened recently leaving the airport of Krakow, Poland, on my way back to Chicago. I stepped out of the airport and onto the tarmac. There it was before me, a sight that immediately struck me as one of the most awesome I had ever witnessed. The jet that would take me back to the US was of an incomprehensible size, a metal replication of the shape of a bird but on an enormous scale and made entirely by human hands.

I tried to think of anything in nature that could compare. I thought of huge animals on safaris, of glorious birds, or gigantic sea animals. I thought of huge mountains, great canyons, and terrifying bodies of water. Nothing compares. Then it dawned on me: humankind has created something truly astonishing here.

What's more, it is not designed to serve a privileged caste but rather to carry average people to the other side of the world and back, soaring through the air while its passengers watch movies and drink wine.

When you think about life, life couldn't be better. Where is the sense of awe? Where is the gratitude for the system that made such a thing come into existence?

The Dreamliner

The plane in question is the Boeing 787, also known as the Dreamliner. As the first airline with a body made of composite materials, it holds 335 passengers and is 20% more fuel-efficient than the 747. Its maiden voyage was in 2009 and now it is an essential tool for making the human population more mobile than ever before in history.

I stood there frozen with my mouth open, and watched the passengers climb aboard from two sides. I waited there for the last person to board, unwilling to give up even a moment in which I could somehow take in the awesome scene. Finally a flight attendant came up to me and said: "I know it is amazing but it is time for you to board now."

I said to her: "What is it like for you to have a job on such a thing as this?"

She answered: "I've been on hundreds of flights, and truly, even now, I can't understand how flight is even possible, much less how this thing carries hundreds of people to the other side of the world, much less how this thing comes to exist in the first place. I'm just along for the ride."

Aren't we all along for the ride? She doesn't understand it and I don't understand it either. You know who else doesn't understand it? Just about everyone else working in and around the plane to guide its motion, load the bags, cater the meals on board, and even those who fly the planes.

The mechanics don't fully understand all its operations. The engineers, specialists in one small aspect of its functioning, don't have the cognitive where-withal to process the whole. The people who sell the tickets don't understand it. The employees in air traffic control don't understand it. Not even the people who make this machine can possibly understand the whole much less recreate such a thing. It is a marvelous example of the immensely productive capacity of the human mind working in cooperation with others.

Where Was This Made?

I looked up the plane to see where it is made. It is assembled in Everett, Washington. But that means almost nothing. Look at the rest of what's behind this.

The wings are manufactured by Mitsubishi in Japan. The horizontal stabilizers are made by Alenia Aeronautica in Italy and Korea Aerospace in South Korea. The fuselage sections are made in Italy, Charleston, South Carolina, by Kawasaki in Japan, by Spirit AeroSystems in Wichita, Kansas, and Korean Air in South Korea.

The passenger doors are made by Latecoere in France. The cargo doors, access doors, and crew doors are made in Sweden. The software that runs the plane is programmed by HCL Enterprise in India. The floor beams also come from India.

The wiring is from Labinal in France. The wing tips, support fairs, and wheel parts are from South Korea. The landing gear is manufactured by Messier-Bugatti-Dowty in France and the UK. The power and management systems and air conditioning come from Connecticut.

And that doesn't even get us to the blankets, food, and drinks for the passengers, the glass on the windows, the carpet on the floor, the music and movies on the screens in front of each chair, plus the tools that made all these things and the tools that made the tools. If it were even possible to add it all up, there would be a hundred nations, thousands of communities, and multiples of millions of people who cooperate together to cause this thing to exist.

What a marvel!

Who Did It?

You have entrepreneurs, dreamers, and capitalists who might have imagined such a thing. But in truth, no one person can contain the whole, much less realize the vision. The genius visionary is not entirely a myth but this institution of the singular great man has been greatly exaggerated.

They have always and everywhere depended on others to realize it.

They, in turn, depend on others, and more and more, in widening circles of specialization and expertise, involving ever more people. Their expertise is also dependent on the technological capital built up over time, going back centuries, to realize what we call human progress. Even then, it is not enough to have an idea; every idea that comes to fruition must depend on saved capital — real resources — to deploy on a risk.

And what is that risk? The risk is that customers won't finally show up to commit real resources to make the project pass the ultimate test, which is profit and loss. Accounting is the economic brick wall that every enterprising dreamer must confront. It works or it does not. And the only final determining factor is whether the consumer is willing to forgo his or her own property to buy your product.

Big and Small

The sheer scale of the 787 itself makes the point. Our lizard brains are impressed. But what about the smaller things around us? I could cite the obvious: the smartphone that has more computing power than the rockets that landed on the moon. It provides access to most all human knowledge, from inside our pockets! It is a marvel.

But let's consider something even more mundane, something like the paperclip. You can't remember ever saving one. It is not valuable enough; each costs less than a penny. But a similar process is involved in making one of those tiny things. If you doubt it, just think through what it would be like to make one yourself. You could never do it, much less achieve it and make your money back.

And yet through the process of human cooperation, the paper clip comes to be. So does the Dreamliner. And why? It's all for you and me, regardless of our political views, gender identity, race, national origin, religion, or any other category that politics uses to exploit our differences rather than bring us together.

Markets are the key to prosperity and progress. We are surrounded by the evidence, provided we are willing to pay attention. It's sad that it takes something as breathtaking as the Dreamliner to jar our minds into realizing it.

76

Mattresses Signify Our Astonishing Prosperity

How did you sleep last night? If not well, it's not for lack of mattress choice. If you are still sleeping on the thing you bought 20 years ago, it's time to rethink. With a few clicks you can have a glorious new sleeping surface brought to you in a few days. You spend a third of your life in bed. The experience determines a major part of your life quality. Market competition has dramatically improved it.

The mattress market has changed over the last 5 years. There is more choice. Prices keep falling, to the point that you can get a solid mattress for a tenth of what it cost ten years ago. There's no more slogging down to your local mattress store, being intimidated by a salesman who pushes you to spend more than you can afford, and then paying another $40 for delivery.

For generations, the $15 billion mattress market was dominated by Sealy and Serta. Then in the blink of an eye, there were all kinds of new choices: Tuft & Needle (my favorite), Casper, Purple, Leesa, Saatva, Sapira, Helix, Bear, Eve, 4sleep, PangeaBed, and I've probably left out many others. Most of these had what early in 2017 were considered fantastic prices: a twin bed for $300-$600. This is far better than the $1,000 and up you used to pay.

You thought you knew cheap and good. Then at some point in the last 6 months, a new name blasted on the scene: Zinus. Apparently, it is an older company that just jumped into the mattress industry, with the help of Chinese manufacturing. Maybe the company is using its mattress as a loss leader. In any case, you can snag a twin bed for $180 delivered.

Mic drop. The reviews are excellent. Now it is the #1 seller on Amazon, just in another blink of an eye. Isn't market competition beautiful?

The Bad Old Days

Before we get too comfortable with the wonders of our age, consider the plight of our ancestors. What did people sleep on in the ancient world? Most people slept on the hard ground. The nobility could perhaps find some cloth stuff with reeds, hay, dried peels or beans or leaves or, if you were really lucky, maybe feathers wrapped in animal skin.

Fast forward 1,500 years to the first signs of progress and prosperity. In the Renaissance, mattresses were made from "pea shucks, straw, feathers, stuffed into coarse ticks, and covered with velvets, brocades, or silks." I can't even imagine how many tiny bugs lived in those mattresses. We think we have a problem with bed bugs today! Then there were the problems with varmints, snakes, scorpions, roaches, and other unthinkable things.

Two hundred years later, cotton was more common but then there were the lumps. After one night, the thing would take on your body shape, such that it probably felt like your coffin after just one week.

Even the highest luxury of the 18th century no one would stand for today.

Coils and Water

Then came the late 19th century with the invention of coils. For the first time, we could sleep with actual support on our backs! What an amazing advance it must have been.

Nothing much changed until the late 1970s, when this strange thing called the waterbed came along. True confession: I was briefly a waterbed salesman when I was a kid. It was a hilarious experience because while they were strangely popular, it turns out that people didn't like them very much. They would come back to the store and report, well, they don't like sleeping on water. Too many waves.

So the floor manager instructed us to trade them in for one with "baffles" which were rubber layers designed to reduce the motion of the bed. We ranked the level of baffles from 1 to 10. People would get one with a level 5 baffle and come back. Finally they would buy a 10 baffle waterbed, which pretty much had no movement at all. It was very nearly a normal mattress.

(I was also responsible for installation. So I would go to people's houses and drag their garden hose through the window and start filling the thing up. The weight was amazing, as much as 2,000 pounds. Yes, in those days, I did indeed meet some strange folks who wanted these things. I see now you can still buy a waterbed but all of them are advertised as "waveless.")

After the waterbed craze, everyone went back to springs but with ever more layers of foam. But the big problem with foam in those days was that it was too hot to sleep on. It took a lot of innovation to deal with that problem. Now that problem is mostly gone, with nearly every mattress on the market claiming not to sleep hot at all. In any case, we have wonderful mattress pads now.

So here we are, with fantastic mattresses, pillows, and sheets available to all, sleeping in rooms that are heated and cooled, free of bugs and snakes. And this lifestyle is within the means of nearly every living person in the developed world. Today I see old mattresses sitting next to dumpsters all the time. Only 50-100 years ago, these would have been treasures. Now they are trash that no one wants.

Again, consider our good fortune. A third of our lives are spent on mattresses. A solid sleep is determinative of a good life. And get this: you didn't build that mattress. Someone else is working right now for you, in the hope that you will buy. That's called the market at work: endless progress, a beautiful community of work, ever better quality, ever lower prices.

Forget counting sheep. Count your blessings instead.

77

Why Drug Dealers, Rappers, and Pimps Wear Their Wealth

A proposed principle: don't ascribe to culture and morality what is better explained by economics. The principle is difficult to apply because the economic forces at work in any given situation are sometimes invisible from the outside. It is easy to see the results, but much harder to see the rational calculations behind what drives people to make the choices they make.

So, for example, you can search Quora for an answer to the question about why rap artists, pimps, and drug dealers are so obsessed with wearing signs of wealth, like gold chains, furs, gold grills on teeth, and carrying serpent-head canes and the like. The most liked answers are all the same: it's about displaying signs of virility and status. To be super flashy with your clothes and jewelry is part of the culture of these industries, a way to show off your successes to others.

This has long been assumed to be true, especially as the tendency is traditionally attached to African-American urban culture. Consider "Puttin' on the Ritz," a song with lyrics and music by Irving Berlin from 1927. The purpose of the song (in its original version) was to poke fun at the signs of prosperity in Harlem, and, in particular, the way black people of the period spent their money on clothes to party in, showing every sign of wealth.

The song presumed that this was a racially based behavior, reflecting not real achievement but rather merely profligate spending.

> If you're blue, and you don't know where to go to
> Why don't you go where Harlem flits?
> Puttin' on the Ritz

Spangled gowns upon the bevy of high browns
From down the levy, all misfits
Puttin' on the Ritz

That's where each and every lulu-belle goes
Every Thursday evening with her swell beaus
Rubbin' elbows

Come with me and we'll attend their jubilee
And see them spend their last two bits
Puttin' on the Ritz

It's a fun song but there is real bite here, especially the last line. The implication is that these people (catch the line about the "high browns?) can't save money, don't understand thrift, are only interested in superficial displays, and, therefore, will never really amount to anything. It was the conventional line in a time of cruel zoning and segregation designed to exclude and keep down non-whites in social and economic status.

Today when people look at the gold-chain culture of rap stars and dealers, the assumption remains the same. And there is a grain of truth to the idea that, by now, this is a microculture attached to a certain demographic; the real question is: what are the economic forces that gave rise to this culture?

What if there is another reason for wearing wealth that speaks to a different economic calculation? Rap and hip-hop originated from a gangster culture of marginalized groups that do what is necessary to survive. People in these professions are dealing with a high degree of legal risk (or singing about people involved with such risk). The laws against prostitution, drugs, and so on, mean that the people who do these things are facing constant risks for entanglement with the law, police, and courts.

They've also learned to distrust official institutions like banks and third-party intermediaries. They couldn't get accounts, couldn't get credit, and probably didn't want them in any case. This song was written in 1927, and it turns out that only 6 years later the distrust of banks proved well founded when FDR closed the banks and devalued the currency. Holding your wealth in gold and other high-end products was wise.

But there is more to the story. In the tradition of American policing and corrections, the police have no trouble freezing your bank assets, taking your car, and even surrounding and confiscating your home. When you are arrested, however, what you have on your person is given back to you later. It remains your property and you are given a voucher for it in standard police practice. But this is contingent on it actually being on your back or in your hand at the time of arrest.

I recall this from the time I was arrested after failing to appear to pay a traffic ticket. The police were extremely reluctant to let me get back anything inside my car. Even my car was impounded. But what I was carrying at the time came with me, and then went into a box at the jail that I easily recovered after bail was posted.

Police will take and keep large amounts of cash but they won't take and keep jewelry, furs, grills, and the like. It's a peculiar feature of American arrest logistics but one that is well known in communities in which illicit activity thrives. It makes sense, then, to carry as much of your high-value assets on your person as possible, so as to mitigate against their confiscation at the time of arrest.

National Public Radio interviewed the famous pawn-shop owner Rick Harrison. He provided more detail as it relates to posting bail.

> "When you get arrested for pandering, they take your cash — because the cash was obtained illegally — but they don't take away your jewelry," Harrison explains. "And a pimp knows that if he buys jewelry in a pawn shop, if [he] brings it back to a pawn shop and gets a loan against it, [they'll] always get half of what you paid for it — as opposed to buying it in a jewelry store, when [they] don't know what [they're] going to get. So, when they get arrested, they will always have someone bring their jewelry down to me. I will loan them half of what they paid for it — and that's their bail money."

You can see, then, that this behavior, now long established, has roots not in race or even class but rather in the way law forces certain economic decisions on whole communities, by necessity. It is a matter of pursuing your self-interest, something everyone does. The habit then catches on and becomes part of the culture of the group, and is even exported abroad to different nations where the music and ethos are adopted.

Thus is there a reason to the rhyme of why dealers, rappers, and pimps wear their wealth. It all comes down to the legal gulf that separates their professions and art from civic practices. If you want to keep what you have earned, and take every precaution against having it pillaged by the police, it's best to carry it with you.

78

This Toilet Plunger Reveals the Secret of Civilization

T here are many wonderful things in the world, but right now I want to talk about a product of the human mind that is a material celebration of the potential for creativity to overcome and rise above the state of nature. To put it briefly and simply, I've found a toilet plunger that embodies the essence of the human drama and reveals why humanity, despite every strong-armed attempt to stamp out progress and subvert the good life, somehow manages not only to survive but thrive through the ages, including even our own.

The product is the Python Plunger, and before you dismiss this as just another household good, you have to consider the background here. Nearly a quarter century ago, a small government regulation in the US declared that your flushes can only use 1.6 gallons of water. It thereby ruined the best single aspect of indoor plumbing, namely the ability to drive human waste far from the human experience and wash away all evidence that it ever existed in the first place.

The Romans understood how to do this, but somehow the US Congress got confused, and imagined that you can improve water efficiency with a wish backed by a gun.

Broken Toilets

The result was a gradual change in a core functionality of the American bathroom. As old toilets were replaced with new ones, everything became worse. You had to have a plunger nearby. People switched from thick toilet paper to one-ply. You had to flush several times under some conditions. Overflowing toilets were common. With less water flowing through, the apparatus in the tank began to collect sediment and rotted. Bleach cubes to keep the bowl clean became essential. After a while, everyone began to think this was normal. A whole generation has now been raised to think that flushing the toilet is an iffy experience.

It's true that every manufacturer has experimented with new designs, new pressure methods, new materials. This is why sometimes you flush and it sounds like a gun. These models are available now for domestic use. They splash everywhere and break easily. The truth is that nothing quite works as well as a typical toilet from the 1980s. We had it right and then we broke it.

You say you like your toilet? I say you don't remember or never knew the good life. There has been a deep downgrade in quality. Now we acquiesce to the idea that every toilet needs a plunger close by. That's kind of pathetic and kind of gross, but it is the way it is.

But there is an additional problem, and you know it. Often the plunger doesn't work. You work it and work it, but still it doesn't quite fix the issue. In desperation, you flush again. Then the ghastly mess begins. The whole scene is unspeakable and terribly embarrassing, not to mention truly unsanitary.

This is why I'm just so impressed by this new plunger technology. It is truly simple, as all brilliant ideas are. It builds a metal snake into the handle and gives the user a lever to push it through. It thereby breaks through the clog with a hole that allows the passage of water.

To be sure, had government never intervened at all, never passed these ridiculous regulations, this innovation would not have been necessary at all. We could have continued to use old-fashioned plungers with no problems. But the brilliance of free enterprise is that it inspires the production of solutions to problems. It is a fix-it machine. It seeks problems and inspires a race to overcome them.

Problem Solving

And this is why free enterprise brings progress to the world. It has always done so.

There is a body of water and we need to get across it. Build a boat. Build a bridge. Make it out of steel so it can hold tremendous weight. Invent an airplane to fly over it. Never let the problems of nature get in the way of the human aspiration to master the elements and triumph in the name of living a better life.

Sometimes the problems in life are created by governments that claim to be solving problems. They introduce rules, bureaucracies, systems of control, blocks to enterprise, barriers to entrepreneurship. Governments have done this since the ancient world. They do it every day now. How to respond? You figure it out. You make something new. You sell it and make a buck. Everything becomes a profit opportunity, and a chance to make the world a better place.

This is precisely why the Python Plunger is such a magnificent human achievement. But there is more. Notice how this is a small company that needs some big financing. Lots of companies are in this position. Thanks to the Internet, private enterprise innovated some fascinating new tools to raise money from people in a democratic way. Countless products have come to market that would otherwise have been stopped. And even here, government regulations restrict what can be done because to sell stock this way would violate securities regulation. Private enterprise to the rescue: your stock will be a product. Presale the whole thing! Problem solved.

Progress Is Not Automatic

We dare not take this process for granted. It doesn't happen automatically. It happens when there is a window of freedom to make progress possible. It happens when people take the initiative, take a risk, stick their necks out there, and dare to invite people to make a choice for what they have done, all in the hope of making a profit. What a system! What a solution!

And take a look around you. Everything you see is a solution to a problem. Take a look at your smartphone. It is the same: solutions to problems. Chances are that 99.9% of them come from the same source: private enterprise. Without it we would still be living in a state of nature, or, worse, in a state of government.

The tragedy is that once this plunger is in a million homes, and it sits there ready to go to work for us when bad things happen, we then take it for granted, presuming it has always been there and always will be there. Not so. It exists only because humans are claiming their rights to invent and serve others in the marketplace. The system that permits this deserves our admiration. And so do those who step up to the task of making the world a better place.

In this particular case, we are talking about fundamental technology that makes life livable: the ability to move human waste as far as possible from human activity. You might think we would have mastered this long ago. Thanks to government, we keep having to re-master it. All hail to those who accept the challenge.

79

They Are Coming for Your Paper Towels

I've always suspected it would come to this.

The uplifters of society, the scolding specialists who loathe our consumer comforts and want to use the law to de-materialize our habits and minds, the descendants of the colonial-era pastors who banned buckles on shoes and the preachers of the public good who banned beer by constitutional amendment, the puritan decriers of our household happiness, now have a new target in mind: paper towels.

The literary cloud no bigger than a man's hand appears in the Atlantic. It decries Americans as uniquely evil for having an obvious obsession with paper towels. This year we will spend $5.7 billion on paper towels, which is as much as the rest of the world combined. Per capita, we will spend $17.50 on paper towels — which is less than I would have predicted but vastly more than the rest of the world's people still attached to rags, mops, and sponges.

As for waste, the EPA keeps this data: 7.5 billion pounds of "tissue products" are disposed of yearly, and paper towels are part of this. But note that the figure here also includes toilet paper, paper napkins, and nasal tissue too. There is an ominous hint in this aggregation: first they will come for your paper towels, but other tissue products are on the list.

Top five countries by overall spending on paper towels
Total U.S. dollars spent on paper towels in 2017, in billions

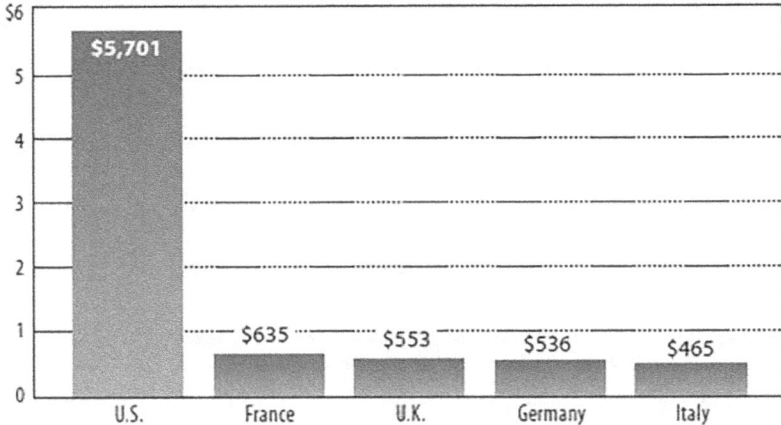

Source: Euromonitor International

The article theorizes that this outrageous overuse of paper towels is symptomatic of a deep moral problem. The author names and shames the "uniquely American desire to be immediately rid of a problem, whatever the cost." We seek instant gratification. Out with this damn spot, now!

The author also worries that we are having undue influence on the rest of the world, citing the prediction that by 2022, global spending on paper towels will rise by 4 percent.

This is just what you needed, yet another planetary disaster to worry about. It will surely require the intervention of public-spirited scientists and statesmen. Maybe a global paper-towel commission will be formed with the United Nations heavily involved. The studies and rhetoric are just beginning but make no mistake. This has all the makings of a movement. They are coming for your paper towels.

On the Other Hand

It's true that there is something of a physical mystery concerning why anyone would throw away a paper towel rather than wash it out and let it dry. Ask yourself why you do it. Maybe the answer comes immediately. It's all about the price. I'm looking at Amazon right now and find prices between half a penny and a penny and a half each, depending on design and thickness. That's truly incredible.

And think of the engineering behind its creation. The tree takes years to grow. It must be cut and milled, pulped, cleaned, and reshaped, with the addition of strengthening agents, perforation, embossing, and packaging. Then it needs to be ported to the store and backed by a clever marketing campaign. Thousands of people are involved in making a single paper towel, with dozens of stages of production and some extremely fancy equipment constructed by the best engineers and maintained by highly trained specialists. No man can make a paper towel.

The Mighty Price

If you were a central-planning intellectual or statesman, and were tasked with pricing the final output, and you otherwise knew nothing about prevailing market conditions, how high would you think the price should be? One dollar? Two dollars? There's no way to know. But I would suggest to you that it would not likely be half a cent.

The halfpenny price is precisely the signaling system that tells consumers to throw it away. That one price conveys vast information that informs our buying and consumption habits. Here is a fantastic example of F.A. Hayek's theory concerning pricing: they provide awesome guides to action, rationing scarce goods in a socially optimal way, while granting us permission to do something that would otherwise be wildly implausible: tossing this thing in the trash after one use.

Let's say that tomorrow there was a huge shortage of paper towels and prices went up by 100 times. Your household habits would change immediately. They should. And keep in mind that this price system only works in the presence of real markets, which in turn only work in the presence of private property rights and competitive enterprise.

There is no reason to speculate about the moral failings of Americans here and our base desires to be immediately gratified with the absence of spills. It's all about economics. Economic forces have made a miracle, an enormously complex and long production structure ending in a product that costs truly next to nothing. All hail the market!

There's another mystery here as to why anyone is in the industry at all. Paper towels were invented in the 1920s and the prices gradually fell over time. Let's say your great uncle came to you and said: "Hey, I have a great idea for a product that will take months and millions to produce and then we sell it to consumers for less than a penny." You would run, not walk away from that idea.

And yet, the industry is still huge and mighty.

It's Recycled Too!

There's another remarkable fact. Trees are not cut for paper towel production directly. Paper towels are made from recycled office paper, cardboard, envelopes, and other already used paper products. It is a clear case of market-based recycling, taking what would have been a complete waste and turning it back into something valuable. Our tut-tutting, moralizing, know-it-all journalist for the Atlantic didn't happen to mention this fact!

Keep in mind that this is genuine, economically sustainable recycling, unlike much else that goes by that name. We have a profitable industry here that is able to make treasure out of trash, solely devoted to improving our household lives.

They want us to use rags, sponges, and mops again for all our small spills in the kitchen? Forget it. We don't want cross contamination. We don't want stinky sponges around our food. We don't want to drag out buckets and rags just to remove that spilled milk on the counter. We don't need a new paper-towel tax; such a thing might inspire riots in the streets, and should. Our hands will be cold and dead before they pry the paper towels from our fingers.

80

Why Ketchup in Mexico
Tastes So Good

You know those little packets of ketchup that come with french fries at a fast-food joint? Imagine if they were delicious. Or maybe you think they are already. The instant I tasted one in Mexico last week, I could tell something was different. Why was this ketchup unusually clear and flavorful? I looked at the ingredients. It's four things: tomatoes, vinegar, salt, and sugar. The last ingredient is the key. The brand is Heinz, the world leader in this ketchup industry. Look at the same thing in the US and you find the inevitable as the replacement: corn syrup. The same brand, same packaging, in the United States is a different good from what you get in Mexico.

You probably know that it is the same with Coke. Mexican coke uses sugar whereas in the US, apparently uniquely in the world, sugar is replaced by high-fructose corn syrup. Once you become aware of this, the reality sets in. What in the US isn't made of corn actually? And perhaps this has something to do with the diabetes epidemic and the stunning obesity rate in the US, both of which have soared since the 1990s?

There is a growing awareness that we have a major problem. What is the source of this fixation on putting some variation of corn in everything we make and eat? From an economics perspective, it stems from two main sources.

The US has a mighty import quota for sugar that limits imports to keep the price as high as possible for American consumers. "Imports of sugar into the United States are governed by tariff-rate quotas (TRQs), which allow a certain quantity of sugar to enter the country under a low tariff," says the USDA. "The USDA establishes the annual quota volumes for each federal fiscal year (beginning October 1) and the U.S. Trade Representative allocates the TRQs among countries."

As a result, US consumers and producers pay approximately three times the world price of sugar. This discourages its use relative to substitutes. Yes, this is happening to you and me every day, and these price signals have dramatically affected our diets. This is because the decision of producers to use corn syrup instead of sugar in a highly price competitive market makes economic sense.

Try to go without corn syrup for a few days. It's not easy. It's true, for example, that Heinz offers a product called Simply Heinz that uses pure sugar, not high-fructose corn syrup. But that product costs nearly $1 more than the standard bottle of ketchup. You are at the grocery aisle. You are price conscious. One bottle costs a dollar less than the other, and the taste difference between the two seems barely discernible.

Only high-end, fussy, conscious consumers go for the high-end product. You can see why people desire to pay less. Prices matter. Central planning has caused this, and massive numbers of American health problems along with it.

Why corn syrup and not honey or some other sweetener? The US government offers a complex and varied panoply of subsidies for agriculture of which corn is the top beneficiary. This is why "corn is the single most important commodity for retail food," says Richard Volpe, an economist for the USDA. "Corn is either directly or indirectly in about three-quarters of all food consumers buy."

The American Midwest has a new mountain range to compare to the Rockies except that it is made of corn, which is plentiful and vastly cheaper to use for everything than what it replaces, including sugar, animal feed, and even gasoline. This is why, when you go to the store, no matter what food you buy, or think you are buying, you are basically buying corn.

America is the land of history's most innovative uses of corn. For example, you buy a pie. The crust uses corn oil. The filling uses corn syrup. It seems like a pie but it is basically corn. Once you become aware of this issue, it is actually difficult to find anything that doesn't use corn as the core of the ingredients. It is sugar substitute. It is oil substitute. It is the thickener. It is everything. Take a look at the fare available in the typical convenience store. It should be called the corn store.

Even the gas. The ethanol mandate came about in 2005 and 2007. It mixes nearly all the gas we can buy with a sticky product now in rather short supply. Of all the government regulations I've looked at in detail over the last 15 years, the ethanol mandate is, by far, the worst. There are no grounds on which it is defensible.

I don't recall much debate in 2005 and 2007 when these draconian laws were imposed in the name of the environment and security. Organizations like the Institute for Energy Research were trying to draw people's attention to what was taking place, but most people figured this was just some wonky and forgettable concern.

Looking this up and examining the history, it appears that government has been trying to put corn in our gas tanks (and mouths) for decades, even back to the 1960s. There were tax breaks, subsidies, lofty national goals, smiley stickers for executives who publicly backed this nonsense, but none of it took. Finally, our masters brought out the brass knuckles and everyone shaped up, culminating in a coercive mandate imposed a dozen years ago.

Now we are stuck with this de facto mandate that we have to put corn in our gas tanks, all based on the kooky idea that fossil fuels are just too primitive, that we have to mix our gas with a movie-theater treat to make it truly clean and efficient.

But clean and efficient are two things that ethanol is not. The reason your edger and weed whacker don't fire up in the spring months is most likely due to the presence of corn in the tiny gas tanks. The fuel mixture does not stay durable over time and tends to gum up engines. This is why the store shelves are filled with gas-tank additives of all sorts that did not used to exist. The whole point is to correct for the mess that ethanol makes.

Now let's look at what's happened to crops since 2005. The percentage of crops devoted to corn have gone from 24% in 1999 to 30% today, more than 96% of all grains. Meanwhile, the crops devoted to soybeans, hay and wheat have all gone down, thereby increasing feed costs for ranchers and consumers. Again, this is not the market talking. This is not what any actual market players are pushing. This all results from government mandates and subsidies. Government intervention has created corn nation. We feed it to our cars, our animals, ourselves.

Meanwhile, the price index of Illinois farmland has tripled in the same period. Even though every price signal would otherwise indicate to farmers to plant less corn, they plant more. And even though land values all over the U.S. went into a major bust in 2008 and following, Illinois farmland goes up and up. This is a result of government intervention, building artificiality into the system and creating unpredictable distortions.

It almost seems hard to believe. It's a scandal that government has degraded home appliances, indoor plumbing, paint, cosmetics, gas cans, pies, cokes, candy bars, and ketchup. Yet the ethanol nonsense, and corn subsidies combined with limits on sugar imports, might be the worst of all, because it represents a fundamental attack on the dietary habits of all Americans. Public awareness is growing but, in my experience, most people have no idea what is being done to them.

Meanwhile, researchers have discovered the truth about diet. It's not about calories. It's about the quality of food. This is what American agricultural policy is against, and has been for decades. The US government is all about forcing corn on you. It is up to you and me and everyone to resist, in your own interest.

Either that or move to Mexico.

81

Why Unhealthy Food Is Cheap and Plentiful

Every health nut will tell you the reason why the US food market is such a mess. It's fast food and corporate farming. We need to get back to local food and organics, they say. And no processed foods ever.

Let's look more closely, based on an experience I had just today.

The waiter in this airport bar walked by carrying huge plates of food, piled high with fries and burgers on puffy golden buns, then another with a gleaming plate of chicken wings covered with barbecue sauce and along with side dishes of more fries, then another with a massive pasta dish covered in white cheese, followed by another carrying a gigantic wedge of chocolate cake topped with ice cream and a caramel sauce.

My goodness, this place is generous with portions!

So it came time for me to order. I picked the catch of the day, which was Mahi Mahi, along with some asparagus and some slaw. Sounds great! The other plates were $15. Mine was $29. Ouch. That's annoying but sometimes you have to put aside price to get what sounds right.

But when it came, my plate looked nothing like the other plates of food around me. It had a very small piece of fish. There were six asparagus spears. The slaw was fine but limited. There was a small relish for the fish. And that was it.

I ate it all in about six minutes. There goes thirty bucks down the drain. And I look around and see happy customers chowing down on glorious plates of food, dumping ketchup (sugar) over everything, delighting in the excess.

Good for them. Sad for me. Or maybe not.

The Science Was Wrong

If you pay even the slightest attention to all the latest research on diet, you know of the emerging consensus. The famous "food pyramid" of the 1970s, along with the dietary recommendations by the federal government, were completely wrong. The war on fat, the huge emphasis on grains (and corn!), the minimal place of fresh vegetables and fruits, the attack on eggs and meat, and all the rest of what was once conventional science, seems to be melting away.

Meanwhile, the American obesity problem, along with all associated health issues, is out of control. The obesity rate has doubled since the 1980s. It is the second leading cause of premature death. Some data show that nearly a third of Americans can be classified as obese. Even our pets are developing an obesity problem. Maybe they are eating what we are eating.

You don't have to read the science to know this. Stay abroad for a few weeks and return to the States, and you notice, perhaps for the first time, that Americans look, ahem, different from other people in the world. You also notice that the food choice — I don't mean at farmer's markets or stores with a philosophy but rather the mainstream fare — is very different in the US.

For example, I've spent the last several days in the Caribbean. The food is fresh and healthy, with all kinds of fruits and delicious veggies plus wonderful meats. Breads are there but play a minor role in the overall offerings. Desserts are yummy but not that sweet. The same is true everywhere I've been lately, outside the US.

In the US, by contrast, the diet is driven by the market but it's a deeply distorted market, where the poor choices get the subsidies and the better choices are left to face competitive cold winds.

The Economist explains "American farm subsidies are egregiously expensive, harvesting $20 billion a year from taxpayers' pockets. Most of the money goes to big, rich farmers producing staple commodities such as corn and soyabeans in states such as Iowa."

The Centers for Disease Control actually funded a massive study on the whole topic. The question: what is the link between the foods that make us fat and sick and the foods that are subsidized by the federal government? The result is just about as clear as empirical science can be.

> Among the justifications for the 1973 US Farm Bill was to assure con-sumers a plentiful supply of food at reasonable prices. Four decades later, the US population is burdened by substantial obesity and cardio-metabolic disease. Suboptimal diet quality is a leading factor associated with death and disability in the United States. Specifically, diets that are high in calories, saturated fats, salt, and sugars but low in fruits and veg-etables have been implicated in the development of cardiometabolic risk

factors (obesity or adiposity, elevated blood pressure, elevated lipid levels, and diabetes) and diseases.

Why Does this Matter?

Many people who are curious about this relationship — I would even say nearly all! — explain the whole problem as tracing to "corporate farming" and "processed foods." Or to put it in brief: fast food. The problem here is that this is imprecise and comes close to blaming industrial progress itself for the problem.

The real root is deeper. It is not corporations or technology. They have made it possible to feed 7.6 billion people, in complete defiance of every Malthusian prediction of disaster dating back centuries. Nor is it the method or speed of delivery. The core of the problem is the massive price distortions in the market that have been brought about by government intervention.

The power of the corn lobby, for example, is legendary. And mixed with that is the power of the sugar lobby, which keeps out imported sugar that would sell for half as much as we pay at the store, thereby incentivizing producers to seek out a substitute in corn, which turns out to make us fatter, thereby panicking do-gooders who try to ban products and limit consumption, so that our bad health will stop driving up health-insurance rates.

I don't even need to look at the ingredients of the dessert that passed by my table to know the high likelihood that the cake, ice cream, sauce, and whipped topping contains corn at all levels. It's actually not easy to find any mainstream American food that is not built from some corn product. Take a tour of your local convenience store and look at the ingredients: observe the ever-malleable presence of corn. The food you seem to be looking at is not the food you are eating.

Blame Not the Market

The market is being blamed, once again, for a problem that traces to government itself. Remarkably, all of this has happened only since the 1970s, before which there was no such thing as high-fructose corn syrup, to say nothing of corn-based gasoline. It's one intervention piled on top of another one.

Foreign peoples find all of this mystifying. Indeed it is, until you look more deeply and see just how important the grain states are in winning elections. It turns out that the main and most valuable products generated by all this strange bad-food activity are political careers.

It's for this reason that we have corn coming out of our ears. We have french fries stacked to the heavens. We have breads, grains, and corn syrup taking over our lives, stuffed in our animals, and porking us all up to the point of rampant disease — all made available at absurdly cheap prices to the point that eating a healthy diet seems economically irrational.

Now, to be sure, this is, as they say, a "first world problem." For most of our 150,000 years of scraping by, humans have mostly struggled to get a bite to eat every day. It's the number one problem that has defined our existence. That we've somehow solved this problem is amazing. That we've replaced that old problem with a new problem — eating too much of the wrong kind of food — is extremely strange.

If we had a genuine free market in food — and the market is doing its best with the Amazon acquisition of Whole Foods — we would also likely see a greater alignment between what is affordable and what is actually good food for human consumption. It would be nice at least to be able to test this, starting with an end to the farm program.

82

It's the Small Things, Like Hershey's Kisses, that Matter

Have you followed the unfolding of the great mystery? Some months ago, the tips of Hershey's Kisses were commonly broken off. You unwrapped them. No tip. The entire sweeping flow of this edible piece of commercial art is thereby interrupted. You put them in cookies and the melting top doesn't look right. The cook doesn't like the result. Consumers are disappointed, just slightly, on the margin.

All of this unfolded during the holiday season of 2018. The company makes 70 million Kisses per day. All of them in these fateful weeks were shipped without tips. Customers complained. It was all over social media. The company looked into the problem. They discovered a problem with some new machines used in the manufacturing process.

Then happily, on the last day of January 2019, the company made a great announcement. They found and fixed the problem. All new Kisses will be shipped with tips.

Hurrah! All's right with the world again.

Now, in light of this news, I'm putting myself in the mind of any number of great thinkers of the past. It could be G.W.F. Hegel, Karl Marx, Leon Trotsky, Oswald Spengler, Carl Schmitt, or Werner Sombart whether in his Communist or Nazi period. All of these people — how we studied their thoughts so hard in college — can be classified as left or right or both. What unites them is their complete lack of interest in the small material concerns of life.

Thus would these "great" thinkers all be thoroughly disgusted by the above paragraphs. Why are we focussing on such absurdly stupid bourgeois concerns (chocolate indeed!) when the very theme of history stands on the precipice of dramatic upheaval? Do we not realize that thinking about the shape of candy is a gigantic distraction from our existential obligation to become part of the meta-narrative of historical transformation currently underway?

Do we not see how the commercial economy has dumbed us down, made us a petty and silly people, tricked us into numbing our consciousness so that we can't even discern what the great thinkers find so obvious? And for what? So that a handful of chocolate kings can make money — mere money! — from our personal desire to have a well-shaped morsel of candy on our tongues.

And these merchants, where are their loyalties? Not to the nation, not to the toiling masses, to the race, to the grand dialectic. No, they are obsessed with... customers, balance sheets, and supply chains. The intellectuals are disgusted.

It's fascinating to me how the thinkers we regard as mighty and decisive interpreters of the world around are actually profoundly uninterested in the actual way all of us conduct our lives in the real world. They care nothing for our discrete motivations and our desire to live a bit better each day, not live as a group or a nation or a class but as individuals in the particulars of our lives that we inhabit, each of us in slightly different ways.

No two individuals experience exactly the same life. There is no one solution that pertains to any large group. All improvement in life extends from tiny choices we make with minds that only we as individuals fully control.

They Hate Gum

Here's an example of intellectual blindness that fascinates me. Leon Trotsky came to New York for 10 weeks in 1917. He came to observe and interpret. He was standing in the subway, watching the masses of workers come and go. He spotted some gumball machines. He noted that people were putting money in the machines and sticking gum in their mouths.

Why was this happening? My explanation: people like gum and are willing to pay for it. This was not his point of view. He wrote a letter:

> Capitalism does not like the working man to think and is afraid...
> It has therefore adopted measures ... It has put up automats in each
> station and has filled them with disgusting candied gum.... And they
> grind it with the automatic chewing of their jaws... It looks like a
> religious rite, like some silent prayer to God-Capital.

Basically, Trotsky hated gum. In his 1934 essay on the shape of a future communism in America, he put a fine point on it: "In the third year of the Soviet rule in America you will no longer chew gum!"

This is not to pick on Trotsky alone; the same bad attitude toward consumer habits was shared by his supposed nemesis the Nazi jurist Carl Schmitt. That list of great intellectuals a few paragraphs before could be expanded with hundreds, thousands, of names, fanatics left and right who have been trying to get our attention for two hundred years. One thing that unites them is a persistent disgust at the sheer plainness of commercial culture; in a word, snobbery. These are people who imagine themselves to be in touch with the meaning of everything gigantic but would be utterly at a loss to explain the appeal of the magazine rack at the typical CVS.

Liberalism Is Different

Think about the difference with the liberal tradition that has always celebrated commerce as an emancipatory force in history. Think of Adam Smith's Wealth of Nations. Students pick it up and expect to read some big claims about the system we call capitalism. Instead what they find is a long series of discrete stories about people's lives, their talents, the incentives they have to improve, and the magic of the interests that cause them to work together to make life better.

Smith's only big claim — and it is a core claim of the liberal tradition — is that the best institutional framework to enable people to live the best possible life is one in which they are given the freedom to choose. But you can only understand that claim by getting your head out of grand meta-narratives and focus instead on how people actually live their lives.

The difference between people who believe in liberty and those who want to replace it with state control comes down to this. Do you think the small things matter or do you believe that the petty concerns of everyday life are a distraction from developing a higher ideological consciousness?

I think too about the many politicians today who are endlessly hectoring us about gigantic issues: national unity, inequality, what they call health care, a guarantee of security for everyone, all of which are said to be provided only by the state. But do these same people really care about how you are going to pay the rent next month, whether your holiday cookies are going to turn out right, whether your Uber driver knows your location, whether your wifi speeds allow for streaming the latest Netflix series you are desperate to watch?

The latter concerns are best addressed by allowing people to keep the money they earn, granting them freedom to choose, making sure technologies are available for the purchase on demand — all the small issues that make our lives slightly better on the margin. These are the only kinds of issues that genuinely impact on whether we live better lives. This is why liberalism cares about them and why illiberalism has always done its best to disparage and denounce them.

So yes, it really does matter whether our Hershey's Kisses have their tips broken off. The solution is the same here, there, and everywhere, not a grand narrative of history but a specialist, paid with wages paid in anticipation of profits, who can fix the machine in the factory so that the results better meet our expectations.

Want to become a champion of liberty? Eschew historicism. Be suspicious of grand millenarian eschatologies. Learn to love the little things in life. Celebrate every individual's right to choose how they live their lives. Smile when you think of every box of chocolate given and received this February 14th.

The tips on the Kisses are back and this is glorious.

83

What Is Your Coffee Cup's Country of Origin?

The trade deficit just soared to a record $891 billion. This is said to be a setback for the US President. By Trump's own standards, that's true. But there is another sense in which it is not a setback for anyone. The calculation is not only unscientific; even if it were possible to label everything as being from somewhere, it just doesn't matter for any reasons that are economically significant.

Branding products with national origin dates to the ancient world. The purpose was marketing. It's nice to know that this urn came from Greece, that wine from Australia, and these stacking dolls from Russia. Silk from China! Fruit from Latin America! As mass prosperity began to dawn in the late medieval period, the market for things from all over the world was exploding as never before, and that meant telling where things are from.

Even today, we are thrilled to own little things from different parts of the world. To do that requires we continue to establish a country of origin.

That's fine until the bureaucrats start mandating such reporting. And that's been happening for the better part of a century. When states got involved in this business, that came with silly data reporting, e.g. the trade deficit. It's supposed to measure the relationship between imports and exports, presuming that all goods come from only one place.

National origin designations are essential for its very calculation. Here is where things become extremely tricky, so much so that the statistics become meaningless, especially in a global economy with supply chains so complicated that it would require a dissertation to deconstruct the full origins of any household product.

Let's consider the coffee cup on my desk. It is a branded mug for the American Institute for Economic Research. I love it so much!

Let's think this through. It is pushing an institution founded in 1933 as an American institution. It is called the American Institute for Economic Research. Employees at this American institution thought of making it. We tapped an American supplier to manufacture them. We Americans are marketing it. We are selling it mostly to Americans.

This is obviously an American cup. Right? Ah, but turn the cup upside down. What does that little sticker say? "Made in China." Wait, how did China get into this mix? The supplier we used for ordering the cup wholesale sought and found the most economically viable way to manufacture this thing. It can, therefore, sell it to us in a way that we can sell it to the consumer for $10. Everyone is happy.

Believe it or not, this thing is considered an import with China as its country of origin. It has thus contributed to the trade deficit, which Trump has cited as a disaster and evidence that China is "raping" this country. True story. I'm pretty sure this mug is doing no such thing.

If the mug was conceived in America, marketed in America, sold to Americans to push an American institution, why is China considered its country of origin? According to trade regulations, it must be counted that way because China is the country in which it experienced a "substantial transformation."

That this is true doesn't matter in the slightest bit to you, me, or anyone, except to the extent that we are thrilled to sell such a nice product for only $10 and the factory in China that put it together is happy to have the business.

And let there be no mistake, these regulations are seriously enforced. The mattress company Nectar was just read the riot act by the Federal Trade Commission for claiming that its products are "designed and assembled in the U.S.A," when in fact they experienced "substantial transformation" in China. The company had to roll back its technically accurate claim. Basically, they were accused of fraud even though their mattresses truly were designed and assembled in the US.

The same fate befell three other businesses in recent months. The Democrats on the FTC have complained that the penalties are not severe enough!

There is another silly issue that is rarely mentioned here. As economist Donald Boudreaux points out constantly, the trade deficit only covers goods whereas 80% of American trading relationships consist of the exchange of services. In other words, the trade deficit describes nothing real. It is a statistical artifact as inaccurate as it is irrelevant.

National economic statistics in a global economy are already suspect, even more so when we are talking about products that depend for their very existence on international supply chains. At this point in history, where trading relationships cover every nation and production structures are infinitely complex, such data literally make no sense. To manufacture national data from globally manufactured commodities is to cram a large square peg in a very small round hole.

And yet here we have this one number built from a limited range of highly suspect data, signifying nothing meaningful at all, being massively misunderstood by the American political class and thereby causing havoc in US trade policy.

Fake economics in the wrong hands can cause an incredible amount of damage.

84

Regulators Are Not What
Makes Food Safe

Romaine lettuce was the big food panic of November 2018, with the FDA, the CDC, and tens of thousands of news reports, including many issued by the industry itself, warning against it because of E. coli. The product vanished from shelves and restaurants within a day.

(Lest we think this is just a private sector problem, I'm writing from Atlanta, where the city is telling residents to boil their municipal water because of some contamination.)

Take a step back from the temporary lettuce mania and consider the risk factors here. At the time of the product recall, 43 people might have been affected, maybe from romaine but one can't know for sure. At worst, the probability you would be hospitalized from eating a contaminated product was 1 in 28 million.

As Jim Prevor observed in the Wall Street Journal, "The probability of getting a royal flush in poker is dozens of times as great, at 1 in 649,740.... If this outbreak were active every day, and you ate one salad a day, on average you would be hospitalized for E. coli once every 77,000 years."

So, yes, everyone got carried away, and it was a disaster for the romaine industry, one that it hopes never to repeat. A panic earlier in the year cost the industry $77 million and a 44 percent decline in sales. This latest one will be even worse, and the industry is scrambling for solutions, even to prevent one infection, as low as the odds are. Some are even talking about using blockchain to better trace provenance.

Food Regulation

It's one of the most puzzling claims of the pro-regulation ideology: food makers and sellers have a weak incentive to make sure their food is safe for consumption. The briefest look at the dynamics of this food panic reveals the opposite. Selling an unsafe product is catastrophic for industry. And yet it is nearly universally presumed that we would all be buying and consuming poisons daily were it not for food regulators in Washington who tell people how to keep food safe. They must stand ready to issue recalls, the thinking goes, else we would be doomed.

The myth was born in the early years of the 20th century, with Upton Sinclair's The Jungle of 1904. It was fiction, but very compelling. The horrors of the meat-packing industry described therein (including scenes of workers falling into vats of boiling fat) inspired the first large-scale federal regulation on food safety: the Meat Inspection Act of 1906. Theodore Roosevelt saw this as a necessary first step "to do away with the efforts of arrogant and selfish greed on the part of the capitalist."

And that's usually where the historical memory ends. The federal government rescued us from unsafe meat, and that's it. Now it keeps us safe from poisonous lettuce. This story accounts for the wide support for government's involvement in stopping food-borne illnesses today. It is the founding template for why government is involved in our food and health at all.

Did the Regulation Work?

Let's look back at this meat-packing history. Did the regulations achieve their aims? Did the situation improve, and, if so, was this improvement due to the regulations or to private innovations? Or did the problem get worse, and, if so, can the worsening be traced to the regulations themselves? These are the sorts of questions we need to ask.

There is something in this little-known history that speaks to the entire basis for government management of health. The legislation required federal inspectors to be on-site at all hours in every meat-packing plant. At the time, regulators came up with a shabby method for detecting bad meat, namely poking a rod into the meat and smelling the rod. If it came out smelling clean, they would poke the same rod into the next piece of meat and smell it again. They would do this throughout the entire plant. This was the supposed fix.

But as Baylen J. Linnekin points out in "The Food-Safety Fallacy: More Regulation Doesn't Necessarily Make Food Safer," (Northeastern University Law Journal, vol. 4, no. 1), this method was fundamentally flawed. You can't necessarily detect pathogens in meat by smell. It takes a long time for bacteria to begin to stink. In the meantime, bacteria can spread disease through touch. The rod could pick up bacteria and transmit it from one piece of meat to another, and there was no way for inspectors to know about it. This method of testing meat almost certainly spread any pathogens from bad meat to good meat, ensuring that an entire plant became a house of pathogens rather than having them restricted to just one carcass.

As Linnekin explains: "USDA inspectors undoubtedly transmitted harmful bacteria from one contaminated piece of meat to other uncontaminated pieces in untold quantities and, consequently, were directly responsible for sickening untold numbers of Americans by their actions."

He continues:

> Poke-and-sniff — incredibly a centerpiece of the USDA's meat inspection program until the late 1990s — was, in terms of its sheer efficiency at transmitting pathogens from infected meat to clean meat, nearly the ideal device. Add to this the fact that the USDA's own inspectors were critical of the inspection regime from the start, and that the USDA abdicated its inspection role at hundreds of meat processors for nearly three decades, and it becomes quite apparent that instead of making food safer, poke-and-sniff made food and consumers less safe.

That's a very long time for a bad regulatory practice to persist. This is the way it is with regulations. Once a rule is in place, no one can seem to stop it, no matter how little sense it makes. This is why you can't get a decent gasoline can anymore. And you know this if you have ever been in the TSA line at the airport. The sheer irrationality strikes me every time — and it strikes the TSA employees, too. They are taking away bottles of shampoo but allowing lighters on planes. Sometimes they confiscate a corkscrew and other times not.

Whenever government imposes a rule, it begins to operate as if on autopilot. No matter how brainless, damaging, irrational, or outmoded it happens to be, the rule ends up trumping the reasoning of the human mind. This becomes a very serious matter regarding health. Ruling this sector of life, you don't want an overlord who is unresponsive to new information and new evidence and innovation — a regime that specializes in following a routine, no matter how bad, rather than improving itself with a testable goal in mind.

This is why in societies where governments rule, things slip into a frozen state. This is why even today Cuba seems like a tableau of the 1950s. This is why when the curtain was pulled back on East Germany and the Soviet Union in 1989-91, we found societies that seemed stuck in the past. This is why the postal service can't seem to innovate and why public schools are still structured as if it were the 1970s. Once a government plan is established, it tends to stick, even when it is not achieving its aims.

The case of poke-and-sniff in meat packing should serve as a warning for all government regulatory measures, whether designed to protect us from disease or bring us safety or any other reason. We live in a world of change and of growing knowledge. Our lives and well-being depend on economic systems that can respond to change, extract that growing knowledge, and enable it to be used in ways that serve human needs. A competitive market economy specializes in doing just that.

If I had to choose to trust either (1) a self-regulating lettuce industry that pays dearly for any mistakes made in food safety, or (2) granting special powers to far-away and detached public sector employees with no localized or specialized knowledge in any particular industry, the choice seems rather obvious. As the latest case of romaine lettuce demonstrates, the contribution of regulators here can be dubious, redundant, generative of unnecessary panic, or even contrary to the goal of safety.

It's been going on for more than 100 years with no end in sight.

85

The Miracle of Canned Tuna Salad

I was feeling the munchies and found a vending machine, which, to my amazement, would take credit cards for a purchase as low as $0.50. I stood before a cornucopia of delights from all over the world (candies, nuts, muffins, dried fruit, beef jerky, energy shots) each available with the push of a button, and had to choose. When I face such a situation, I can't help but recall the discoveries of historians and anthropologists of how the largest swath of all known history has consisted of human beings struggling for the next meal. Instead of running around fields, digging in the dirt, or risking life on the high seas, we stand in front of machines and swipe a plastic card.

Clothing and housing were easy by comparison to the great problem of getting food — especially when it had to come mostly from what was available in near proximity. If there was no meat, you would have to do without. The first great improvement in packaging, shipping, and storing meat (without refrigeration) came only in 1937 with Hormel's great product called Spam, short for spiced ham. Now we use the term to mean emails we do not want. The progress we've made in food technology over the last half century absolutely boggles the mind.

Tuna for Nothing

Back to the vending machine. My eye fell on a box of Bumble Bee Tuna Salad. It included crackers. It cost $1.50. It's just sitting there in a machine awaiting my purchase. It's not refrigerated. It even comes with a plastic spoon! Within minutes, I'm eating what would have been regarded by anyone anywhere throughout history as an incomparable banquet of delectable eating perfection.

Just think of the core ingredient, the tuna itself. Somehow we think of this as no big deal. But I don't know anyone who lives anywhere near a place where you can catch a tuna. You have to travel by boat to the Atlantic Ocean, the Gulf of Mexico, the Mediterranean, or the Black Sea. If you time it just right, you might find them off the North American coast. This is because these amazing fish are always on the move.

You have to be in a boat on the high seas for weeks following these beasts around. And it turns out to be one of the most dangerous jobs. The Center for Disease Control lists commercial fishing of this sort as "one of the most dangerous occupations in the United States." To avoid injury and survive requires special training.

Even if you had a sea in your backyard, it takes special equipment to snag one of these beauties and reel it in. They weigh between 300 and 1,000 pounds! I have a hard enough time with a 3-pound bass.

My Benefactors

Fortunately, because of the division of labor, there are people who do this for me, full time. I've never met a tuna fisherman and none has ever met me. But I benefit enormously from their labors: catching, cleaning, storing, preparing, packaging, delivering, and waiting in the hope that someday I will get the munchies and spend one dollar and fifty cents.

Talk about good fortune!

But there's more than just the delicious tuna in this can. It also includes salt. We think nothing of salt today, but we forget that salt was once so valuable that it was used as money. Have you lately tried your favorite food, whatever it is, without salt? I've variously made bread or cakes without it, and it's absolutely shocking how lifeless food is without salt. Today it is so ubiquitous that there is a big market in extremely fancy salts with snob appeal, whereas plain-old salt gets no love or appreciation from anyone.

Also, this tuna salad includes eggs. Everyone knows where they came from. But think of the improbable coordination that has to happen to have a chicken farmer come together with a tuna fisherman to combine the ingredients into a single food, each complementing the other. Then also have the addition of vegetable oil, which itself requires a completely different process of production.

I Don't Want to Grow Celery

Where does the "salad" part come from? This small can also contains both celery and carrots, meaning that an entire growing season is necessary. I became curious about the celery part, in particular, to discover that celery turns out to be extremely difficult to grow, according to the University of California Vegetable Research and Information Center.

"Celery seed is very small and difficult to germinate," say the experts. For this reason, "all commercial celery is planted as transplants grown in green-houses and nurseries." It requires constant watering. It is mostly harvested by hand. Further, the costs are high. "Celery is one of the high-cost crops in the coastal regions of Southern, California."

The Amazing Can

My most immediate worry when I opened the package was the can. I don't have a can opener. It turns out that I didn't need one. It is a can with a peel-off top. I have no idea who invented this but it is absolutely brilliant. The top has this small tab that easily lifts off, requiring no skill at all. We don't often think about packaging but consider how perfect it has to be. This can has to sit in a vending machine for months on end without being bought and then still be fresh when you open it.

How can this happen given that it also contains mayonnaise and eggs? Well, the ingredients specify that the mayo is "heat stable" which I am supposing involves some high-end processing.

Truly, I can't even fathom how all this comes together to provide me this wonderful snack. We are talking about a dozen different industries, thousands of processes, and potentially millions of inventions once you include all the boating, growing, shipping, canning, and even the making of the cute little spoon that is included, not to mention the machine that gave me the tuna and processed my credit card too.

What am I leaving out? Oh yes, the crackers. Picture wheat fields in the Midwest, grain silos, giant mixers, ovens, machines for shaping and cutting. It's a massive production just to give me these five small crackers.

No Planners

Here is what is so amazing. It all happens without any central direction from the top down. In fact, we can go further to say that it could not happen under central direction. No government bureaucrat made this possible. They only get in the way. You need owners, marketers, manufacturers, prices, markets, banks, millions of people, and thousands upon thousands of rounds of trading across dozens of countries, plus many years, decades, and centuries of economic development, all ending in a sweet little healthy snack just for me.

And here's the kicker. It all works at all levels thanks to human choice. Every worker along the way is there by his or her own volition. None of it works at all if, at the last stage of consumer choice, I would decide to get the Snickers bar instead. I didn't. I bought the tuna salad. It set me back one dollar and fifty cents. And we don't even need to express gratitude. We buy, eat, and forget it. This is why it is called the miracle of the market.

86

How Instant Coffee
Became Wonderful

The hotel room in Sydney, Australia, didn't have a coffee pot. But there was a water heater and some packages of instant coffee. Blech, right? That's what I remember from the old days, meaning some uncertain point in the past. But desperation forced experimentation. I heated the water, poured the packet of Moccona "Indulgence" in the cup. No stirring.

You know what? It was just wonderful. Ok, sure, it was not as great as you might get from fresh-brewed coffee, but this does just fine in a pinch. Not just fine. I could get used to this. It was not as I remembered from years ago, all bitter and hard to take, something you force down if only to get the caffeine injection. This instead was truly enjoyable. And it's not just this brand; there are now great instant coffees everywhere.

I got curious about this whole thing we call instant coffee. It turns out that product predates the American revolution. There is this prehistory:

> The earliest version of instant coffee is said to have been invented around 1771 in Britain. The first American product was developed in 1853, and an experimental version (in cake form) was field tested during the Civil War. In 1890, David Strang of Invercargill, New Zealand invented and patented instant coffee. In 1901, the first successful technique for manufacturing a stable powdered product was invented in Japan by Sartori Kato, who used a process he had developed for making instant tea.

The product got better and better, and became mainstream only in the 1960s. Even then, there is more going on. The process of making this stuff is enormously complex. It is a matter of grinding up the roasted beans into a fine powder, freezing it at extreme cold, and then drying it to suck out every last bit of moisture. Obviously there is a lot to go wrong in this process, and much to tweak to get ever better. That's where the free market comes in, always striving for a better way for people to live better lives.

The Great Coffee Controversy

These days, producers have it almost to the point of perfection. What's fascinating to me is the way it has grown up alongside the development of economic prosperity. In 18th century Europe, many products and services reached a newly emergent middle class for the first time in human history.

The capitalist age was maturing, and that meant that average people had money for the first time and lots of choices on how to spend it. One of the new products they could buy was coffee. With that came a great deal of social suspicion and even dread.

Yes, coffee was the marijuana of the 18th century, a substance loved and feared for its physiological effects and its social dimensions. None other than Johann Sebastian Bach satirized the puritanical fear of coffee in his delightful and witty "Coffee Cantata." It was one of the few times he ever tried his hand at pure pop entertainment. Of course he succeeded brilliantly; he was Bach after all!

The "Coffee Cantata" tells the story of a daughter who scandalized her father due to her devotion to coffee. She couldn't stop singing about how wonderful it is, while her father corrected her constantly.

"You naughty child, you wild girl, ah!" the father yells at his daughter. "When will I achieve my goal: get rid of the coffee for my sake!"

"Father sir, but do not be so harsh!" she responds. "If I couldn't, three times a day, be allowed to drink my little cup of coffee, in my anguish I will turn into a shriveled-up roast goat."

She happily agrees to do everything he says in every area of life except one: she will not give up coffee.

And then follows a beautiful tribute to coffee: "How sweet coffee tastes, more delicious than a thousand kisses, milder than muscatel wine. Coffee, I have to have coffee, and, if someone wants to pamper me, ah, then bring me coffee as a gift!"

The father threatens her: "If you don't give up coffee for me, you won't go to any wedding parties, or even go out for walks."

She still refuses.

Then the daughter plays a little game. She has a husband in mind and extracts from him a promise that if she marries him, he must allow her to drink coffee. He agrees. Then she goes to her father, who opposes the marriage, and makes a deal: if she is permitted to marry him, she will give up coffee. The father is delighted, and agrees.

Thus does the daughter gain a new husband, and, much more importantly, a permanent right to drink coffee whenever she wants!

Coffeephobia

What was this fear of coffee? Why was this such a big deal? It does have some narcotic properties to it, as we all know so well. It can give you a delightful lift.

But that alone does not account for the early opprobrium with which coffee-drinking, particularly for young girls, was greeted. For a fuller account, we need to understand something larger and more socially transformative: the advent of the coffee house itself.

The coffee house was one of the earliest public institutions, operating on a purely commercial basis, that brought a wide variety of social classes, not to mention a mixture between men and women, in a market-based social setting. In the 18th century, coffee houses spread all over

Europe and the UK, attracting young people who would sit and drink together and discuss politics, religion, and business, and exchange any manner of ideas.

What the father in the Cantata is actually objecting to is not coffee as such but unapproved, unchaperoned social wanderings, all made possible by the new prosperity.

The Loss of Control

This was a huge departure from the tradition that entitled parents and other social authorities, including governments, to determine what kind of associations their children would have. Coffee houses introduced a kind of anarchy to the social structure, and raised new risks of randomized contact with ideas and people that parents could no longer control. Coffee represented freedom itself — the freedom to mix, mingle, and consume what one wanted.

Indeed, coffee houses became a great source of public controversy. In England, in the 17th Century, Charles II tried to ban them all on grounds that they were "places where the disaffected met, and spread scandalous reports concerning the conduct of His Majesty and his Ministers."

Even a century later, women were banned from attending them, and this was true in France as well. Germany had more liberal laws concerning women and coffee but public suspicion was still high, as the "Coffee Cantata" suggests.

Women who were banned from coffee houses developed a very clever response. In the famous "Women's Petition Against Coffee" of 1674, women said that coffee was responsible for the "enfeeblement" of men. Historians say the campaign contributed to the gender integration of coffee houses.

We see, then, that the commercial availability of coffee actually contributed to the advance of women's rights!

Looking back at the astonishing success of every mode of coffee delivery in our own time, it doesn't seem surprising. Coffee houses serve as gathering spots, social mixers, places of business, and centers of conversation and ideas. We are more accustomed to it now than centuries ago, and yet even today, how much political controversy is engendered by access to products and services of which social authorities disapprove?

And today, we have the glorious improvement of even instant coffee. Fully half the world's coffee beans are being used for instant coffee. We can have it anywhere, even without access to a coffee pot or fancy espresso machine. Now no one can stop us.

> As the Coffee Cantata says:
> Cats do not give up mousing,
> girls remain coffee-sisters.
> The mother adores her coffee-habit,
> and grandma also drank it,
> so who can blame the daughters!

87

The Sock Slider, It Turns Out, Is a Godsend

Afriend sent me an image of a hilarious product he found in the aisle of some store. I laughed hard. It immediately struck me as something ridiculous. It is a plastic contraption that helps you put on your socks. Like we really need that.

My immediate thought was: this is surely a ripoff. Some people will make anything to ply a few bucks from your wallet. My mind went back to my childhood fascination with Ronco kitchen gadgets like the hotdogger and patty melt maker. These are things we buy based on our fascination with convenience but they only end up junking up our cabinets.

Surely the SockSlider was the same. Lol, as they say.

Some commentators caught the spirit.

"Is this what Foucault and Baudrillard meant by late capitalism?" one person asked.

"Peak capitalism," another commented.

But then others introduced a slight complication.

"I got one for my mom with mobility issues. I love capitalism."

"If you've ever been injured and unable to move, you'd understand how useful these things are."

"Seriously though, this is great for people with bad hips. It's hard to get into the end range flexion that we healthy people take for granted."

I Was Completely Wrong

I got curious and went to Amazon product reviews. They are over the top, plus lots of customers reporting that they are thrilled.

See here: "My husband is a disabled veteran. He is not able to bend his legs and also has difficulties bending his back. He required my help putting on his socks and pants! I was skeptical when ordering your Sock Slider, but I can honestly say: this Slider is the best thing that has happened to my husband in a very long time! He is able to put on his socks AND pants without my help! Thank you so much for making a Veteran happy!"

The use cases are many. Pregnancy, back issues, obesity, arthritis, and any mobility issue that prevents a person from reaching all the way down to one's feet to put on a sock. On reflection, I realized that this product is enormously useful. It might be the very thing that allows some people to get fully dressed and wear real shoes.

I, of all people, should have known that this product is real. The market does indeed provide. If something is a racket, it will get weeded out, provided there are free information flows, accountability, and means of spreading knowledge from consumer to consumer. Fortunately we are in the golden age of product reviews, so much so that it makes the government-based system of consumer product regulation look either redundant or ridiculous.

There is another matter too. When we look at products, our first impulse might be to think that if I don't need this, it shouldn't even be for sale. We have a hard time with economic empathy; that is, putting ourselves in another's person's socks, so to speak.

Disdain for the Public

As it turns out, many people have needs that cannot be appreciated or discerned in advance by intellectuals. Many times, they cannot even understand them. This has been obvious since the late 19th century, when the socialist critique of the capitalist market underwent a huge shift. The Marxists had predicted that capitalism would impoverish the working class while enriching the class of capital owners. When that turned out to be obviously false, the critique shifted: now the system was being attacked for providing too much in the way of frivolous luxury goods to the middle class.

The classic work advancing this theory was the quasi-socialist Thorstein Veblen and his influential book The Theory of the Leisure Class. To give you a sense of the whole tedious treatise, consider his analysis of how and why the middle class likes new clothing:

> "The law of conspicuous waste guides consumption in apparel, as in other things, chiefly at the second remove, by shaping the canons of taste and decency. In the common run of cases the conscious motive of the wearer or purchaser of conspicuously wasteful apparel is the need

of conforming to established usage, and of living up to the accredited standard of taste and reputability. It is not only that one must be guided by the code of proprieties in dress in order to avoid the mortification that comes of unfavorable notice and comment, though that motive in itself counts for a great deal; but besides that, the requirement of expensiveness is so ingrained into our habits of thought in matters of dress that any other than expensive apparel is instinctively odious to us. "

Do you see what's going on here? Veblen imagines that the average consumer is a rube running around making choices with the instinct of animals. It has nothing to do with satisfying real human wants. These are illusions imparted in a brain by a misbegotten need to fit in. It's all just a waste, he says. We should just be content with our lot in life and stop trying to look the part of our betters. The core problem of capitalism, he suggested, was precisely our obsession with living a better life. Capitalism is indicted because it makes that possible.

Such is the mind of the socialist intellectual from time immemorial, combining snobbery with disdain for the intelligence of the buying public (but these same people should be intelligent enough to overthrow capitalism and replace the whole consumer marketplace with a vanguard of a collective made from workers and peasants).

Revolution in Marketing

For centuries, people have misunderstood power relationships within the structure of capitalism. The conventional wisdom was and is that the people with the businesses (the capital) are in control. The on-the-ground reality is that consumers are in a position to make or break any business and drive the production decisions through their choices. This is the system that William H. Hutt called consumer sovereignty. Producers are beholden to the masses of people to make things that people show themselves willing to buy.

This logic of the marketplace overthrew the old order in which the powerful made the decisions over the use of scarce resources. This is why Ludwig von Mises said that the great innovation of capitalism was in its principle of marketing. No more would the well-to-do determine the course of history. Now everyone in the position to buy had the driving influence over what is made, how much is made, who gets rich, and who does not. Competition exists but it takes a different form: it is all about striving to be the best in the service of others.

Remarkable. All of us are too quick to dismiss products merely because we happen not to need them. If the product is a success, that indicates that someone needs them. Someone is benefitting. For someone, even the silliest sounding thing could be a life saver. That is certainly true for the SockSlider. And it is truly for millions and millions of other things out there that you and I might not need or understand.

Economic empathy consists in the habit of mind to realize that none of us, as individuals, are in a position to know all things. This is the job of great entrepreneurs and marketers. It is a better system for organizing the use of social resources than anyone has yet imagined. Certainly our friend Professor Veblen did not or could not.

88

Why the Sudden Frenzy
Against Plastic Straws?

If you took a nice summer vacation, you might have missed the latest frenzy in American political culture: the huge movement to ban plastic straws. It's real. Several cities in California have passed "straw-on-request" laws. Companies such as Starbucks have promised to eliminate them in two years, though one wonders how paper is going to fare when sucking up a hot latte. Signature petitions are alive all over the county.

I've even noticed that the wait staff at restaurants is reluctant even to give them out, as if giving you a convenient, clean, and effective way to drink your water is treading on dangerous territory.

My first theory was that this is the American prohibitionist culture run amok. We've seen this before. Never forget that this is the country that actually believed that an amendment to the Constitution could achieve the complete banishment of alcohol production and consumption. Several generations later, the attempt was made — without an amendment — to ban a weed that people like because it makes people feel light headed.

Then there is the penchant for pointless restrictionism, which has led to the ruination of our plumbing in our homes. Toilets don't work. Showers are terrible. Our washing machines barely function. Our pipes are clogged because not enough water flows through them. Our hot water heaters are more like tepid water warmers.

What leads to this political culture of bans, restrictions, controls, and micro-management of our lives from above? You could say it is the boredom that comes with hyper-prosperity. Maybe it is some innate desire to control what other people should do, something shared by both the left and right side of the political spectrum. Maybe it's the unleashing of the unconstrained vision, in Thomas Sowell's memorable phrase.

Academy Award

Reflecting on all of this, I finally watched the video. It's the one with the turtle getting a straw removed from its nose. You couldn't produce a more compelling, dramatic, and emotionally manipulative video by the best Hollywood producer. It has all the ingredients that make for viral videos. It has a homemade quality. It is spontaneous. It has the gradual reveal. It features a stunningly beautiful sea turtle with a nice personality.

It's hard to stop watching. When the nose of the turtle starts to bleed, even the most hardened heart begins to break. The turtle makes sneezing noises. Its eyes are big and beautiful. You feel the turtle's pain as if it were your own. You are with the rescuers as they decide what to do: clip the straw, leave it in because it might be embedded in the brain, or keep pulling until it is set free.

To top it off, the battery on the phone that is doing the recording is dying. It's the perfect combination to cause wincing and heart racing.

The film is so good that I'm actually reluctant to give away the end. So spoiler alert: they get the full straw out. It is the most glorious moment. You just smile. You want even to cheer. The whole experience is absolutely unforgettable. And the researchers end with a call for a complete ban on the plastic straw.

You can watch it now if you haven't already. But I warn you: you cannot unwatch it.

The film was released in 2015. Today it has 33 million views! It took three years to go from obscure to mainstream.

What we have here is an amazing example of politics via viral video.

We are making decisions affecting the lives of millions of consumers and businesses based on a politically powerful video about a straw in the nose of a single sea turtle.

I both get it and I do not. You can watch this and think: how incredibly uncanny that such a straw ended up in the nose of this turtle! How enormously fortunate it is for this pretty animal that these researchers found it and fixed the problem! We could leave it at that, and also not reflect on the reality of sea life. Every minute is a calamity of suffering and bloodshed, as billions of creatures devour other creatures constantly.

But we don't leave it there, as rational people might. Instead we go from "sad/happy fate of one turtle" to "let's massively impose on the liberties and property of every business and reverse the forward path of market-based products to cause an overall downgrade in the quality of life."

Market Failure?

Now we have a whole industry of writers who are glad to tell us that we've all made a mistake. We don't need plastic straws anyway. Paper and steel are just fine. "On rational grounds, the plastic straw can't be justified, at least in the vast quantities that they are currently used," writes Bee Wilson in the Wall Street Journal, as if she is personally wiser than the whole of the market and every consumer.

Let's march through some myths as discovered by the Competitive Enterprise Institute.

- 500 million straws are not used daily. Instead the number is closer to 175 million;
- Plastic in the oceans is a problem but only 1% comes from the US, and a tiny percent are straws;
- The vast majority of straws end up in landfills;
- People with disabilities absolutely depend on plastic straws;
- Nearly half the plastic waste in oceans is from fish nets;
- Plastic is more sanitary than the alternatives;
- Plastic is better for the environment than the alternatives;
- Plastic is more economical than the alternatives.

At some level, it seems preposterous to have to make such arguments. The market is better at selecting the products we use, based on resource availability and functionality, than governments or activists. But some people need a cause, and government is there to entice them to believe that through the right uses of power, the world can be made a better place.

And yes, I'm glad that sea turtle no longer has a straw up his nose. I hope he wasn't quickly eaten by a shark, which is the leading predator of these animals.

Conclusion

89

The Perfect Book to Lift Your Spirits

I'm absolutely loving Hans Rosling's posthumous book Factfulness: Ten Reasons We're Wrong About the World (Flatiron Books, 2018), which, to my further delight, has become an Amazon bestseller. If you need a break from the mainstream media message about how the world is falling apart, I can highly recommend this fact-filled and super fun book.

In fact, I might even suggest that this book should be the starting place for any kind of discussion about economics, politics, and the state of the world in general.

It opens with 13 multiple-choice questions about the state of the world today. Here are a few examples. Test your knowledge with just these five.

1. In the last 20 years, the proportion of the world population living in extreme poverty has a) almost doubled, b) stayed the same, c) almost halved.

2. How many people in the world have some access to electricity? a) 20 percent, b) 50 percent, c) 80 percent.

3. How many of the world's 1-year-old children today have been vaccinated against some disease? a) 20 percent, b) 50 percent, c) 80 percent.

4. Worldwide, 30-year-old men have spent 10 years in school, on average. How many years have women of the same age spent in school? a) 9 years, b) 6 years, c) 3 years.

5. In 1996, tigers, giant pandas, and black rhinos were all listed as endangered. How many of these three species are more critically endangered today? a) two of them, b) one of them, c) none of them.

Here are the correct answers: c, c, c, a, c.

Surprised? If not, you are unusually informed. Most people are not.

Those are five of the fifteen but all of them involve the standard of living, which is the topic of the entire book. His goal is to prove through an unrelenting series of facts that we are living healthier, wealthier, safer, cleaner, and longer lives than ever — and the increases in all of these factors are so astounding that we should all sit around being amazed by them.

Consider just the first point: the percentage of the world population that is living in extreme poverty has fallen by half in the last 20 years. That's thrilling news! But did you know that? Do you understand what this implies about burning issues like globalization, markets, and technology?

And yet we don't really pay attention. In fact, most people get most of the questions wrong. I tested this on my colleagues before writing this article. The best score was 5 correct out of 13. The worst score was 2. I'm a pretty optimistic and informed guy but I missed fully four of the questions, even though I knew the idea behind the quiz. Essentially I was not cheery enough. None of us are.

We further find out that disease, death, airline crashes, oil spills, HIV infections, and hunger are all dramatically down. Harvests, immunizations, access to clean water, electricity, education, cell phone ownership, and new music and movies are all up. Again, dramatically.

Why So Sad?

The purpose of the book is not only to reveal facts about the world around us and the trends that are driving it. Rosling seeks to explain our unwillingness to face and incorporate into our thinking good news about the world. He lists a number of biases, which he calls instincts. We have an instinct to be drawn toward negativity, fear, and generalizing from single cases. We like blaming things and people and look for problems to feed that desire. We think only about bad news we just hear rather than long term approaches. The media feeds this desire for ratings.

All of this sounds right to me but there is a simpler explanation too. Our minds are shaped by the narrative of our own lives. We live now and forward in time, whereas the past is an abstraction we either didn't experience or have already forgotten. It's true that one thousand years ago, most of us would be living in huts, sleeping on straw, threatened by violence, stuck in our own communities, dying young, suffering in pain from disease, unable to experience anything like what we call progress — if we would be alive at all.

We can say this, imagine it possibly, but we don't actually live it. We only experience our prosperity that we take for granted while grousing about the various problems we have in life, and it is these that consume us. The upside of this way of thinking is that it makes the human mind aspirational, which drives us to try to make a future more to our liking.

What is the point of adopting a fact-based worldview? Rosling says that it is essential so that we can better navigate life, the way a GPS helps us navigate a city. Further, knowing the facts about life around us brings us more comfort. We are less alarmed at the news. We are less likely to be manipulated by panicked political promises. We see through the fog. We can be more calm, rational, and perceptive.

Most of all, realizing the progress that has been granted unto us by markets and human cooperation makes us skeptical of wild plans to bring about progress via force and central planning. If you look at the fabulous trends of our time carefully, you can see that they are not the results of impositions but rather better human cooperation, technology, and the spread of knowledge. This is the way to improve the world.

90

Changing the World
Requires Patience

A common theme in Jordan Peterson's lectures concerns the difficulty of changing virtually anything. You say you want to change the world? Maybe you can. But you should practice on changing something within your direct purview.

The spouse with a bad habit you can't stand? Figure out a way to raise the subject. Those two uncles that fight incessantly? Figure out a plan to help them get along. Have a brother who can't hold a job? Help him develop a work ethic. Dad has a drinking problem? See what you can do to point him to moderation.

He uses this as a class exercise. Everyone picks some problem in their life that concerns some other (or another) person or institution. Several weeks later they report back on their progress. They are surprised to discover just how deeply difficult it is to change the smallest thing about other's behaviors and values, much less whole institutions, much less whole societies and world orders, and do it without making things worse rather than better. Change is hard. And, he adds, the best way to practice changing the world is to start with changing yourself. See if you can do that and work outwards from there.

A Check on Utopianism

The message is not supposed to be demotivating. It is meant to be a dose of reality, and a check against the wild utopianism and arrogance that infuses ideologically driven political activism. Above all else, goes the lesson, serious change requires wisdom, discipline, patience, vision, and a willingness to work slowly and carefully a bit at a time.

Change doesn't usually come about through threats, screaming, signs, and intimidating demands, much less unhinged dreams of how you think the world should work. If the movements gathering around the country to demand this and that in front of the Supreme Court reduced their ambitions to immediate family and friends, they might discover the truth of what Peterson is teaching. Making a loud fuss can be satisfying but it doesn't get the job done.

That said, one possible downside to his message might be to discourage anyone from trying to achieve anything that makes the world a better place. This is not a good takeaway. The truth is that it is possible to make a positive difference, whether in your own life, the lives of others, or even in the path of history itself. Social change is the reward of tenacity, courage, and patience above all else.

Mises's Exile

I want to cite a case in point to illustrate how it can happen, and I'm drawing here from the life of Ludwig von Mises, because it is a subject about which I spoke last night at an annual dinner that honors his memory.

He wrote some sad words in 1940, while on a boat leaving Europe for America, coming here with nothing at the age of 60 following an illustrious career that had ended in his exile. He wrote that he had "set out to be a reformer but only became a historian of decline." Had he made a mistake when he started out as an idealist who would fight for sound money, free trade, peace, and the liberal order? He clearly wondered. He lost most battles and now Europe was being torn apart by war and destroyed by totalitarianism.

Let me take you back six years earlier. Mises was the chief economist for the Vienna chamber of commerce, and ran a seminar for economics graduate students at the University of Vienna. He also had a great circle of friends, mostly scholars who got together in the evenings to discuss ideas and forge bonds of friendship.

By 1934, the rise of Hitler in Germany appeared inexorable, and everyone knew that he had his eyes on Austria with a plan to annex the country based on imperial ambitions to unite German-speaking countries. Worse, there was support for this idea within Austria itself. Mises could see the Hitler youth marching in the streets, an actual welcoming movement for German armies. They were calling for an end to liberalism and for driving out the Jews, whom they had come to scapegoat for all existing problems.

Mises made the exceedingly difficult decision to leave the country. Fortunately, there was an institution in Geneva, Switzerland — the Graduate Institute of International Studies — that was taking in scholars such as himself, in order to keep them safe and give them an opportunity to teach and write so long as the trouble in Europe persisted. He was given a desk, a solid income, colleagues, and access to books. He was given no "performance metrics," no target demographic, no obligation to show results from his work, no demands from a board pushing him to do this rather than that.

A Book for the Ages

It took fully six years to finish his mighty treatise on economic theory, a notably dispassionate book of theory (until the very end where he warned that civilization was at stake). I can't imagine the personal discipline it took to write such a thing in wartime, doing his best to tune out the world around him and write for the ages. He completed his task and the book went to print. But a German-language treatise on economics appearing in 1940 had, how shall I say, a limited market.

At this point, the Graduate Institute was overwhelmed with requests for academic sanctuary and Mises was encouraged to find another home. That's when he left for America — somehow getting past the very tight immigration controls that had long targeted Jews in particular for exclusion. He made his way here, managed to cobble together enough funds to live on, and put together a friend circle.

Among those friends was Henry Hazlitt, then an editor at the New York Times. He had a friend at Yale University Press. Mises published a couple of smaller works there, and they were successful. Then Hazlitt broached the topic: how about Mises undertake to translate his great 1940 treatise into English? Mises was reluctant to revisit that failed project but he did in any case. At the age of 68.

The book in question became Human Action, which was titled after many attempts to come up with something to characterize one of the great books in the history of economics. By the way, it almost didn't happen simply because Yale couldn't find an employed economist in American academia who was willing to vouch for it and recommend it. In any case, it finally happened, and this book helped build the pro-liberal, pro-market movement in the postwar period. The ideological shift it brought about did indeed change the world, however slowly, however intermittently, however much on the margin.

But think back now. Mises left Vienna in 1934. His massive treatise didn't come out for another 15 years, and it would be another 15 years beyond that before it really took hold and made the difference. It's hard to imagine today how life might have been different. That book is part of our lives, integral to how we think. But it might have been otherwise.

Mises did the hard work, without celebration and without obvious effect. The crucial point is that it wasn't achieved by committees demanding metrics or bureaucrats demanding instant results, much less mass movements screaming and demanding for change.

It happened because a genius was given the freedom and space to do his work. He wrote with reason, passion, determination, and elegance.

There's another factor that I think Peterson would cite as an essential precondition for a plan to change the world: it must be consistent with real-world conditions. You can't cause pigs to sprout wings or scarcity to disappear, which is precisely why socialism is nothing more than a fantasy. Ambitions for social change must deal with people and the material world as they really exist, which is precisely why changes on the margin are such an important check on the intellectual imagination.

Also part of reality is terrible evil, oppression, injustice, immorality, waste, disease, all of which require work to eliminate from human experience, though perfectionism will never exist this side of heaven. The conditions have to be right to change the world. It takes men and women of great courage and patience. But it can happen. We owe everything to those in the past who have been willing to take that difficult road and dare to both dream and act on those dreams.

91

The Good Guys are Winning This

Two important items are worth celebrating right now. Indeed, we should all be swooning with joy, raising a glass with the toast: "To rising so far above the state of nature!" The lives of each and every one of us have been made better off because of this news.

First, Apple, a consummate American company with massive and complex international connections to global supply chains, just passed $1 trillion in market capitalization.

Second, Amazon, the online retailer that twenty years ago was dismissed as a ridiculous idea that only benefited from a financial bubble, also passed $1 trillion in market capitalization (it is down, of course, as of this writing).

These companies are solidly digital-age enterprises, symbols of the gradual refashioning of our economic lives according to cutting-edge technology that departs from anything we've known before. Nothing like either of them or the services they deliver on this scale were imagined twenty years ago.

Apple has sold more than 1 billion iPhones over the last ten years. It employs 50,000 people in the US but is indirectly responsible for supporting 10 times as many. It has total assets of $367.5 billion. Meanwhile, Amazon employs half a million people. It processes an amazing 35 orders per second or 1 billion per year. It posts $20 billion in liquid assets.

These numbers were once unthinkable. They are now becoming more common. The one-trillion mark seems huge but the overall market capitalization of US public companies exceeds $30 trillion. Not only that, the US easily leads the world in high-capitalization public companies. No one else is even close.

Wealth Creation

But these aren't just numbers. They point to the great achievement of human-kind: we've learned how to create wealth. Aristotle, as smart as he was, couldn't make heads or tails out of economics, and even declared with great certainty that "retail trade is not a natural part of the art of getting wealth," and is "justly censured." He was stunningly wrong on this, and this is precisely why economics emerged as a science in the late Middle Ages, to explain where and why wealth comes from.

All of this wealth has been created out of what? Out of the creativity of the human mind, the drive to serve the needs of others toward the mutual benefit of everyone involved. The more we cooperate peacefully with each other, and so long as property rights are secure and trade is unencumbered, wealth can be created. The Industrial Revolution taught us just how awesome this can be. The flourishing of commerce means the flourishing of everything we call civilization.

The rise of prosperity is not baked into the logic of history. It requires heroism and faith because nothing is certain about enterprise. It relies on the freely-chosen decisions on the part of everyone involved. The business must speculate on the needs of others, and the consumers they serve must make the choice, every step of the way.

Consider too that every profitable company faces formidable foes to its own success. It deals with competition from others who are free to emulate its every move, which means that every company must innovate constantly, daily, hourly, just to stay ahead. It deals with the uncertainty of the future; everything must be built in the hope that people will buy but one can never be sure. And every enterprise must deal with an unfathomable amount of government regulations and taxes that get in the way.

It's one thing for such wealth creation to take place in the Gilded Age, when there was no income or corporate tax, and government did not regulate wages or products and services. It was a world of laissez faire. Today, it is different. The state knows no limits to its power, and looks for every opportunity to pillage both individual and corporate wealth makers and holders. The obstacles in compliance are stunningly daunting.

Given all of this, it is the highest tribute to the human mind that this has happened, despite every attempt to stop it. It is nothing short of heroic.

So where is the celebration? At the political level, the great achievement is being put down. Donald Trump never misses a chance to threaten Amazon with regulatory action. Vanity Fair sums it up: Donald Trump will not rest until Amazon is a smoldering pile of radioactive ash. That article was published in May 2018. He has since posted a dozen more tweets against the company.

Meanwhile, on the left side of the political spectrum, there is a growing movement, stemming from a similar hatred of these companies, to tax them to the extent that workers receive welfare benefits. Bernie Sanders is already introducing legislation, based entirely on a simple economic error over what determines wages.

Workers are paid not based on their household income (whatever that would mean) but rather their contribution to the productivity of the firm. There is absolutely no relationship between wages at Amazon and the benefits workers receive from the welfare state. It's even the opposite: the more job experience these workers gain, the more they can work themselves into an income bracket that makes them ineligible for welfare.

Faced with this left/right attack, I decided to conduct a poll on my Twitter feed. Which side of the political spectrum represents a greater threat to these companies?

I have no idea if the poll results are correct. Politicians can do terrible damage to companies. However, if I were to place bets this time, I would predict that they won't get away with it. The larger and more impressive is the private sector, the better position they are in to fight off the attempt by political actors to pillage and smash them. And these days, the sheer might and resources of the private sector is growing at a remarkable rate. This speaks well of the prospects for human freedom.

Meanwhile, if you are a seriously political person, you are right now watching the incredible antics taking place over the nomination of a new Supreme Court nominee. You have chosen your sides based on the media you watch. You are convinced that the enemy of your enemy is necessarily your friend. It's a dog-eat-dog world.

You might see the whole frenzy about the control of the powers of government as the key struggle of our time, an existential crisis that will determine the fight over the future of civilization itself.

You know what? You might actually be paying attention to the wrong thing. What matters more is the battle that is taking place that gets very little public attention at all: the private vs. the public sector in overall wealth. Here the good guys are winning.

Despite every conspiracy against wealth creation and wealth creators, despite a bipartisan attack on enterprise that dates back 100 years, despite every attempt to stop the material advance of humanity, commerce is still flourishing, still showing us better ways to do things, still inventing what no one thought possible, still lifting us further out of the state of nature, still giving us hope in a brighter future.

About the Author

Jeffrey Tucker is Founder and President of Brownstone Institute, a daily columnist at Epoch Times, Senior Distinguished Fellow of the Austrian Economics Center in Vienna, Austria, Research Affiliate for the RMIT University Blockchain Innovation Hub in Melbourne, Australia, Honorary Fellow of Mises Brazil, and a fellow of the Acton Institute and Mackinac Institute. He speaks widely on topics of economics, technology, social philosophy, and culture.

About the Publisher

The Brownstone Institute is a nonprofit 501(c)(3) organization founded May 2021. Its vision is of a society that places the highest value on the voluntary interaction of individuals and groups while minimizing the use of violence and force including that which is exercised by public or private authorities. This vision is that of the Enlightenment which elevated learning, science, progress, and universal rights to the forefront of public life. It is constantly threatened by ideologies and systems that would take the world back to before the triumph of the ideal of freedom.

The motive force of Brownstone Institute was the global crisis created by policy responses to the Covid-19 pandemic of 2020. That trauma revealed a fundamental misunderstanding alive in all countries around the world today, a willingness on the part of the public and officials to relinquish freedom and fundamental human rights in the name of managing a public health crisis, which was not managed well in most countries. The consequences were devastating and will live in infamy.

INDEX